For Susie and James
Who, like nearly 30,000 other families in the land
sat and watched the Falklands War unfolding,
and tried not to think about that knock on the front door.
They also serve…

…and in happy and proud Memory
of those former colleagues from
'The Red and Green Life Machine'
who have 'crossed the bar' since 1982:

Jim Pearson
Scouse Davies
Kev Frankland
Neil Blain
Brian Apperley
Bill McGregor
Phred Newbound

Dr Rick Jolly OBE, the author, hereby records his love
and thanks to his wife Susie, together with his gratitude for
the support and friendship of Mrs Rosalie Dunn, and all the
Deltor team, especially Darren McVeigh.

BRITAIN'S FRONTLINE MEDIC IN THE FIGHT FOR THE FALKLANDS

DOCTOR FOR FRIEND AND FOE

CONWAY

A Conway book

© Rick Jolly OBE 1983, 2007, 2012

First published as *The Red & Green Life Machine* in hardback in
the United Kingdom in 1983 by Century Publishing
Reissued in paperback by Corgi Books in 1984

Revised edition published by Red&Green Books in paperback in 2007

This new edition published in the United Kingdom in 2012 by Conway,
an imprint of Anova Books Company Ltd.
10 Southcombe Street
London W14 0RA
www.anovabooks.com
www.conwaypublishing.com

The author's royalties from sales of this book will be donated to *Combat Stress*,
the unique national charity devoted to the treatment and care of British
veterans with psychological problems that relate to active service
in the Armed Forces of the Crown.

ISBN 9781844861545

Printed and bound by CPI Group (UK) Ltd, Croydon, CR0 4YY

Image credits: All photographs taken by the author, unless specifically acknowledged otherwise. The paintings in the plate sections are by **David Hardstaff**,
courtesy of the author's collection.

CONTENTS

The Conflict: 1982

THE CONFLICT: 1982

Friday, April 2nd

Just before five in the morning, the bedside telephone rang, and my Falklands campaign began. It took me a little while to come to my senses, because I wasn't supposed to be 'duty doctor on call'. The voice on the line was not that of an anxious patient. Instead, it belonged to Lieutenant Colonel Ivar Hellberg, the Commanding Officer (CO) of the Commando Logistic Regiment, Royal Marines. Incredibly, the rumours of yesterday were not part of some elaborate April Fool's Day joke after all. The Argentines really *had* gone and done it!

Late on Thursday night, the Cabinet were told in London that an Argentine invasion force had landed from the sea and taken over Stanley, the capital of the Falkland Islands. The small outgoing and incoming garrisons of Royal Marines belonging to Naval Party 8901, who were just changing over after a year's duty, had put up a good fight, but eventually succumbed to the sheer weight of numbers and heavy weapons ranged against them. Ivar had no information in response to my inevitable question about casualties, but we could be sure that there must have been some Royal Marines wounded, perhaps even killed. He was now summoning me, and all his other Squadron commanders, to a pre-dawn O (Orders) Group. I got up and dressed hurriedly, kissed a sleepy Susie goodbye, and went in to work.

The CO told us that he had already been to the Mount Wise offices of HQ Commando Forces RM. There, he'd been informed that a British Task Force was being prepared to sail, with all despatch, down to the South Atlantic. Our normal NATO commitments were to be suspended, because this was very much a private matter. The Sovereign territory of the Falkland Islands had been sequestrated, and the residents of the Islands, through their Governor, had cried out for help...

Like all the other units of 3rd Commando Brigade, the Logistic Regiment's Easter leave had now been cancelled. Furthermore, Ivar had then been told to activate the standing plans to collect and deliver the many thousand tons of War Maintenance Reserve stores held in various depots around the country. Rations, fuel, artillery ammunition and a range of engineering spares had to be identified and delivered to a series of out-loading ports. This huge effort was going to be even more demanding than usual, because the task had to be completed in 72 hours instead of the more normal planning targets that assumed a lengthy period of tension over several weeks before escalation to actual war.

The CO's normally cheery face was now distinctly grim. It was going to be very difficult to meet this time requirement, particularly as British Rail had warned the military of their inability to help. The weekend was approaching, and moreover none of their rolling stock had been pre-positioned – as it would have been in time of tension. It seemed that this forcible Argentine seizure had caught everyone, including the Foreign and Commonwealth Office, completely on the hop. The episode had all the makings of a complete and utter shambles, but I was pleased to note both from the signals coming in and the tone of most subsequent telephone conversations, that throughout the Brigade our general reactions were all much the same. There was a quiet anger about this invasion of Sovereign territory, coupled with a palpable and growing determination to redress the grievance of initial defeat.

We simply had to get down there and push the invaders off. Whatever their reasons for taking the unprecedented step of invading a neighbouring country, an independent territory that existed under the protection of the British Crown, the Argentine forces had to be repelled.

I remembered some of the stories that I had been told about the Royal Marine garrison and their long and happy relationship with the Islands. Some of the men who had spent a year's tour of duty in Naval Party 8901 had settled there in retirement. The Argies knew just who those men were, and we all wondered if they had been selected, by a cruel and implacable *Junta*, for an especially hard time. I knew that several of my own Medical Squadron boys had served in the Islands, and that two of them had actually married Falkland Islands girls. Their families were now under the Argentine yoke. This high-handed Argentine *coup de main* had now become a very personal matter indeed...

Our little Regiment was unique in the British Armed Forces. The Royal Marines, with their usual clear thinking, had identified 'combat logistics' as a key feature in the maintenance of fighting efficiency. In our daily lives we are almost unaware of the procurement, delivery and storage procedures for what appears on our supermarket shelves. 3 Commando Brigade could be tasked to be ready to fight in a variety of global locations, with that versatility further complicated by four main climatic conditions – hot dry, hot wet, cold dry – and cold wet. In 1972 the Corps decided to create a hybrid formation of specialist Army and Royal Marine personnel to cope with the various logistic needs that would result, with every key position within the Commando Logistic Regiment, whether at officer or NCO level, filled by an individual who had earned the green beret.

The Commanding Officers alternated between the Army and Royal Marines, with the Army candidates coming from either the Royal Army Ordnance Corps (RAOC – ammunition, explosives, fuel and combat rations), the Royal Corps of Transport (RCT – delivery to the front line), the Royal Electrical and Mechanical Engineers (REME – repair and maintenance of all equipment) and uniquely, the Royal Navy Medical Service, responsible for combat casualty care.

I'd actually been part of 'Commando Logs' at its inaugural

parade in 1972, and although it took a while to get the tentage and equipment scales of a 'Light Field Ambulance' properly sorted, you could see that Medical Squadron was a sound concept, and a key component of the versatile replenishment and repair system that now operated in support of 3 Commando Brigade. All that planning and specialist training was now on the line. It was time to prove ourselves.

Transport Squadron began grinding up the M5 motorway to various ammunition depots around the country. Advance parties were dispatched to the various Royal Fleet Auxiliary ships that would be carrying us and all the War Maintenance Reserve stores of rations, fuel, ammunition and spares. There were something like thirty thousand tons of all these combat supplies to collect and load, and a new acronym entered our vocabularies. 'STUFT' was shorthand for *Shipping Taken Up From Trade*, so there were lots of jokes about being told to 'get STUFT' if you needed a vessel to meet your specialist requirements. Over sixty such merchant ships were eventually requisitioned for HM Government service in the South Atlantic.

For me, there were a few different buttons to push. The Defence Medical Equipment Depot at Andover had already been alerted, and was packing and dispatching Naval medical war stores for the Fleet as fast as it could. Despite this existing workload, my request for the Royal Marines' medical specialist supplements was met with a cheerful 'can-do' attitude by Captain Chas Kirton, the Mobilisation Stores Officer at Ludgershall. By noon on Saturday, we had all the extra surgical kit needed for our two Naval Surgical Support Teams on its way down to us in Plymouth.

These teams were also alerted and mobilised, one from the Royal Naval Hospital (RNH) in Plymouth and the other from RNH Haslar, near Portsmouth. The Haslar team also arrived that night, handicapped by the absence of their Administrative Officer who was abroad, on leave. There was also another problem. Because we were likely to deploy to war in Royal Navy ships, a really high level Command decision had to be taken on the issue of whether there could be any women in the surgical teams.

Nobody had given this matter any real thought in peacetime. If the ladies had to be replaced at this late stage, such an action would remove the female nursing element at a stroke, and would also create big problems in finding suitable male replacements in time. Needless to say, the girls (who had trained hard in peacetime) were a bit upset as well. While we awaited a final decision from on high, events moved swiftly. The Senior Medical Officer at HQ Commando Forces was also away somewhere, so I had to call in regularly at Mount Wise, to give technical advice and be made aware of further developments.

The senior staff officer in charge of Logistics and Personnel, Colonel Ian Baxter, then took me aside there on Saturday. He told me that the Ministry of Defence were requisitioning the luxury liner *Canberra*, then on the last leg of a round-the-world voyage. She was due in Southampton on the following Wednesday, but meanwhile I was to join a small advance party that would leave UK the next day, fly to Gibraltar, and join the ship there. There was no-one else with the right seniority or medical experience to send, so there had to be more frantic preparations before I put the reins once more into the capable hands of my deputy, Lieutenant Fred Cook RM.

There was just enough time for an updating brief to the two Surgical Support Teams back in our Medical Squadron lines. Outside my office, all our stores were being transferred into wooden logistic containers nicknamed 'chacons'. We began to realise just how serious Her Majesty's Government was being about the whole endeavour when we asked for over thirty of these chacons to be delivered. Normally the delay between ordering and receiving would be measured in months. On this occasion, a stream of dockyard lorries produced the full order the next day.

Sunday, April 4th

My family rose and breakfasted early, as we had over a hundred miles to cover before 0930, my reporting time for the Gibraltar flight. The journey up to Somerset was uneventful, apart from a stream of lorries heading the other way to Plymouth. Some were recognisable by their battle-plate numbers as Transport Squadron vehicles; most of them were right down on their axles, moving slowly with heavy loads of artillery ammunition.

Despite all the secrecy that was supposed to surround our departure, the Royal Naval Air Station at Yeovilton was throbbing with activity, and the main car park by the Fleet Air Arm Museum already filled with interested spectators. Parked near them on the apron, a four-engined Belfast freighter was ingesting two stripped-down Wessex helicopters into its massive belly. I visited an aircrew friend in Station Flight for a chat, then heard the familiar whine of Sea Harrier jet engines. A flight of four fighters taxied past and then lined up on the main runway. James, my nine year-old son, decided that they had laid on the whole performance just for him, and we waved as the quartet rolled forward into a very noisy stream take-off.

Then it was my turn. As our Hercules freighter trundled sedately down to the end of the duty runway, I caught a glimpse of Susie and James standing by the car. It was no use waving back. We had said our farewells already, and had taken those last fierce hugs and kisses that were so bitter-sweet. I was off to war. The possibility of death was a very real one, and I was well aware that this might have been my very last sight of them. Minutes later we were accelerating down a broad asphalt ribbon, then climbing steeply above the patchwork fields of England and setting course for the south.

The flight crew were very friendly and invited us up to the cockpit. Leading our group was Captain Robert Ward, a Royal Marines officer who was a free-fall parachuting enthusiast. The

Canberra liaison officer was Sammy Bradford, a Deputy Captain who knew the ship intimately, having actually commanded her. He was also a Captain in the Royal Naval Reserve and therefore understood the needs of the Senior Service. Our aircraft was eventually destined for Ascension Island, a pimple of volcanic ash and rock positioned just below the Equator. Its hold was loaded up with engineering spares and support crew for the two Wessex helicopters which were due to follow on behind us in the much bigger Belfast.

Four hours later we let down through cloud, well clear of the Pillars of Hercules, then turned in towards the Rock. Our cold, dry aircraft was now scudding along over a grey Atlantic, through warm moist air. The tricky turn on to finals along the edge of Spanish airspace demanded intense concentration, and I watched, fascinated, as several large drops of condensed moisture fell from the overhead panels straight down onto the pilot's neck.

Suddenly, the co-pilot increased power and we overshot the tiny runway, then climbed and began to trundle around the Rock again. We had a nose wheel problem apparently, but it was the cockpit indicator light at fault because the engineer climbed down underneath the flight deck, fiddled with something, and all was well. There followed another smooth approach, full flap as we turned in over the fleets of ballasted tankers and the Russian fish factory vessels, then a steep descent angle and suddenly we were down on the ground with a roar of reversing propeller blades.

A party led by the local P&O agents greeted us, and, while the others went to a hotel to relax, Bob Ward, Sammy Bradford and I were taken to Flag Officer Gibraltar's residence for a G&T and a quick briefing. I then went and paid my respects to the Medical Officer in Charge of the RN Hospital, and we discussed likely routes of evacuation for casualties. The harbour below us was nearly empty in the evening sunlight, the storage depots in a similar state. Rear Admiral Woodward's Task Force had just been through for replenishment before steaming south. Even for a Sunday, Gibraltar was strangely quiet.

Later on, under cover of darkness, the agent's cutter took us out of the calm inner harbour into a gentle swell. Suddenly she was there – a huge white cathedral of lights that moved in close and then stopped, waiting for us to come alongside. The rails were crowded with passengers in evening dress, all wondering about this unscheduled diversion. They watched as seven men with short haircuts and military bergen rucksacks climbed the rope ladder that had been lowered from a baggage port.

The passengers' curiosity later turned to anxiety when the rumour was leaked, quite deliberately, that we were Customs and Excise rummage officers, boarding early for the final part of the voyage! The plugs on the satellite telephone switchboard were then pulled, as a counter-rumour began to circulate about our true purpose. No-one back in England was allowed to know that the ship had been taken into Government service, until the Prime Minister had made an announcement in the House of Commons.

Up in the Captain's beautifully appointed Day Cabin, Bob Ward broke the news. There were sighs of relief that P&O would not have to fly all the passengers home there and then. As the impressive-looking, official requisitioning document was carefully inspected by all those present, I could detect excitement and anticipation in some of the younger Merchant Navy officers. The Purser, a charming individual sporting a set of 1939–45 miniature medal ribbons on the lapel of his white mess jacket, looked thoughtful and reflective. He was a veteran of the Atlantic convoys, and had seen active service in his early career.

War, with all its attendant confusion, risk and danger, was about to threaten his well-ordered life again.

Monday, April 5th – Tuesday, April 6th

A quick look around *Canberra*'s public rooms, followed by a much slower and more careful inspection, confirmed that there were only two real possibilities for the medical areas. Our casualty handling and treatment priorities were for wide, open spaces – plus rapid access to these areas from the helicopter arrival point, wherever that was going to be. Right aft lay the Peacock Room, with a small swimming pool just outside. The weight of steel girders and plates for a helo platform here would have seriously affected the ship's handling, so that possibility had to be abandoned.

The next choice for the casualties' arrival point involved a change in level, between the midships swimming pool (which was now being converted into a flight deck platform), and the deck below. Here, the starboard waistdeck led along into a pair of doors that opened into the Stadium Theatre and night club complex. This proposal was not as easy to create as it first sounded. We could see at once that the nearby passenger lifts were designed for two couples in evening dress, not for a loaded stretcher, or 'litter' in American parlance. Therefore, some sort of sloping ramp was required; this had to be designed and constructed. Whatever scheme was adopted, such a steeply tilted descent might pose real problems when getting injured casualties up and down, and we also needed to think a bit more about that.

Despite her length and bulk, *Canberra* began to roll and pitch in a choppy Bay of Biscay, and I began to feel sick! Dr Peter Mayner, the ship's surgeon, came to my rescue with an injection. He was a great character and, like the rest of the ship's officers and crew, could not have been more helpful and friendly as we tried to imagine preparing their lovely liner for her new 'fast troopship and floating hospital' role. In fact, our working relationship became so good that we decided one lunchtime to form the *Canberra Medical Society*.

My instinct was that a social as well as scientific programme would help to ensure that all the medical, dental and nursing staff (yet to be embarked) would be pulling in the same direction when the balloon eventually went up. Peter became the Society's Chairman, with me as Secretary, while Dr Susie West, Assistant Ship's Surgeon, 'volunteered' for the post of Treasurer. Meanwhile, as the various resources in the ship were being allocated, I also managed to requisition the former massage parlour as the new Medical Squadron office!

The final night at sea for those passengers who had circled the globe was a grand affair. The dinner tables in the Pacific Restaurant sagged under multiple courses of an impeccable standard, and there was a lively cabaret to follow. Looking around the Stadium night club with its plush fittings and thick carpet, it was very difficult to imagine bloodied operating tables and groaning wounded positioned there. Were we really going to war? At the back of my mind I knew the answer already. All the rhetoric and diplomacy in the civilised world would not be enough to shift the Argentine troops from the Falkland Islands.

We were going to have to shove them off ourselves.

Wednesday, April 7th – Friday, April 9th

Southampton degenerated into something of a nightmare. *Canberra* lay alongside a narrow wharf that was opened on to by a series of large baggage sheds. The drizzle fell from a leaden sky as Vosper Thornycroft's skilled workforce began to cut metal and clear away any upper deck fittings that would obstruct a helicopter's approach to the midships area. Tons of steel girder lengths with mysterious chalk markings appeared in and amongst the quayside jumble of freight and stores. These were lifted carefully up and across into the empty main swimming pool, then bolted together. The weight of water in the pool, when full, had been calculated as about seventeen tons; the new steel forest that would underpin the welded flight deck plates had to be about the same.

The edge for the midships flight deck was the aperture cut in the upper deck for the pool; concept and design soon became reality thanks to some rapid engineering drawings and the diverse skills of the workforce. By dusk, on the day they started, all traces of the swimming pool on the upper deck had disappeared, and a quarter of the old gap had been replaced by a flush-fitting deck surface which was completed the next day.

The next problem concerned how to get casualties (received on the flight deck) down one level to the Stadium night club, which had been selected as the only suitable area for their Triage, Resuscitation and Treatment. The main passenger lifts were smooth and silent, but quite incapable of taking a loaded stretcher. We had to make some different arrangements.

This time, the men from Vospers, plus one of the RN medical officers and a Royal Marine carpenter, combined forces to come up with a fantastic solution. A vertical bulkhead was surveyed and then cut out, to reveal a storage locker behind. Some more sheet steel was acquired and used to extend the length of the original piece. The whole assembly was then angled away through 45 degrees to form a sloping steel ramp which was firmly secured, and sheathed in plywood.

Next, it was fitted with a Southampton dock porter's trolley, which was tilted backwards to rest against the slope. At the bottom end, a buffer stop was fitted and the trolley made to run in the space between two 3" high wooden edges fitted to the ramp, and which extended all the way up to the flight deck above. At the top lip, a wide roller mechanism was installed, around which was fed a long manila rope, in turn secured to a pulley on the top cross-bar of the trolley. The rope had a decoratively knotted end which, when pulled towards the stern of the *Canberra*, caused the trolley to move smoothly up the ramp, and had the benefit of some mechanical advantage as well.

When I showed the transparency of our 'funicular' trolley ramp in the Pentagon a year later, it produced gasps of disbelief. Apparently, what we Brits describe as being created by 'Heath Robinson' they label over there as being derived from the drawing board of a chap called 'Rube Goldberg'! One US Marine Corps voice growled about 'a million dollar problem and the ten-cent solution'. It really didn't matter, because the design worked perfectly, and was absolutely typical of many successful 'lash-ups' and 'bodgits' that were devised at various levels throughout the Task Force.

Along with ammunition and other bits and pieces, boxes and boxes of medical stores were also delivered to the quayside, then carefully netted and lifted up on to A Deck aft. The wharfies and crane drivers were tireless and cheerful – but almost religious about their tea breaks. Eventually, after moaning about this apparent waste of valuable time, we realised that they were absolutely right. I learned an important lesson from them, which proved vital later on – hot sweet tea, at appropriate and regular intervals, leads on to more productive working hours when coping with a crisis.

A pallet load of Argentine corned beef was then delivered, causing great hilarity amongst the shore parties. In the other direction, piles of furnishings materialised from the bowels of the ship to be piled up on the quayside, all to be replaced later at the Ministry of Defence's expense.

The Royal Marines of 40 and 42 Commando arrived, laden with kit, followed by 3 Para disembarking from their buses, their camouflage smocks contrasting sharply with the blue dress uniforms of their Regimental band. On the medical side, Surgeon Captain (Frank) Roger Wilkes also joined as Medical Officer in Charge, accompanied by the newly-created Surgical Team Three (SST 3).

His team looked dejected and tired. I had very little idea of the 'stop-start' routines that they had been subjected to throughout the day; orders and counter-orders had washed over them, combined with rumour and misinterpretation of national and world events. The main news was that all their female members *had* eventually been removed from potential front line service, and it was a thoroughly hacked-off Roger Wilkes that finally boarded the *Canberra*.

He was a short, stocky firebrand. As a young medical officer in an aircraft carrier he had been awarded the MBE for his initiative and determination in caring for a Naval Air Mechanic who had suffered a 'flail chest' in a flight deck accident. The man's breastbone had been crushed as a jet fighter's cockpit canopy closed without warning. By inserting six thick catgut sutures around the ribs to each side, Roger Wilkes had managed to stabilise the chest by securing it to a wooden frame hastily constructed by the Chief Shipwright. His actions played a key part in saving the man's life.

I had worked for him previously when doing a recall from the Royal Naval Reserve in the hospital at Stonehouse, and had liked what I saw. He was a rumbustious, no-nonsense sort of consultant who enjoyed teaching, loved his patients and would leave no stone unturned in his efforts on their behalf. I greeted him personally, and told him excitedly about everything that had happened – the way we had advanced our plans for designating the medical areas within the ship, and how well I was getting on with the ship's surgeon, Dr Peter Mayner.

When I had finished, FRW (as we all knew him) eyed me coldly and said that he very much resented being talked down to by a subordinate officer (I think he meant figuratively rather than literally, as I was over a foot and a half taller than him) and that he did not take kindly to either my attitude or approach. I was rather surprised and disappointed – but knew from past experience that FRW could be difficult at times.

That bit of unpleasantness over, I greeted the rest of my colleagues, trying to welcome them on board. Some were old friends from time in the RN hospital at Stonehouse, and the links were quickly re-established. However, one chap, an oral surgeon, looked at me with a rather disdainful expression on his face and refused to shake my extended and welcoming hand.

That surprised and rather hurt me. He obviously blamed Rick Jolly for the lengthy period of being messed about that he and the rest of SST 3 had been subjected to. Of course, the indecision and vacillation had occurred way above my level, but with this calculated slight coming on top of Roger Wilkes's public dressing-down, my heart was sinking fast. We simply had to get on in a spirit of co-operation and shared effort, but this was not really happening. I went back to my cabin and sat down to think about the problem.

Twenty minutes later, there was a knock on the door. One of the SST 3 ratings stood outside, and his message was blunt. Surgeon Captain Wilkes wanted to see me *immediately* in his cabin, which was one deck below. I swallowed hard and went down to get another bollocking. When I knocked on FRW's door, a gruff voice shouted from within. As I entered, I noted that the cabin's only occupant had his back to me. His terse order that I should shut the door was obeyed. Roger Wilkes then turned round to face me, with a sparkling gin and tonic in each hand. In a genuine and contrite way he apologised for being so sharp with me, and said that he very much appreciated the preparatory hard work that I had put in on his behalf, and that I did not deserve any of the bad things that he had said on arrival. He then offered me the gin with a big smile on his face.

The relief that washed over me was so strong that I can still remember the sensation. It may have been a deliberate management ploy, but I was now ready to die for him. I learned so much from that wonderful man. He was a joy to serve, and the whole experience of working for him, from then on until we went ashore in the Islands, proved to be stimulating and happy. He was tough, uncompromising, devoted, thoughtful and utterly loyal to his team. Why the system subsequently missed him out from the South Atlantic Honours List remains another of those strange mysteries that are beyond the understanding of us ordinary mortals.

And the 'gnasher-basher' (dentist)? He did not apologise or explain – but luckily, I never had to speak to him again.

To my surprise I then discovered that although we now had the Plymouth-based Surgical Support Team Two (SST 2) embarked, someone had ordered their colleagues in SST 1 to return to their base at Haslar, in Portsmouth, and then take passage south in HMS *Hermes*, instead of remaining with us. It was a strange decision, because they were supposedly earmarked and dedicated to the Royal Marines, and had been given both the appropriate equipment and training for this task. I assumed that this unforeseen dilution of our surgical capabilities had been authorised by the Brigade Commander in my absence. After all, he was the ultimate 'owner' of this wartime asset, but it later transpired that Julian Thompson had *not* been consulted at all. As a result, half of our surgical capability and expertise had been chopped out without his permission...

I tried to console myself with the thought that they would be available to the 'Carrier' part of the Task Force in the event of some disaster before we got to the Falklands, and indeed was delighted later on that they proved useful in the aftermath of the attack on HMS *Sheffield*, but it was the first inkling of the kind of attitude that Julian and I would encounter later on, when the Brigade's medical organisation was subject to a hijacking attempt by another senior Naval medical officer who suddenly turned up as we sailed down south.

The medical officers (MOs) of 40 and 42 Commando were Surgeon Lieutenants Mike Hayward and Ross Adley respectively, both green-bereted. 3 Para's MO was Captain John Burgess of the

Royal Army Medical Corps (RAMC); as his reinforcement, he had a charming Ulsterman named John Graham, also a RAMC Captain. Worryingly, I noticed that neither JG nor his staff were Airborne trained; they had not completed P Company, or acquired their parachute 'wings'. This would seriously limit my options to deploy them forward as battle casualty replacements in the event of death or injury in the 3 Para medical team.

An amusing incident then took place which resulted in disciplinary action having to be taken later on. Five Royal Marines driving heavy lorries in 42 Cdo had brought the embarking unit's baggage up from Plymouth, and also brought their own kit along as well. They parked the vehicles neatly, handed their 'work tickets' in to the military Command Post that had now been established on the dock, and then smuggled themselves on board. They owned up eventually, and were paraded in front of their CO who, while trying to keep a straight face, sentenced them to 'stoppage of shore leave' for a month!

Finally, and almost unbelievably, everyone was over the brow, inboard – and we were ready to go. As the sun dipped below the horizon and daylight slowly faded, we cast off. The Para and Royal Marines bands struck up *Sailing* and *Land of Hope and Glory* as the liner edged out into Southampton Water. Cars honked their horns and flashed headlights as *Canberra* gathered way, her decks lined with thoughtful men, some shedding silent tears as the town of Hamble slipped slowly by along the port side. It was a most emotional moment. Twenty-seven of us would never see England again.

Saturday, April 10th – Friday, April 16th

At sea, a routine began to shape up. The men paraded at 0830. We discussed the detail for the day then, and tried to integrate our training requirements with the space available. The medical officers also met at the same time, but separately under John Williams, a consultant physician. Following this, John and I would descend to C Deck for our morning brief with the Boss. FRW was a good host and had an amusing and original mind. In particular, his memory for the detail of past events was incredible. When necessary, we also discussed signals of medical relevance that had come in, and then drafted our replies.

The 'crazy ideas' phase was obviously underway back in London. Some clever, desk-bound chap had dusted off a large tropical medicine textbook to warn us about the tick and louse-borne diseases that were endemic to Argentina, and therefore, in *his* opinion at least, now liable to be encountered throughout the Falklands. We gently enquired how substantial this conclusion could be, in view of the cold and wet conditions prevailing in the Islands compared with the hot and dry *pampas* of the South American mainland. Personally, I thought that high-speed metallic fragments would form a much greater potential hazard! However, a cloud of signals then started flying around in response from other ships in the Task Force, mostly demanding gallons of disinfectant and delousing powder by the first available airdrop.

John Williams also got going on working up *Canberra*'s medical Organisation for Action. He beavered away, filling a large bound book with clinical policy notes and sudden ideas, which eventually distilled down into two concise typewritten pages. Drama ensued one day when the book disappeared along with the sheets, to be returned by a sticky-fingered culprit soon after John made a broadcast to the ship emphasising the nature and life-saving importance of its contents.

There were also several arguments over priorities for training areas, fuelled by ignorance among some of the embarked military about our role. I was well aware of the fact that we were travelling southwards with our potential customers. At the same time, as thinking medics, we were not anxious to point out that piece of brutal reality too bluntly. As usual, a few of the Para and Royal Marine officers refused to see beyond the requirements of their own training programmes.

This issue came to a head one day at a ship's meeting when the Training Officer of one of the two Commando units embarked insisted that as his men would be the first ashore in the Falklands, their needs were far more important than those of the 'bloody medics'. I asked him to spell out his surname (which I actually knew perfectly well) and pretended to write it down with exaggerated care. In response to his query as to why I was doing this, I explained that Medical Squadron always had a *'NOT TO BE RESUSCITATED'* name board hung up in the Admissions Area, and that I wanted to be sure that *his* name was spelled correctly when we painted it on that afternoon.

Of course, this was all a complete spoof and invention, but quite suddenly, he conceded the point!

All the historical and geographical reference books that we could lay our hands on were being studied carefully. In the ship's library, I looked in vain for any natural, predisposing ill-will towards Great Britain amongst the masses in Argentina. Every part of the British homeland had contributed to the economic and manufacturing history of the distant *pampas*, from the Scottish input to ship building, light engineering and the railways, through the English invention of the *estancia* which divided up and made better use of the estates, and finally to the contribution of Wales to life in Patagonia, where the sheep roamed freely and the Welsh language was spoken with as equal facility as Spanish.

Was it some part of their Mediterranean heritage that had flashed up their dislike of Great Britain so easily? The Italians and Spanish had historical reason to hate the people who had defeated them so often in the past, and we were after all the descendants of Sir Francis Drake, Admiral Lord Nelson and Field Marshal the Duke of Wellington – yet all around them in Buenos Aires were public buildings that bore the stamp of British architecture and design.

One history graduate in our ship described the Argentines as 'Italians who speak Spanish, behave like the French, but wish they were English'. We heard that there was even a Harrods store in Buenos Aires, although not specifically linked with the Knightsbridge establishment. Our hopes were that their love of martial display would not be backed up with any determination or force. However, Marine Garcia, one of our drivers, had been born and raised in South America before moving to finish his schooling in England, and probably had the best insight of all:

'Sir', he said to me one morning, 'these guys will *not* negotiate from what they perceive is a position of strength, and even if you convinced them that they were not as strong as they thought, they would *never* make concessions to a woman...' It was also amusing to note, in the Appendix to the *Navy List*, that the top award for young officers passing out of training at Dartmouth was the Argentine Navy Gold Medal...

Alongside us, the men of the Commando Forces Band trained as hard as anyone. Gradually, they absorbed all the minor military jobs on board, until finally they had a range of over 30 different skills on offer, in addition to the playing of their music that they did so well. They were a wonderful asset with their willingness and good humour, as well as being right up to the mark when it came to the practical aspects of stretcher bearing and First Aid training.

Alternate evenings also saw the *Canberra Medical Society's* programme getting under way, launched with great success by an inaugural 'annual cocktail party' in Peter Mayner's cabin. It was an excellent evening, with barriers broken down on all sides between the hospital types and the general duties doctors. FRW was in particularly good form.

We invited Lieutenant Colonel Hew Pike to speak to us about Airborne Forces, and then wined and dined with him and his 'Centurions' – the company commanders of 3 Para – as our guests. There was similar treatment for the officers of 40 and 42 Commandos, in return for talks about the Corps and Norwegian operations respectively by their COs, Malcolm Hunt and Nick Vaux. Gradually, their collective reservations and concerns about their medical support disappeared, along with our difficulties about training areas. About this time we also made the first emergency broadcast on the Tannoy:

'For exercise, for exercise. Casualties inbound within the hour. Rig emergency medical facilities…'

The boys turned to with a will, and operating tables and anaesthetic trolleys appeared from storage places all around the Stadium theatre. Arctic camouflage netting got strung from the deckhead to divide off the various areas; stores and stretchers were laid out, and the adjoining Bonito Night Club actually began to look like a ward. This evolution was repeated several times, and soon the timings were down to Field Gun levels as the participants became more practised.

Saturday, April 17th

Overnight we lay alongside the refuelling jetty at Freetown, a rather scruffy-looking port in Sierra Leone. There was some suspicion that the Government had only allowed *Canberra* to refuel there because the big white liner was basically a 'hospital ship'! If the local British Consul was therefore a bit surprised to see several thousand 'male nurses' lining the rails to ogle his teenage daughters, he said nothing, and merely contented himself with a rapid tour of our emergency medical areas. Luckily, we had left everything up and rigged, in order to test the lighting systems that night, and our cover story had some credibility. Long before dawn we were at sea again, heading for the Equator.

Sunday, April 18th – Thursday, May 6th

For just over a fortnight, we swung at anchor off Ascension Island. The geology of its thirty-four square miles seemed a little bizarre, with huge piles of brown and blue-grey volcanic rocks and dust that rose steeply in the centre of the island to a cooler vegetation-covered feature aptly named Green Mountain. The ecology was equally strange. Its only natural vegetation consisted of thorn bushes, satellite dishes and radio aerials. The BBC World Service owned some of these, as did Cable and Wireless, while the secret squirrels of GCHQ back in Cheltenham were also quietly active. There were supposed to be nearly a thousand residents, although from our anchorage out in the heavy and unpredictable swell off English Bay, there was very little hint of that.

A single 10,000 foot long runway, built during WW2, maintained and still physically owned by the United States of America was the real match-winning feature here. The Americans had some important missile-tracking instrumentation in position as part of the Cape Canaveral testing range. The airfield was curiously called 'Wideawake', but managed to live up to this name at one point during the campaign when over five hundred aircraft movements were recorded on one particularly busy day.

Rear Admiral Woodward's main carrier battle group had already sailed. Around us on the bright blue sea lay the anchored ships of the amphibious landing force, as well as a large grey

American Navy fuel tanker. This was secured to a buoy off George Town, from which a pipeline ran to the 'tank farm' located next to the airfield. The whole arrangement was a godsend to the Task Force – over twelve million gallons of American aviation kerosene were pumped ashore and used during the campaign.

The water teemed with unattractive little black fish that apparently possessed piranha-like qualities. The stories about the voraciousness of these predators grew in the telling, and I was seriously questioned by one of the journalists on board as to the identity of some unlucky Task Force bather who had actually been torn to pieces by them. This particular representative of 'Fleet Street's Finest' was not the only victim of this lovely 'bite'.

We also had some fun with another hard-drinking and know-it-all reporter from one of the 'red top' tabloids. I solemnly informed him that his luck was in, because one of our trainee surgeons was a real wizard at organ transplantion. We told him that, if he was shot through the belly, we would try to exchange his worn-out liver for a new one – and then he could start his prodigious drinking career all over again. While that was sinking in, we even asked if he had any objection to receiving an Argentine donor organ if one became available. It was all a bit of military black humour of course, but the poor chap went white-faced, and tried to make me swear on the Bible that I'd never arrange such a procedure, and would finish him off with a lethal injection instead. Transplant surgery in a Forward Dressing Station? Come alongside, Jack...

A hammerhead shark flapped lazily by, the sunlight dappling on the grey back as its dorsal fin creased the surface swell. All around us, helicopters, landing craft and Mexeflote pontoons busied themselves with tactical re-stowage. Most of the stores and combat supplies had been loaded higgledy-piggledy into ships to meet the sailing deadlines from Plymouth, Portsmouth and Southampton, and much effort now had to be expended in order to get the right mix of combat supplies into the correct ships for an opposed landing when we reached the Falklands.

I went across to the LSL *Sir Lancelot*, which was hot and stuffy. However, my Medical Squadron boys in No. 1 Medical Troop were very cheerful. Their boss, a Royal Navy Medical Services officer named Malcolm Hazell, had displayed his lunatic enthusiasm for road running by actually completing a full Marathon distance on a small 60-yard circuit of the landing ship's cramped deck. It was an extreme effort of stamina and skill, especially as LSLs possess the stability of a drunken corkscrew in anything other than a dry dock.

Back on the 'Great White Whale', as *Canberra* had now been nicknamed, training continued relentlessly. From dawn to dusk, the marines and paras crunched round and round *her* quarter mile of Promenade Deck in heavy-booted, muscular and sweating squads. Some of them were now carrying loaded bergens, or machine guns and anti-tank weapons in order to increase the punishment. Such was the enthusiasm for individuals keen to do extra training of this sort, the Promenade Deck had to be put out of bounds between evening dinner and breakfast, because the noise of thudding boots kept the senior officers awake in the cabins of C Deck just below. The company commanders, worried about the repetitive nature of this and some of the classroom work, pressed anxiously for a chance to get ashore and march in a straight line for once, and also find a firing range in order to zero their infantry and support weapons.

Over the two week period we were there, everyone got that chance, and it was gratefully taken. On one remarkable day, 3 Para's anti-tank platoon fired 37 training years' worth of 105 mm ammunition from their Wombat recoilless rifles. These weapons were not earmarked for service ashore in the Falklands, and so they simply demolished a twenty foot high lump of volcanic rock with them. Even the medics managed a march across the Island, from English Bay towards Wideawake airfield. The hot tarmac meant a crop of blisters for me after five miles, but the pain was well worth it. Peter Mayner came with us in a vehicle, as did some of the Naval Medical Assistants who were not Commando-trained.

On the range, I watched the Brigade Staff fire their pistols in practice, then saw their renewed (and much improved) efforts after a SAS officer attached to Julian Thompson's staff gave them a short demonstration. It was the most effective piece of military tuition I'd ever seen, but surely something would have gone badly wrong if the Brigade Commander ever had to fire his 9 mm Browning pistol in self defence.

Overhead, Hercules transports and Sea Harrier fighters kept the normally sleepy airfield circuit busy. On several occasions I also took advantage of the empty co-pilot's seat in *Canberra*'s resident Mk. 4 Sea King helicopter. Its two 'Jungly' pilots, Lieutenants Ron Crawford and Martin Eales, were happy to have someone to talk to, and also let me fly many of the sectors as we practiced early morning airborne assaults from *Canberra* to Wideawake's main dispersal area. Some of the boys in the back became a little anxious when they recognised me up front, and then saw just whose hands were operating the cyclic and collective levers! The weather was glorious, and the flying totally exhilarating.

Around the dispersal area, about a dozen RAF Victor tanker aircraft were densely parked. They had refuelled each other, as well as the Vulcan bomber which had put the Stanley airfield out of action – or so we were told at the time. This big beast – codenamed '*Black Buck*' – was parked near the main air traffic control building, with an armed sentry guarding it and at the same time sheltering from the sun beneath its huge delta wings.

Another afternoon was exciting for a different reason. On the ammunition freighter *Elk*, a crewman developed sudden and severe abdominal pain. The Duty Medical Officer from *Canberra* was alerted, went to the aft pontoon, and got into a landing craft.

Unfortunately, he then forgot which ship had called for help, and spent most of the afternoon touring the anchored fleet.

Elk was a P&O ship, so when Peter Mayner heard on the P&O grapevine that one of 'his' crewmen was ill, he commandeered a Rigid Raider, a sort of military speedboat. Then a Wessex helicopter arrived over *Canberra's* deck with some underslung stores, heard about the problem – and offered to assist. Without knowing what was happening elsewhere, I was summoned from my cabin, boarded this aircraft and was then winched down to *Elk's* main deck. There, I found that Peter had already arrived, soaking wet after his high-speed ride. We agreed that the crewman patient was obviously very unwell. He'd probably perforated a duodenal ulcer, and a boat journey back to *Canberra* would have been cruel, and probably lethal. So, we carefully winched him up into the *Wessex*, transferred him as smoothly as possible, and an hour later Phil Shouler was working inside his patient's belly. The provisional diagnosis was soon confirmed, and the hole in his small intestine neatly oversewn. We'd been involved in some real surgery at last!

At about this time a little cloud appeared on my personal horizon, in the shape of a senior naval doctor who turned up and claimed that *he* was now going to be running the medical aspects of the show. Roger Wilkes and I were both astonished by this chap's vision of how the Amphibious Force's casualty treatment and evacuation arrangements were going to be altered. According to him, all the medical assets of 3 Commando Brigade were now to be made available for his plans, and because he was the senior MO in terms of rank, there would not be any argument about his intentions.

It was immediately obvious that this chap had no real understanding of the subtle difference between '*seniority*' (a quality based on time in rank) and '*command*' (a specific set of powers and responsibilities vested or delegated, by Her Majesty's authority, in an individual). My own take on this little difficulty was that as the Senior Medical Officer of 3 Commando Brigade Royal Marines, I was the lawful custodian of a set of medical support assets which belonged, not to me, but to Brigadier Julian Thompson. While as his medical adviser I might well 'propose' a scheme of casualty treatment and evacuation in response to his operational plans, in the end it was he who would actually authorised how they were 'disposed'.

Sadly, my attitude was regarded as 'obstructionist' and 'difficult' by the new arrival, and a crisis was looming. I went across to HMS *Fearless* and discussed my problems with the Brigade staff officer responsible for day-to-day management of all logistic assets. Major Gerry Wells-Cole was a long-standing chum from 42 Commando and active service in Belfast, some eight years previously. He and I knew each other well; he was also sympathetic to my point of view but at the same time reluctant to burden Julian Thompson with yet another problem. I quite understood.

A day later I came back to him and said that we really needed clarification on this issue, because I was finding it difficult to refuse a senior officer who, although I called him 'Sir' because of his rank, I had absolutely no respect for – since he was trying to give me unlawful, and potentially dangerous orders. We found a gap in the Brigadier's programme and went to see him.

JHAT (Brigadier *Julian Howard Atherden Thompson*) was in his cabin, poring over various charts and land maps of the Falklands. He was obviously under strain, but at the same time (as his personal physician) I could sense that he was quite up to the task of grappling with the myriad problems of deciding where he was going to put the Brigade ashore.

I explained the nature of my problem as succinctly as I could. Julian Thompson's eyes flared when he heard of this latest attempt to hijack his medical personnel and their stores. He had already been angered by the arbitrary decision by a higher formation to remove SST 1 from his Order of Battle – without any one asking him.

Julian fixed us both with his clear but tired eyes. 'Let me make this clear', he said, 'you – Rick – are my *personal* physician. You are also the Brigade's staff medical adviser and, furthermore, I have delegated to you the command of all my medical second line assets. When a Brigade operation is planned, you will discuss with me the best way for all the casualty handling and evacuation teams to be deployed...'

He paused, then turned to his Logistics adviser: 'Gerry, when Rick and I have been through all these options, and I have made my decision, you will be the instrument through which my orders are executed. Do I make myself clear?'

We both grinned at him in our relief, saluted and made to leave the cabin. I was then summoned back, and ordered to close the door. In a state of some trepidation, I awaited what we used to call an 'interview without coffee'. My Brigade Commander stood up from where he was leaning over the table, stretched luxuriously – and laughed: 'Rick, I think I've met this chap, but he hasn't said anything to me about stealing my Dressing Stations. From what you say, I suspect that we're going to have a few more problems with him...' Relieved that my ultimate boss wasn't angry with me for wasting his time, I nodded as JHAT continued: '...so, we had better agree on a radio title for him, so you can contact me if he causes us any more problems!'

I laughed out loud at his suggestion, which had to remain classified and personal between us, and then left the cabin in high spirits. From here on in I would think of this interloper as 'NE', or 'Not Entitled'. The chap would indeed cause me further difficulties (more than the Argentine Air Force in fact), but I can now recount these facts without prejudice or malice. Indeed, thirty years later, I have almost forgiven 'NE'! The point was that I now had the 'top cover' that was needed to resist any further interference. What a man Julian was, and what a *leader* of men as well!

The Hospital Ship *Uganda* had joined up with us, but was causing problems. Because of her Red Cross markings, and her protected status under the terms of the Geneva Convention, any of the ship's communications equipment with military potential had been stripped out. Indeed, apart from a Marisat satellite link, which 3 Cdo Bde were not actually equipped with when ashore, there was no way I or anyone else could actually talk to her. Additionally, a policy of severe restriction in all radio transmissions had now been imposed. The Argentines were undoubtedly 'sniffing' the airwaves electronically, and trying to fix our positions. We had probably sold them all the the right kit to do this – and with an instruction package as well! What a juicy target *Canberra* would have been for one of their three remaining submarines, deployed on a last ditch and desperate long-range mission...

Poor *Uganda* seemed rather out of it all, and although we were still getting an absolute torrent of signal traffic from Northwood, no-one seemed to be very sure about the hospital ship's exact role or positioning. Would she come close in, brightly lit, or float around at a safe distance north of the Falklands, and use the converted hydrographic survey vessels, HM Ships *Hydra*, *Hecla* and *Herald* as hospital ambulance vessels to bring our patients out to her?

We were trying to wrestle with problems like these while the keen medical advisers back in London, anxious to make their personal contribution to the war effort, continued to bombard us. One warning concerned the dangers of constipation, and the need for COs to ensure that their crews remained 'regular'. A rather stylish Captain who had already been in anti-air action had the wit to reply that Northwood need not bother themselves too much on that subject, because close attention from Argentine Skyhawks had been having a powerful stimulant effect on his crew's bowels. I think he got an electronic reprimand...

Edith Meiklejohn left us to become the Matron of *Uganda*, and FRW escorted her across and looked around the big white hospital ship. He reported back that the atmosphere on board there was a little stiff and stilted, with something of an 'us and them' divide between the senior and junior officers. Later on I would be able to confirm this for myself, but at the time I was just grateful to see that our third-line of medical support was actually down and physically present with us in the South Atlantic.

During our time off Ascension, *Canberra* also hosted the newly-arrived CO of the Second Battalion of the Parachute Regiment. 2 Para had been due to travel to Belize for jungle warfare training, but were now coming south in the North Sea ferry *Norland*. 'H' Jones had been ordered to fly out early for briefings and familiarisation with the 3 Cdo Bde staff, and simply slotted into *Canberra's* training routines alongside 3 Para and his good friend Lt Col Hew Pike.

One evening, I met 'H' on the staircase, and introduced myself. He had been the UK Land Forces SPEARHEAD staff officer, and I'd been the recipient of one of his briefings two years previously. This fact broke the ice, and he began bombarding me with detailed questions about Medical Squadron's size and capabilities. He was a sharp cookie, with an excellent grasp of the fundamentals of battlefield medical care, and hinted that he was really positive about his own battalion MO and medical staff.

I tried to reassure him that all our Royal Marines medical doctrines were based on the Army's teaching and experience, and that we were used to delivering a high standard of care in some pretty harsh environments – like Northern Ireland, and Norway. H shook his head: 'I'm glad to hear that, Rick, and thanks for your positive attitude – but I've got a feeling that this particular fight is going to be very different. I'm reassured by what you're saying – but I hope that if "push" does come to "shove", you and your teams will all turn out to be good enough...'

He grinned at me – and was gone. I was to remember those words nearly four weeks later, when I examined his stiff and lifeless body after the battle for Goose Green.

During our time at Ascension much had happened else-where, both back in England and further down in the South

Atlantic. General Al Haig was shuttling back and forth between Buenos Aires, Washington and London, trying to persuade Galtieri that the Brits were serious – and that American support lay with with their historical allies rather than the *Junta*. The South Georgia element of the Task Force disabled an Argy submarine on the surface, and then re-took Grytviken in Her Majesty's name.

The Total Exclusion Zone (TEZ) around the Falklands was established at the end of April, and to emphasize the point that 'Big Boys' Rules' were now in operation, a lone RAF Vulcan bomber awoke the Argentine garrison at 0400 on the first of May with a stick of twenty-one 1000lb bombs onto the airfield, followed up by a huge 20 ship gaggle of Sea Harriers in a triple-wave dawn strike. All the aircraft returned safely, and the Falkland Islanders suddenly realised that the rumours were true – *'The Force was with them...'*

On the next day (Sunday, May 2nd) the flagship of the *Armada Argentina*, a Pearl Harbour-vintage cruiser named after the Argentine hero General Belgrano, was sunk by a torpedo salvo fired from HMS *Conqueror*. There was a wave of noisy good cheer throughout *Canberra* – followed by a quiet sadness at the thought of the inevitable casualties that would have resulted as the cruiser sank. These sentiments became much more poignant two days later, when the Argentine riposte was delivered in the shape of an air-to-sea Exocet missile that smashed into the side of HMS *Sheffield*.

From here on there was to be no more 'Mr Nice Guy', and for all of us it had now become 'Game on'...

Friday, May 7th

The Amphibious Task Group had sailed from Ascension Island the previous afternoon, and we were now 250 miles south-west, on a zig-zag course. From my frequent visits to HMS *Fearless*, I was hearing on the grapevine that the number of serious landing options had been whittled down from eight to three, and that a final selection was imminent. Julian Thompson was under huge pressure to get the various decisions absolutely right.

Meanwhile, on the medical side we continued to carry on planning and training in pursuit of common sense and maximum effectiveness. Apart from our local difficulty with 'NE', the medical plot was clearing a bit. The official word was still that *Canberra* would remain located close in to any amphibious landing area, and with my Medical Squadron teams well integrated into Roger Wilkes' own efficient and effective ship-based organisation, there was even a possibility that the Royal Marines' medical support might remain on board *Canberra*, if this actually remained an option. We had however retained our capability of unplugging the green beret elements to go ashore in the Falklands if, when, and wherever the land battle dictated.

In reality, it all depended on the Argentine Air Force, or *Fuerza Aerea Argentina*. My private worries about the enemy air threat seemed to be shared by all the Brigade Staff, but Northwood kept reassuring us that the two British aircraft carriers and their 28 embarked Sea Harriers, armed with the latest version of the Sidewinder air-to-air missile, would be enough to have total air superiority established by the time we got down to Total Exclusion Zone (TEZ). Despite early success in air-to-air combat when two RAF exchange officers downed a Mirage each early in May, Northwood's optimism began to look a bit thin when news came in that two other Sea Harriers had not returned from a night patrol, in bad weather, near the area of HMS *Sheffield's* sinking. There was speculation about a mid-air collision. Both Fleet Air Arm pilots were listed as 'missing' while helicopters searched for them.

Saturday, May 8th – Tuesday, May 12th

On the *Canberra*, in sharp contrast to the mood in *Uganda*, harmony was very much the name of the game. The specialist training for the embarked surgeons, in particular, was of a very high order. As well as receiving tutorials from the Boss, who had genuine operational experience, they repeatedly watched and discussed excerpts from a consignment of Vietnam and Korean War medical training films that had arrived for us in Ascension. These constituted an interesting mixture of practical and realistic advice, combined with a somewhat faded Technicolour fantasy.

For the embarked units, we set up a 'Self Aid' training programme based on the Brigade Commander's instruction to me. He was anxious to avoid over-dependence, up in the front line, on external medical help. During exercises on Salisbury Plain, or in Arctic Norway, genuine casualties were dealt with very quickly using every possible resource. Exercise 'play' would be suspended, a helicopter flown in to evacuate the patient to the nearest (civilian) hospital, and only then was the 'war' allowed to continue. JHAT's instincts were right on the button, as ever. Service in Belfast was an unrealistic preparation for fighting in a remote location devoid of any civilian infrastructure such as the Royal Victoria Infirmary.

Each rifle company was therefore refreshed in the basic aspects of battlefield medical care, and I completed this course with a lecture on *'The Injuries of Urban Guerilla Warfare'*. This had the Corps-wide nickname of *'Doc Jolly's Horror Show'*, but the aim was the same. If you knew what a gunshot wound looked like, from viewing a colour slide, then you were in a better position to cope with a real one than someone whose knowledge was theory-based.

One Company Sergeant Major advised his OC to decline this presentation, on the grounds that it would 'put the blokes off wanting to cross the Start Line...' Afterwards, he admitted to me that this had been a bad decision, because they had all seen much worse things than the bullet wounds and blast injuries featured in my presentation. His views changed so radically, in fact, that when he was commissioned as an officer later on, Cameron March became the Corps' expert in the early detection and treatment of PTSD (Post Traumatic Stress Disorder).

I'd also been involved in a little wager with one of the embarked Blues and Royals officers whose light armoured vehicles were being deployed with the Brigade. Lieutenant the Lord Robin Innes-Ker was a delightful young 'donkey walloper' (the generic nickname for all cavalry officers) and seemed surprised when I commented that HRH Prince Andrew could soon be involved in some real action. He told me that there would be no question of exposing Her Majesty's second son to any real danger, which I countered with the fact that, as he was a professional Fleet Air Arm officer and helicopter pilot, no-one in the Royal Navy (and least of all the Prince himself) would expect anything less. The stake was £10, which Lord Robin paid most gracefully when news came of an Exocet missile passing close to the Prince's Sea King!

The young Lord was a dedicated polo player; his colleague, Lt Mark Coreth, was a sculptor with a growing reputation for his work. They would both end the war with a 'Mention in Despatches' each (from 3 Cdo Brigade's limited allocation) for their first-class fire support in a number of engagements.

We were still looking for other ships that might have a surgical capability, so one morning I flew over to *Norland*, the P&O

North Sea ferry that had also joined us in Ascension. She now carried the Second Battalion of the Parachute Regiment (hereafter referred to as '2 Para'), as well as the Army medical men of the Parachute Clearing Troop (PCT), and some of the RAF aircrew and maintainers whose Chinook helicopters and ground-attack Harriers were stored over in the big Cunard freighter *Atlantic Conveyor*.

The embarked RAF Harrier pilots were all a bit glum. The identities of the two still-missing pilots had now been released – they were Al Curtis and John Eyton-Jones. Both men were graduates of the same training pipeline that they had passed through. Al was a former Royal New Zealand Air Force pilot who had already managed to shoot down an Argentine Canberra night bomber. 'E-J' was well known to everyone in the RAF Harrier and Fleet Air Arm Sea Harrier communities. He had flown Sea Vixens in the early days, and then F-4K Phantoms off the old HMS *Ark Royal*, and was a cheerful, good-looking, cocky and a fantastically able fast jet pilot. I had met and partied with him while he was on exchange duties with the US Navy in California. One of the RAF chaps observed to me that if E-J really had gone, it did not bode too well for the survival chances of less able mortals like him…

Space in the old North Sea ferry was a bit cramped, but her new flight deck aft opened into a large public room that was close to the existing operating theatre. The PCT personnel came from the Royal Army Medical Corps, and were all parachute-trained. That didn't just mean jumping out of static balloons and moving aircraft. They had also completed the gruelling 'P Company' selection course. Like the Commando medics' green berets, their maroon berets and parachute badges signified that they were worthy of the honour of serving with their Airborne infantry colleagues.

I took to them all instantly, and was very pleased that they were with us. The size of the PCT was out of all proportion to the unit that it was supporting. It was now revealed that 2 Para had been allocated a hitherto secret 'hostage rescue' role, based on the fantastic success of the French Foreign Legion and Belgian Army paras who had saved countless European lives at Kolwezi, in 1971. The PCT's size and capability equalled that of the Haslar Naval surgical team that had been taken from us earlier on, so by a happy and quite unplanned piece of serendipity, the medical support for 3 Commando Brigade was back up to somewhere near its planned and proper strength.

To add to this slice of luck, all but one of the PCT doctors, even the surgeons and anaesthetists, had also been Parachute Regiment battalion MOs in their earlier days. That meant I could reinforce either 2 or 3 Para with a doctor who had been part of the same unit within the last five or six years. This is an issue which outsiders don't understand, but which is hugely important in any Airborne or Commando unit's preparation for battle. These doctors and medics had the same genuine affection for the 'Toms' (as they called the private soldiers) as we, for our part, had for 'Royal'. Little did I suspect just how well this affection would cross-operate when we all ended up together in the mutton refrigeration and packing plant at Ajax Bay.

2 Para's Regimental MO was a young RAMC Captain named Steve Hughes. With typical 'Airborne initiative' this fair-haired young tiger had been very busy. He was a real enthusiast, highly receptive to sensible new concepts as well as up to speed on proven ideas, but also absolutely determined that his First Aid training and preparation of his 'Toms' would be of the very highest standard. Having read about soldiers in the Israeli Army each carrying a bag of intravenous fluid into battle, he realised that this was the way to solve his own replenishment stores problem in the field. He persuaded 2 Para's Command that each paratrooper should carry his own bag of saline, and that some of them would also have the necessary polythene tubing infusion sets secured within their clothing.

The patrol medics were trained to insert intravenous needles, but for the others, in case they were cut off from medical help, he also demonstrated the principle of *rectal* infusion. The Toms all laughed, and volunteered each other for this procedure, carried out after a period of intense physical training on the upper deck of *Norland*, in the heat of a noonday sun. The witnesses were all surprised how quickly the fluid was absorbed after being run in, and just how soon the 'patient' felt comfortably rehydrated – in contrast to their own thirst and discomfort. It was, and still is, an important survival technique. None of the Toms had yet heard of a place called Goose Green.

Phil Shouler and John Williams flew across to HMS *Intrepid*, which had also rejoined the Fleet and arrived in Ascension after an incredibly rapid mini-refit in Portsmouth. Somebody, and we thought we knew who, had suggested the conversion of her Wardroom (the equivalent of an officer's mess) and Gunroom (the same, but for the more junior officers under training) into a surgical operating theatre. Indeed, work had actually begun on cutting away bulkheads to create this concept before Phil and John could stop them.

To reach the Wardroom by stretcher from the flight deck required the negotiation of two sharp corners and a near-vertical ladder. It was all palpable nonsense, and wholly impractical. We thought no more of it, and explained why this was so in a detailed signal to Northwood, copied as well to Commando Brigade HQ.

During one of the many live-firing exercises that were being conducted over the stern railings, a machine-gun team from 40 Commando managed to destroy the wooden towed target in a storm of bullets. This elaborate device had been constructed by *Canberra's* chippies, and it was a rather anxious pair of Royal Marines that was sent along to apologise to these craftsmen. Their reaction was that as long as these items were helping the marines to shoot like that in defence of the ship, they could have as many towed targets as they wanted!

Thursday, May 13th

On this sunlit morning we had gathered as usual for the morning parade and a confirmatory repeat of daily orders before dismissing. One of the marines then came up and asked to see me privately. We moved across to the rail and I asked him what the problem was. The young stretcher-bearer hesitated before explaining that he had been in the Corps for over four years, and the only thing that he had ever really set his heart on was proving himself to be a good infantryman on active service. He was desperate to put his Commando training into practice, and show his ex-RM father and two uncles that he was good enough to be in their company – despite their collective experience of Aden, Borneo and Suez.

It was a frequently heard complaint from the fit young men who found themselves in the Logistic Regiment, well away from the front line, doing something a bit 'pacifist' like carrying one corner of a stretcher instead of a rifle and ammunition. I tried to reassure this fine young man (and colleague) that there were places to be filled all over the Commando Brigade and while some positions might apparently lack the glamour and impact of front-line combat, what we were preparing to do was *really* important.

Throughout our discussion I tried to be gentle with him, but he was quite upset, particularly when he realised that I was going to be unyielding in my refusal to lose him. Over his shoulder I signalled the Sergeant Major to come and lead him away before he could do or say anything stupid. I could understand his feelings, even sympathise with him, but Medical Squadron was where he was going to stay, for this war at least. Something else then came up to occupy my attention, and so I forgot all about his problem.

Elsewhere the pace was quickening. An important series of decisions had now been made, and in the afternoon, key officers were summoned to HMS *Fearless* for Brigadier Thompson's landing Orders Group. As his medical adviser I went along too, and as we took our seats in the LPD's crowded Wardroom, we were all conscious that this was an historic event. The main briefing for Operation MUSKETEER, the landings at Suez some 25 years before, must have been something like this.

There was a lot of preliminary information to get through. The weather and terrain were covered once again by Major Ewen Southby-Tailyour, with his excellent portfolio of slides and cruising notes. He looked thinner and more tired than his usual extrovert self. The strain of being responsible for finding an assault force landing site had obviously been telling on him. An immaculately delivered Intelligence Brief followed from Captain Viv Rowe, a tall, fair-haired and strongly-built veteran of infantry operations in Oman. There were some admitted gaps in his presentations however, particularly as to the operational strength and capabilities of the *Fuerza Aerea Argentina*.

The Brigade Commander then stood up, looked hard for a moment at his Commanding Officers sitting in the chintz-covered front-row chairs, then donned his reading glasses. In a quiet but very clear voice he gave his orders, beginning with the classic preamble: 'Our Mission, gentlemen. To land in Port San Carlos, San Carlos Settlement and Ajax Bay, and establish a beachhead for mounting offensive operations, leading on to re-capture of the Falkland Islands...' There was absolute silence. He repeated the sentence, then carried on: 'Design for Battle. A silent, night attack by landing craft, with the object of securing all high ground by first light...'

The crisp instructions followed, one by one, until every angle and problem was covered. Many of the details were classified *Secret* and probably still remain so, but eventually all the questions were answered, either by the Brigadier himself, or by the Brigade Major, John Chester. Then there was a rustle of papers as people made their preparations to leave, anxious to write their own orders as soon as possible.

'Gentlemen...' Julian Thompson's voice had a whiplash edge to it as his narrowed eyes scanned the audience: '...may I remind you once more – this will be *no picnic...*'

Saturday, May 15th

A rough day. We now had a little more information about the San Carlos area, including the location of a large abandoned building suitable for setting up my expanded Main Dressing Station. On the western edge of San Carlos Water lay a shallow indentation called Ajax Bay, now codenamed 'Red Beach'. Just up from this beach was a sheep slaughterhouse, with an attached refrigeration and mutton packing plant. Built as a joint venture between the Falkland Islands Company and the British Government, it seemed to have foundered because of a lack of local labour, and had lain derelict and abandoned since the late 1950s. The whole Ajax Bay feature, with its gently sloping beach, looked like becoming the main logistic support area for the Brigade, so part of the mutton plant was pencilled as a potential site for Medical Squadron when (and if) we disembarked from *Canberra* and RFA *Sir Lancelot.*

Feeling a bit queasy, despite *Canberra's* bulk and her efficient stabilisers, I then managed to keep down enough medication to give my own operational and landing brief to the medical men. For security reasons we were in FRW's large cabin, which was immediately below the Promenade Deck. The horizon kept vanishing from the tall panoramic windows, so the Boss very kindly drew the curtain, seeing that otherwise the audience would probably have received a bit more than just my verbal contribution into their open notebooks.

Sunday, May 16th

A quieter day, thank goodness, and a calmer sea. Major Terry Knott, the Second in Command of the Logistics Regiment, came onboard for a look around. He was a tall, slim Royal Marines officer who had won the Military Cross in Aden as a young and rather lethal young subaltern. He'd also been unlucky enough to be in Denmark on a recce when General Galtieri invaded the Falklands, and although recalled rapidly, had been left behind to look after the rear party. Repeated letters and daily threatening phone calls around the Corps bazaars resulted in something of a late 'regain', and now he was in charge of a composite rifle company on board HMS *Intrepid*. I was glad to see him and, as a result of a long chat about the niceties of staff work, was then able to write an accurate medical Operation Order.

Roger Wilkes and I had been thinking hard about a blood transfusion policy. We knew that blood replacement would be an absolutely essential feature of our battlefield medical care, but trying to estimate casualty numbers and their likely degrees of seriousness was a very difficult business when there were so many unknown variables to account for within the equation. The pathologists reckoned that we would be able to store fresh blood in the special citrated Fenwal plastic bags for about five weeks, but only if a 4 degrees Celsius temperature in the associated chilling boxes was carefully maintained.

We were however constrained by the fact that the day planned for our landing in the Islands was an 'Official Secret'! So, we decided that the taking of blood would begin a week before the landing (which the whole world now knows to be May 21st) and that this one week interval would allow the donors to make up that lost red cell volume in the interval before D-Day. Each of the three embarked Units were therefore invited to participate as donors.

There must have been some sort of inter-unit rivalry going, because eventually the medical staff were actually turning away potential donors. We ended up with nearly a thousand half-litre bags of high quality red stuff on tap. Sadly, the men only got warm lemonade as a rehydrating gift for their contribution to this mutual life insurance policy, although over in *Norland*, a tin of beer was the more appropriate local reward. The timing of these sessions had been a tricky piece of judgement for me, and I was relieved to have had FRW's common sense and practical wisdom in support.

Later on, I was to note just how quickly those who had donated blood, and had then been wounded, managed to recover their health. Had we tickled their immunological and repair systems into a state of greater efficiency by causing this earlier 'damage' through blood donation? It was a wholly subjective and personal observation, and it is not backed by any special laboratory investigation. The theory remains a speculative piece of 'blue-sky' thinking that has never been properly investigated.

You work up to athletic competition by challenging your body with training, and by demanding an improved response even when in serious oxygen debt. So why not challenge the body's repair processes in the same way too? Or was the fast recovery from traumatic wounds just another hidden benefit that came directly from supreme aerobic fitness, of the kind achieved by most of the marines and paras before they landed?

In mid-afternoon we joined up with the HMS *Antrim* group and the five LSLs (Landing Ships Logistic). Our convoy was now nineteen strong, travelling south and west at twelve knots. There were just under four hundred nautical miles to go.

Monday, May 17th

Clearance was signalled from Brigade HQ in HMS *Fearless* to begin briefing audiences about the landing plan, initially down to junior NCO level. As my temporary boss, FRW suggested, correctly, that we started with our medical, dental and para-medical officers, as well as the command structure of the Band. Bryn Dobbs was my Medical Admin Warrant Officer, and a Naval medical branch rating of over 17 years service with the Corps. He opened proceedings by describing the Naval part of the landing plan to an attentive audience. Bryn was (and still is) a great character with a wickedly dry sense of humour, and repeated the joke that he had first tried on me one evening as we leaned on *Canberra's* Promenade Deck railings, gazing out at a lovely sunset. We were chewing things over, just after the loss of HMS *Sheffield*: 'I spy with my little eye something beginning with E* – and you've got exactly six seconds to answer…'

Tuesday, May 18th

Today it was the turn of Medical Squadron, the Surgical Support Teams and the Band to get all the facts. The Bonito Room was full as once more we ran through the brief, which had now become fairly polished in its delivery. We told our audience that *Canberra* was still 80 miles outside the TEZ, and although the actual date of D-Day itself had not yet been promulgated, I was now allowed to divulge it. Most of the boys had been smart enough to work it out for themselves anyway.

*Exocet missile…

The first 'war' casualty was also received onboard. An idle idiot of a fire sentry in *Europic Ferry* had been playing with a grenade detonator that he had picked up out of a broken wooden storage case. Out of boredom, he removed the firing pin, then tried to replace it. The explosion blew several fingers off, and also drove metal fragments into his face and chest. Phil Jones and Nick Morgan did a beautiful tidying-up job.

Later in the evening, some urgent messages over the Tannoy system indicated that something was up. It turned out that the Brigade planners had become very worried about the submarine and air threat to our ship. With two Commando units and one Para battalion onboard *Canberra*, they definitely had the majority of their eggs in this one large white basket. Plans were made to cross-deck 40 Commando and 3 Para into other ships the next day.

Wednesday, May 19th

It was a beautiful morning, with clear skies and only a light swell to interfere with the difficult business of transferring 40 Commando to HMS *Fearless*, and, a bit later on, 3 Para over to HMS *Intrepid*. The marines and soldiers were in their full assault rig for this operation, leaving their suitcases and other personal kit in the liner's baggage store room. Some of the smaller individuals were dwarfed by their loaded bergens. The unit medics were also rather more heavily laden than most, since they had to tote ammunition as well as medical stores. Top weight was carried by the mortar and anti-tank sections. For the former, an 81 mm mortar barrel, plus personal equipment, weighed 60 kilograms. For the latter, a bergen, fighting order, weapon, ammunition plus a Milan missile firing post clocked in at an amazing, and back-breaking 64 kg!

I spent a busy day with Scouse Davies and his team, packing morphine syrettes for the various sub units, for issue on a scale of one per man. The logistics were a bit difficult because some units, like the gunners of 29 Commando Regiment Royal Artillery, were scattered between four or five ships. We managed to get most of the stuff delivered before nightfall, and then asked for a helicopter the next day in order to complete these issues to ships out on the periphery of the amphibious group.

Tragedy struck after dark as a Commando Sea King helicopter crashed, killing most of the passengers as it hit the sea and turned over. There were rumours of impact with a large bird, causing the anti-icing shield to break up and be sucked into both engine intakes. The buzz was also that the passengers were mainly SAS men – a rumour that was also confirmed later. It was a bitter blow, since among them were the battle-tested hard men of South Georgia and Pebble Island. The time-honoured and instinctive reaction that I expressed in my diary now had a closer, rather more personal intensity in the light of our impending assault from the sea – *May they rest in peace...*

How many more of us might end up lying in some unknown, unmarked grave?

Thursday, May 20th

The 20-ship Amphibious Landing Force formed up and penetrated the Total Exclusion Zone at dawn. We were now 100 miles east of Stanley – and the gods were kind to us. A Force Six wind and sea state combined with thick mist to hide us from the prying eyes of any Argentine reconnaissance aircraft. Long-range radar indicated that the enemy were certainly out looking for us, but the Sea Harrier fighters sitting at Alert 5 on the edge of HMS

Hermes' long flight deck had no closing customers to intercept.

The powerful Sea Wolf-equipped frigates, HM Ships *Broadsword* and *Brilliant*, fussed around on the flanks of the convoy as it ploughed steadily westwards. The LSLs, with their flat-bottomed and unstabilised hulls, were rolling and pitching badly, their wide bows often obliterated from view by a foaming mass of freezing South Atlantic. Helicopter flying was also very difficult, so my morphine issue by Gazelle was cancelled. There were big problems for me as a result, and I now had to try for a final distribution run on D-Day itself. We had agreed a Brigade-wide policy that there would be no casualty evacuation (casevac) facilities during and immediately after the H-Hour landings, at least until first light. Then I would have access to a Wessex 5 helicopter, allocated to me for casevac purposes. The day dragged on and on, until nightfall came at last.

Precisely on time, the Landing Force then turned up to the north and began the long right hook around East Falkland, heading up towards the top entrance to Falkland Sound. One of the escorts carried straight on towards the Islands, and then together with HMS *Glamorgan*, helped to distract Argentine curiosity by bombarding targets in the Stanley area, We also knew that tonight another group of SAS men would be making a lot of explosive and diversionary noises near Goose Green, further confusing the defending forces.

Most of us 'turned in' early, as D-Day would undoubtedly be a long and tiring one. As I dressed for bed in my survival clothing, the BBC World Service relay from Ascension described how an amphibious landing in the Falklands was now imminent. They even had a tame expert on hand to describe what would happen. By now we had nicknamed these retired officers as 'rent-a-gobs'. The 'former Director of Naval Intelligence' was hopelessly wrong when he described landing craft as outdated, and that British assault helicopters would either land in Port Stanley, or out on the plains of Lafonia. He also stated that, in his opinion, the assault would not be a bloody affair. With the poor casevac facilities at our disposal during the hours of darkness, I sincerely hoped that this particular '*Rentagob*' had actually got something right.

Friday, May 21st

Loud bangs, in pairs, woke me up. The noises had a brassy, metallic quality and seemed very close. Pulling down the blackout curtain on the cabin scuttle revealed a bright flash occurring just before each sound. Then I remembered that the big guided missile destroyer HMS *Antrim* was due to provide naval gunfire support for the initial attack on Fanning Head. An Argentine OP (Observation Post) had been spotted in the area, and the boys of the SBS (Special Boat Squadron) were being put in there just as soon as a preparatory dose of 4.5 inch high explosive warheads had been dispensed.

After putting on more warm clothing, I walked up to the midships flight deck, and stepped out of the red-lit corridor into a chilly darkness. It took a few minutes to gain night vision. The stars of the southern night sky were brilliant and unfamiliar, but all around us was complete blackness. I had brought my binoculars and was feeling my way up to the Officer's sun deck on the port side when HMS *Antrim* opened up again. From my unprotected vantage point the noise was almost painful. The thunderclap of firing rolled unchecked over the flat calm of Falkland Sound, each shell followed by a long yellow tongue of flame that briefly stabbed out into the darkness. Two, maybe three, seconds later came a distant 'kerr-ump' as the shells impacted on Fanning Head.

We were at anchor while the initial assault waves went in from *Norland, Fearless* and *Intrepid*, but the plan was then to move *Can-*

berra into San Carlos Water at around first light. Down in the Pacific Restaurant, breakfast tasted good, with anxiety about today's programme of events fuelling my appetite. The stewards were a subdued lot for once, although it was noticeable that *Antrim's* percussion section was inaudible in the centre of the ship.

The first fingers of light appeared in the east as we then moved silently under Fanning Head to our anchor position. The two picks went down with a rumbling roar of chain paying out from the bows, and I found myself standing next to Lieutenant Colonel Nick Vaux. The CO of 42 Commando RM was obviously fretful at being held in reserve for the initial assault. From the bridge, in the gradually lightening gloom, we could make out the shapes of two LSLs gliding past us, then the familiar outline of RFA *Stromness*. Over on Fanning Head, a machine gun opened up silently, the red tracer blips streaking in a long curving arc before bouncing and ricocheting at the base of the hill. The SBS were obviously in a fire fight, but this 'Brock's benefit' firework show seemed to be a bit one-sided.

Dawn broke imperceptibly, the violet layers next to the skyline gradually brightening through deep indigo to blue, then changing to orange as the sun's disc rose above the eastern horizon. It was going to be a clear and bright blue sky. Good news for our helicopters certainly, but also wonderful flying weather for any Argentine Air Force planes who might be hunting for us. They must have spotted the landing force fleet by now.

On cue, and on time, the Sea King helicopters of 846 Squadron began to line up in the hover out to *Canberra's* port side. Their Rolls Royce Gnome engines had a characteristic whistling roar which was blended to the nasal whine of their six-bladed tail rotors. You could shut your eyes but still be sure of correct identification by listening. The netted loads of first and second-line ammunition were lifted from the midships flight deck, then taken ashore, suspended in cargo nets that swung gently beneath their boat-shaped fuselages.

In the clearer light we could also see little groups of landing craft streaming past, taking the men of 3 Para into Port San Carlos. They were about an hour late, but this seemed to be the only hitch in the complex choreography of an amphibious assault that had otherwise gone like clockwork. The Ops Room was busy, but the airwaves were silent because of the embargo on all electronic communication. No one could tell me if the landings were being opposed or not. If there were any casualties sustained, then Stephen Hughes of 2 Para, John Burgess of 3 Para, David Griffiths of 45 Cdo and Mike Hayward of 40 Cdo would simply have to do their best – until I arrived sometime after dawn with the means to get their wounded out vertically.

An hour after sun-up there was still no sign of my Wessex 5, but then suddenly Lt Cdr Mike Crabtree and his crew were out there and closing. They were marshalled onto the forward deck and then allowed to shut down. The crew had already been flying for more than three hours after inserting the SBS and their kit into Fanning Head, so a quick and restorative cup of coffee and a bacon sandwich were in order before we departed.

The run down to San Carlos Settlement was uneventful as Mike Crabtree checked the map, and Lt Hector Heathcote (co-pilot) flew the aircraft. Turning into wind, we landed on Falklands soil for the very first time, and I ran over to the nearest men who were digging slit trenches. Some of the camouflage-creamed faces were recognizable as Marines of 40 Commando. They reassured me that the landing on Blue Beach had been a piece of uneventful routine so far. Two young children then appeared, and ran out to look at the Wessex, this new phenomenon in their lives. I went over to say hello to them too. They were chubby-cheeked and pink-faced, and one shyly gave me a sweet. I grinned and jerked my thumb at the noisy helicopter, 'burning and turning' on the grass behind me. The elder one smiled, reached into her anorak and gave me another Murray mint – this one for the pilot!

Next, we flew to Red Beach, the Brigade codename for Ajax Bay, and landed on a convenient piece of concrete hardstanding nearby. Our reception here was much less friendly. One of 45 Commando's corporals invited us, in a classic piece of paraphrasing, to investigate '*sex and travel*'; he thought that they were being mortared. I persisted, remembering why we had actually come in the first place, but apparently there were no casualties here either. We needed no second bidding, though doubting if we really were under Argentine mortar attack. The Wessex rose swiftly into the cold air, and turned back over the deserted refrigeration plant.

Jock Inglis, one of my Medical Squadron marines, had told me that the abandoned freezing compartments were big enough to play football in. Interesting, but it would probably take a lot of time and effort to get ready as a field medical facility or dressing station. Hopefully, and with Northwood's promised 'air superiority', the highly capable action medical organisation in *Canberra* was going to be all that we needed.

As we climbed away, I had time to lean out of the door and take in a few details. Along the front of the main building, which was shaped like a 'T', there was a narrow concrete track. This road led down to a broken pier, past a huge stack of red and rusting oil drums. The ground looked horrible – wet, muddy and very stony. The whole place reminded me of a long disused municipal rubbish dump.

After refuelling the aircraft on the *Fearless* flight deck, we distributed the last of the morphine to the various ships. Minutes after returning to *Canberra*, the first formal casevac request also came in to her Ops Room. The grid reference made very little sense until we asked for it to be repeated, and then found that the figures were in a form of code that we did not possess! Some rummaging in an adjoining stationery store provided a potential correct answer, and away we went. Right at the head of San Carlos Water we then saw a discharging red smoke grenade, and landed on the foreshore nearby. Our customer was a chap from 2 Para who had badly twisted his back after stumbling, in the darkness, into a small creek.

I quickly assessed the patient's condition, agreed with the Para medic's provisional diagnosis, then went back to the helicopter to get a stretcher. Consternation! Unbelievable stupidity! We had actually forgotten to bring one! What the hell were we going to do? Corporal Kevin Gleeson, the Royal Marines aircrewman, was equal to the failures of my planning and common sense. He just disconnected the canvas seating on the starboard side, and ripped the tubular aluminium out of its holding clips to make a crude, lightweight stretcher, onto which we then gently lifted the very uncomfortable paratrooper.

It seemed a slightly crazy thing to do, but in the morning sunlight I then stepped back to take a picture of this historic event. Here was the first casualty of the land phase of the South Atlantic campaign. If you now study the resulting photo carefully, you can clearly see the bewilderment written on the medic's face as he looks up at the camera, with Kev Gleeson crouching beside him. I think that his innermost thoughts at that moment were probably along the lines of 'What the bloody hell is this crazy Naval doctor up to now?'

There was another task waiting when we returned to *Canberra*, but this turned into a wild goose chase. The saga only ended when we queried the grid reference, only to find that it was the first set of numbers once more, only wrongly decoded this time! While refuelling on *Fearless* again, I raced up to the Brigade Ops Room to protest. I asked the Duty Officer responsible for these matters to give any casevac tasking positions to us in an uncoded form from now on. There was a slight risk of enemy interception, but we could accept this rather than be sent on fools' errands by human coding mistakes. The anti-flash hooded figure agreed.

My remonstrations then attracted the attention of the Officer Commanding SBS. He was desperate to visit his men up on Fanning Head, but could not find a helicopter to take him up there. Apparently there were some Argentine casualties up on the feature as well, so I offered him a ride, which he gratefully accepted. He grabbed his M-16 rifle and, after strapping in, we lifted off again.

Seconds later we had a new task. There had been some sort of incident involving helicopters up near the Port San Carlos settlement. We raced up to the scene, but apparently got too close to the forward edge of the battle area. Mike suddenly noticed a line of paratroopers, in attacking formation, advancing beneath him. Some of them were waving him away and back to San Carlos Water. He pulled the Wessex around again in a steep, diving turn that brought us very close to the sea. Having beaten this hasty retreat, we slowed up to collect our senses once more. A closer look at the map, followed by a reduced speed to study the ground more closely, and we were suddenly on top of the reported incident. Mike landed into wind but said nothing. OC SBS and I got out to see what was going on, and were greeted by an awful sight.

With its back broken and the long green tail boom folded back on itself, a Gazelle of 3 Cdo Brigade's Air Squadron lay on the slope before us. I had time to note that the large cockpit transparency must have been destroyed in the air, because there were no Plexiglass fragments on the ground around it, as I had seen in two previous Gazelle training accidents that I had attended. Most of the cockpit contents were strewn over the grass instead, including its two crew members. The pilot and air gunner were intact, but both dead, their flying suits stained with blood. The two paratroopers who had stayed behind had done all they could, but to no avail.

I recognised the pilot as Lt Ken Francis, a bright Royal Marines officer who had flown me down to Culdrose in Cornwall only three or four months before. He had been killed by a bullet that had come up through the cockpit floor and passed on into his flying helmet, nearly severing the chin strap. Death would have been instantaneous, and the aircraft out of control as it plunged to the ground. The crewman also had several bullet wounds to the chest and trunk, and would have also died quickly.

I had some tough decisions to take now. It just seemed morally wrong to leave these bodies out on that beautiful hillside; I was aware of a local predatory rook-sized bird called a Striated Caracara that preyed on sick and injured sheep. The Paras helped me to pick the two bodies up and carry them back to the Wessex. We also removed a machine gun and code books from the wreckage of the Gazelle. Our hearts were heavy as we flew our two dead colleagues back to *Canberra*, where I passed them down the ramp into the care of my Fleet Chief, the redoubtable Bryn Dobbs.

I still don't see how I could have acted differently, and yet retained a clear conscience, but our actions were later to be a source of great sadness and regret for the relations of Ken Francis, because his body, and that of Brett Giffen, his air gunner, were later committed to the sea rather than being returned to the UK.

Next, we flew up to Fanning Head. I was greeted by the SBS Sergeant Major with that classic phrase which I had heard so often (and still hear from time to time): 'Hello sir, what the hell are *you* doing here?' Ted E and I roared with laughter, shook hands and clapped each other on the back – we were old chums, meeting up again right in the middle of nowhere.

There were three Argentine wounded to evacuate after Mike had completed a little stores-shifting job for the SBS Troop. We had also brought them some more ammunition to replace what had been used up in the earlier firepower display. This we were entitled to do, as the Wessex was not marked with Red Crosses. The conscript prisoners looked absolutely terrified, and apparently believed the stories they had been told by their superiors that the British were rather fond of eating any prisoners that they captured! Even though they had been expertly treated by the SBS medics with battlefield splints and bandages for their bullet wounds, they were still *very* wary.

I decided to take the injured Argentines back to *Canberra* as well because, although there were orders saying prisoners should not be flown in helicopters, there was really nowhere else for them to go on this day. Perhaps, also, if the *Junta* HQ in Buenos Aires was told that Argentine wounded were being treated in *Canberra*, it might then leave the liner alone. I took some more photos and we flew back to the Great White Whale in two trips, because cabin floor space for stretchers was very limited. The Argentine lads all had high-velocity gunshot wounds of the legs, so they were definitely going to need surgery.

Somewhere around midday the casevac tasks were temporarily complete, so Mike Crabtree elected to refuel once more, and then return to *Canberra's* forward deck. With its nylon lashings secured, the Wessex helicopter's four blades slowed to a halt and her engines shut down at last.

Deep in the hull of the ship, life went on normally. The Pacific Restaurant was being cleared after lunch, but the staff arranged a quick resupply of rolls and ham for the four of us. Up in the Stadium, things had been more hectic as the resuscitation tasks and detailed assessment of numerous casualties continued against a background of repeated air raids and Tannoy warnings. As we walked from the Stadium theatre through to what was once the Bonito Night club, the metallic voice boomed out again: '*D'ye hear there? This is the bridge. An attack on the anchorage is developing from the North. Two aircraft inbound – TAKE COVER...TAKE COVER!*' All around us people dropped, as if pole-axed, to the shiny corridor floors.

Pressing ourselves into an unyielding surface, arms clutched tightly in protection over our heads, we could hear the reverberating echo of the machine guns up on the bridge superstructure as they engaged the attackers. The noise was a bit like a road-mender's pneumatic drill, and seemed to become amplified as it carried through the ship's aluminium superstructure. There was also a sudden '*whoosh*' – was that the Argentine jet going past?

'Blowpipe', muttered someone in the dim passageway, the name of a shoulder-launched anti-aircraft missile that I had also seen up on the bridge deck. Shortly afterwards, the 'All clear' was given, and I was munching my ham roll when the next Tannoy order came.

'*Launch the casevac helicopter…*'

Captain Chris Burne, *Canberra's* Senior Naval Officer, then gave a brief situation report, much appreciated by his thousand strong and entirely captive audience. The Leander Class frigate HMS *Argonaut* had been damaged in an air attack and was asking for help with her injured.

Up on the forward flight deck the lashings were off the Wessex by the time I arrived, and Mike Crabtee had already started one engine. Moments later we were easing up into the air and away again. The helicopter took a direct line to the damaged frigate, easily visible as she curved around Fanning Head towards the north end of Falkland Sound, her funnel smoking more heavily than usual. Mike positioned the Wessex over her boiling wake, with the cabin door looking down to an empty flight deck. Donning the winch strop and sitting on the doorstep, it all seemed clear for my transfer, but the Flight Deck Officer stubbornly refused us. His arms remained crossed – instead of beckoning the Wessex in towards him with his control bats.

The stand-off seemed to continue for ages – probably a minute or more – before the aircrewman tapped me on the shoulder. l unplugged my helmet electrical lead, and he operated the winch motor control lever to swing me up and out of the aircraft to begin the short descent to the flight deck, about twenty feet below. The Wessex now moved sideways and directly over the flight deck, then suddenly dipped its bulbous nose towards the sea and began to accelerate away from the frigate.

I cursed Mike Crabtree's apparent lack of concern for my welfare, and struggled to regain the cabin. By now we were pulling round to the left in a tight turn at low level, really moving fast over the waves. Plugging in again, I had no time to complain. The crewman saw and heard me join the intercom circuit and said briefly: 'Air Raid Red, sir, enemy aircraft coming in...' I knelt in the cabin doorway again, my pulse racing, and noticed that we were crossing a small beach under Fanning Head and, as the nose reared up to slow the helicopter down, I looked upwards. Two menacing shapes flashed above us, their stubby delta wings easily recognizable as A-4 Skyhawks. We settled in a small gully to take stock of the situation, and as we did so, the air seemed full of snow. It was 'chaff', the metallized nylon fibres thrown up by HMS *Argonaut* in a last-ditch attempt to deflect her oncoming attackers.

A little later, Mike Crabtree lifted the Wessex off the ground, and moved off along and then up the hillside, following the line of a stream coming down a small re-entrant. At one point the gully widened out, about 600 feet above sea level, and with some careful precision hovering he was able to position the aircraft on the ground with its starboard main wheel on the slightly raised bank of the stream. The cabin machine gun could now be swung in a wide defensive arc of fire that would not intersect with the spinning rotor blades. More attacks were developing on the Naval picket line out in Falkland Sound, so we settled down to watch, as well as wait for the chance to get airborne again.

By now, the tactical radio net was very busy as various ships called the developing air strikes. Every so often our faces split into wide grins as the net controller in HMS *Brilliant* announced another downed Argentine aircraft. The Sea Harriers, on their CAP (Combat Air Patrol) stations to the north and south were proving lethal to the Daggers and Skyhawks, whether the latter were inbound to their targets or exiting on their way back to the Argentine mainland. The British successes came as a crisp and laconic radio call: '*Hello all stations, this is the CAP – Splash one A-4*', but to the thin grey Naval picket line in Falkland Sound and the Landing Force ships behind them in San Carlos Water, these words carried huge encouragement.

It suddenly struck me, with total clarity, that I was watching history in the making, as well as the phenomenon of history repeating itself. Here was a group of Royal Navy warships, spread out in a line below us, taking on a well-handled enemy air force and protecting all the stores and troop ships huddled behind them. It had been much the same in Crete, forty-one years (almost to the month) earlier, when twenty RN ships were lost and over two thousand sailors had been killed or wounded to save the British Army Expeditionary Force as it struggled to get off the island, and escape captivity after a dangerous passage to Alexandria. I felt very calm – and very proud.

In the distance we could see another attack begin on the ships at the southern end of Falkland Sound. A black dot appeared above the horizon, then dipped, swooping in low and fast, then left two towering plumes of water where its bombs straddled the elderly Type 12 frigate, HMS *Plymouth*. The dot was now recognisable as a Dagger fighter-bomber which climbed up and turned away from us, towards the distant Argentine mainland. Its jet engine reheat was lit and clearly visible as it twisted and weaved to make good its escape. Too late. A thin white line joined HMS *Broadsword's* foredeck to the fleeing Argentine aircraft, which silently exploded, dissolving into metal confetti.

As Corporal Kevin Gleeson and I punched each other on the arm with excitement and laughter, I did not realise that what we had seen would be very important evidence to the Argentine pilot's family some seventeen years later. Our headphones then crackled again: '*Four bandits bearing 070 at twenty miles inbound at low level and closing fast...*' Kneeling on the cabin floor, I grabbed a handhold and hung out of the doorway for a better look.

Nothing. To the north and east there was nothing but blue sky and puffy white clouds.

It was a very unpleasant feeling to be sitting there, waiting for the air attack to begin, and basically being powerless to do anything about it. I had a very uncomfortable sensation in the pit of my stomach, as if someone had poured iced water into my belly. My mind suddenly switched, quite improbably, to events at the Battle of Trafalgar in 1805. Lord Nelson had arranged the British ships into two columns that bore steadily down on the combined French and Spanish line. Although they would eventually smash through that line in two places and begin its destruction, for about half an hour, the crew of HMS *Victory* were in range of the French and Spanish broadsides, yet unable to bring their own guns to bear. They simply had to endure the wait, and a great deal of physical punishment, before they could fire back.

This was the same sort of scenario, of forced inaction before your own weapons could open up. But what if the attackers saw us first in our little helicopter, sitting on the hillside? Might they go for that easier target rather than engage one of the two Sea Wolf-equipped frigates at centre stage out there in the Sound? Where were these Argy jets anyway? Was I looking in the right direction?

As I swung back in to the cabin in order to check the bearing, Corporal Gleeson pointed upwards past my shoulder. From the north, accelerating as they dived in line astern, four Argentine Daggers began their attack on HMS *Antrim*. Like a mother tiger prowling restlessly in the neck of San Carlos Water, protecting her cubs in the den behind her, the big County Class destroyer began to spit back her defiance. The line of splashes caused by the Daggers' cannon shells now met her tall grey flanks, and for several seconds she absorbed dozens of direct hits. The fourth aircraft had other ideas. Disturbed by the rising cloud of red tracer coming up to meet him, he suddenly broke off to his left and straightened up, heading directly for us and Fanning Head. Without hesitation, Corporal Gleeson reached for his machine-gun, cocked it, and began to fire defiantly at the lethal outline that we now saw expanding rapidly above and before us. I was completely transfixed. Were those leading edges of the Dagger twinkling with cannon fire directed at us?

My decision was reflex. Jumping down, and taking half a dozen strides away from the Wessex, I dived straight into the ditch beside the stream. Better a clean death here from a 30 mm shell through the head, rather than incineration and fragmentation in a whirling maelstrom of ruptured fuel tanks and broken rotor blades...

But the end did not come in the blinding flash of agony that I was half-expecting. Instead, when I lifted my head again, the Wessex was still sitting noisily behind me, and there was no sign of the Dagger. Once again the skies were clear, and HMS *Antrim* began another circuit of her endless racetrack pattern. Picking myself out of the ditch I noticed that one trouser leg was wet and muddy, and that my helmet visor had jammed down after its violent contact with the ground.

I walked around to the front and side of the *Wessex*, and got a 'thumbs-up' signal from Hector to allow me to approach the aircraft again. Climbing back up into the cabin, I was totally ignored by Kevin Gleeson as he made the machine-gun safe. Mike Crabtree's first words to me as I plugged back in on the intercom had a gently sarcastic ring: 'Oh – you back with us then, Doc?' He and his crew had been forced to remain strapped in throughout the incident. Unlike me, they had been given no chance to run away, and I felt very ashamed and humbled at my terror in the face of the enemy. I didn't know it then, but those feelings were to be of great benefit to me a short time afterwards, but just at that moment I was rather miserable about my failures as a warrior.

Down on the beach there was movement near the water's edge, as two heads suddenly popped up above the surface. Frogmen? No, just two seals that played among the kelp beds for a few moments, then dived again to escape the crazy antics of man.

Out in Falkland Sound, the 'Thin Grey Line' of six frigates and the destroyer continued their courageous fight against the Argentine Air Force and Naval Air Arm. We then saw a few more dots above the horizon, then a distant flash and smoke, and we cheered again, thinking that Sea Wolf might have gobbled up another victim. But then the tactical net repeated the four-letter call sign of the ship that had been hit. It was HMS *Ardent* that we could just see at the base of that column of black smoke. Mike and I discussed what to do. We both felt that we must go to her assistance, but were unsure whether or not it was safe to get into the air again. There was no-one else to ask. The decision had to be ours.

The inspirational answer came almost immediately as HMS *Plymouth*'s Wasp helicopter rushed past us, nose down for maximum speed, making the transit to *Canberra* with the casualties from HMS *Argonaut* that we had originally been tasked to collect. This particular Fleet Air Arm pilot, a chap called John Dransfield, had obviously decided that the requirement for his services exceeded the risk associated with providing them. His unsung but inspired bravery was just what we needed at that critical moment. Mike lifted the collective lever, trimmed the cyclic stick forward to gain speed, and soon we were filling our near empty fuel tanks once more on HMS *Fearless*. I ran to the main ramp area leading down to the Tank Deck and grabbed two new-looking, winchable stretchers. The Chief Petty Officer of the Flight Deck came over to query my actions, but waved me on as soon as he heard that *Ardent* had been hit, and that we were on our way to help. A true sailor will give everything he has for a brother seafarer in distress. However, as I discovered later, another individual who thought very little of me had a rather different interpretation for these actions!

We took the direct route to the scene of *Ardent's* bombing, climbing to cross the Sussex Mountains south of Ajax Bay. It was ground still held by the enemy as far we knew, so Mike, a Commando helicopter instructor, hugged the contours of the ground as we sped along. Over the hump of this ridge and descending, we in the back were denied the sight at which they suddenly fell silent up in the cockpit. Downwind of the burning ship, an acrid smell pervaded the cabin as we flew through a thick pall of black smoke. The Wessex came to a hover again, 30 feet above the swell and just off *Ardent's* port quarter. Now silenced ourselves, the crewman and I stared out.

What a sight! The Type 21 frigate lay still in the water, listing and drifting. Her lovely, classic lines had been obscenely defaced by some demented giant who had smashed her helicopter hangar in and also opened up the flight deck edge with a huge tin opener. Deep inside this enormous, blackened hole with its ragged edges, the fires of Hell were burning. The flames had a bright orange intensity that was painful to look at directly. Reaching for my camera once again, to photograph this blazing wound, I found to my disgust that there were no exposures left. While I was feeling in all my jacket pockets for another film, Mike and Hector noticed that *Ardent's* survivors were now mainly grouped on the upper deck, forward of the bridge. Some were already in their Day-Glo emergency survival suits, but almost all of them were pointing at the sea off to the port quarter.

The pilots then spotted two survivors in the water, and Mike immediately moved the Wessex across to get into position above them for a rescue. Corporal Gleeson started the pre-winching safety checks. As a passenger, I had no part to play in this retrieval process, so I continued searching for a fresh roll of film in my various pockets, at the same time watching the seamanship of HMS *Yarmouth's* captain as he put the elderly Type 12 frigate's stern right next to *Ardent's* bow. The survivors began to scramble across and down. Then I realised that Kevin Gleeson was having trouble with the first survivor, so I crawled over on my knees to the cabin door, looked down – and could immediately see why.

The man was drowning. The downwash from the helicopter's rotor blades was whipping the surface of the sea into a thick spray, through which I could see his agonised expression as he floundered helplessly. The lifting strop that was dangling just in front of his face was also jumping around; he just could not grasp the thing, let alone slip it over his shoulders.

In a flash, I knew that I had to do something, and quickly. I'd had some experience of winching during my time at Culdrose, and this part of the problem was down to me to solve. Replacing the camera in my pocket, and still smarting from the moral disgrace of my behaviour at Fanning Head, I volunteered to go down and get this drowning young man. Corporal Gleeson looked at me strangely, then started talking on the intercom to Mike. I was told later that he was expressing his doubts as to whether I'd be able to do anything useful, but Mike knew my Fleet Air Arm background, and gave his command approval for me to try. The aircrewman shrugged, winched the strop back up, grabbed it and placed it around my shoulders and beneath my arms.

The world suddenly went strangely quiet as I made ready, sensing that I was about to face a serious physical challenge. Seconds later, I was descending towards the surface of the sea. A lot of memories came back at the rush. Winchmen were usually properly dressed in immersion clothing, and were always earthed via a braided copper discharge wire before they made contact with the ground or sea, to disperse the likely build-up of static voltage.

There was no time for this nicety here. The discharging electrostatic shock was most unpleasant, and only just preceded the even worse shock of immersion. They told me later that the water temperature was 3 degrees Celsius. All I knew was that a sudden and numbing cold had enveloped my whole body as I gasped for breath. I could also feel my heart slowing, and my peripheral vision began to dim as the heart's output dropped and my retinas became less perfused.

All the while Mike, with marvellous precision flying, was towing me across the swell towards the survivor. The desperate look on the man's face, his frantic thrashings and punctured life jacket said it all. A fresh adrenaline surge kicked in, and I forgot my own discomfort. Our outstretched hands touched, grasped — and then I managed to spin him around in the water, and got him gripped in a fierce bear hug. My fingers locked tightly together in front of his chest, and I waited, unable to look up to the helicopter above us. There would be no other way to lift him.

Very gently, Mike lifted the Wessex up about ten feet, and the strain came on my arms as we left the buoyant support of the sea. It hurt, and I felt something tear suddenly in my left shoulder blade area, but I also realised at the same time that if I could no longer hold on to this survivor, he would drop straight back into the sea, and we would never see him again. I begged my shoulder muscles not to weaken in this moment of crisis. It seemed an agonisingly slow process, but Kevin Gleeson was winching us up very gently. He knew what I was going through.

The aircrewman then displayed genuine skill and real strength in getting us both back into the cabin. He had to raise us almost up into the winch motor housing above the door, making small, precise control movements with his left hand, and then pull hard on my clothing with his right hand as he reversed the winch control and began paying out the wire so he could draw us back in to safety. The blood now flowed back into my arms and shoulders as I collapsed beside the survivor on the cabin floor. We'd done it!

I compressed the casualty's chest hard, looking for some confirmation of life, and was rewarded with a vomited gout of sea water. The young lad then opened his eyes, and was violently sick again. I picked myself up off the floor, sat on the canvas seating, and breathed a huge sigh of pride and relief, realising that I had now done at least one genuinely useful thing in my life. As a team, and against the odds, we had saved another human being from death! I felt really pleased with myself, and especially so that I'd shown my new chum Kevin Gleeson, a Royal Marines Corporal, that although I'd behaved like a tosser up on Fanning Head, I was in reality made of much sterner stuff. Or was I?

I looked across at Kevin and smiled, receiving a warm grin back. He then made a hand signal with his thumb up and a querying expression on his face. I nodded, putting my own thumb up, confirming that I was OK, whereupon he turned his hand into a fist, with the forefinger pointing downwards. Then I remembered. There was someone else down there. In a cruel mockery of the poet John Masefield's famous line – I had to '*go down to the sea again*'...

The aircrewman looked at me anxiously as I donned the winch strop once more, then gave me an encouraging pat on the back as he swung me out of the *Wessex* for the second time. During this descent, a twist that had developed in the winch wire caused me to spiral slowly as the wire paid out.

A mad Cinerama projection unfolded before my eyes. The burning outline of *Ardent*, with her crew watching, was followed by the profile of HMS *Yarmouth*, then HMS *Broadsword*, now close to us for anti-aircraft protection. After that came Grantham Sound, the Falklands shore, and then *Ardent* again. I watched, somewhat stunned and rather chilled, until I was just above the surface, when a new sight appeared on the merry-go-round. Lying there quietly in the swell, arms outstretched and blood streaming downsea from amputated fingers and a huge cut on his scalp, the second survivor watched me with uncomprehending eyes. He later told me that because he could not see the winch wire I was suspended from, he thought I was the Archangel Gabriel coming to collect him!

Bang! The horrid static voltage discharged through my body again, and then I was in the water alongside him. I knew that I was now too weak to lift him out manually, and thought instead about slipping the single strop and placing it around his shoulders. I would have to take my chances in the interim, including the possibility that my helicopter might be driven off if another air attack came in. Such a prospect was not an attractive one.

Instinct saved the day. At the top of each swell, the taut winch wire went slack, flexing sufficiently to allow me to reach up and get the winch hook into a small nylon becket on the front of his life jacket. In reality, it shouldn't have worked, but it did, and together we were lifted up to the safety of the helicopter's cabin. My jaw was now rattling with cold, so Mike Crabtree ordered the door closed, and put the cabin heaters on full blast. Agonisingly, slowly, sensation returned. I could now feel things with my fingers again, and they touched the little Olympus camera still in my combat jacket pocket. It was ruined...

We delivered our customers to *Canberra*, then Mike said: 'Well *done* Doc. Bloody marvellous –' After the events of Fanning Head I felt a lot better, and we were now all square as we flew back to the scene. By this time, *Ardent* had been abandoned because the fire aft had taken such a hold that her main magazines were about to blow. We were ordered clear, so instead I winched down with the two special stretchers to HMS *Yarmouth*, which had taken all the survivors aboard. In the emergency sick bay that had been made out of the frigate's wardroom, the young MO was living up to his name. Surgeon Lieutenant Andy Cope was in complete control, pointing out the seriously injured to me for high priority of evacuation, while calmly suturing two lacerated scalps. It was really terrific stuff, and I was very proud of him. That pride was tinged with sadness however, because HMS *Ardent's* medical officer, Surgeon Lieutenant Simon Ridout, was last seen floating in the sea having been blown over the side. He was missing, presumed dead.

Both stretchers, and some of the men of *Ardent* with burns or minor injuries were then winched up from *Yarmouth's* flight deck into one of the stream of helicopters that had arrived to help. We travelled up Falkland Sound, and then round into San Carlos Water, before slowing to come alongside *Canberra*. The remainder of the subdued, hollow-eyed and tired survivors then transferred onto a moored pontoon, then climbed the gangway up and into the liner's embarkation door. Still damp from my immersion, I joined them.

What happened next will live with me for the rest of my life. The men of 42 Commando RM were waiting patiently in the darkened corridors for their call forward to go ashore. They were all dressed in full battle gear, with camouflage cream on their faces. As the *Ardent* survivors, for the most part still wearing their anti-flash hoods and gloves, and stinking of firesmoke, stumbled past them in the narrowed passageways, the Marines of 42 Commando quietly applauded, patting some of them on the back with whispered thanks. *Ardent's* defiant stand against hopeless odds had not gone unappreciated. Royal owed Jack for that, and Royal was now going ashore to sort the Argies out. Many of the *Ardents* were in tears.

Onboard *Canberra*, they'd been very busy and, as dusk fell, the Action Medical Organisation swung into top gear. Now, with the risk of air attack gone, the surgeons could work on their patients without interruption, and they started on their long lists. A quick tour of the Bonito Club revealed my two rescued survivors asleep but comfortable. Both had injuries of sufficient severity to require morphine, and I noted that the first one, an Able Seaman named John Dillon, was lying next to one of the Argentine soldiers that we had lifted earlier in the day from Fanning Head!

As I stared at the second survivor, a bearded Chief Petty Officer, he opened his eyes and looked at me. His parched lips were moving. I bent closer to hear the words, and his whispered thanks meant a lot. I then remembered that someone had given me a paper cup with a tot of rum in it, so with Dr Peter Mayner's approval, I moistened his lips and tongue with a few drops of rum from my finger. Chief Ken Enticknap's face relaxed into a smile, and an instant later he was asleep again.

Later, as I changed into dry clothing in my small cabin, another message came through. Simon Ridout had, quite miraculously, survived after all and was now warming up in the Captain's bath in HMS *Broadsword*. The relief of that news was quickly forgotten with the next Command bombshell. *Canberra* was being ordered to sail that night, away from San Carlos and any repeat of all the day's danger, away to the safety of South Georgia.

I sought out Roger Wilkes for an urgent discussion. He and his staff had been busy all day, and there was still work to do. We had to get the green-bereted element of the team off quickly, and as there were no cranes or helicopters to unload the freight chacons on the upper deck, it was pointless taking No. 3 Medical Troop ashore, or even the excellent stretcher bearers from our Band. He asked if he could keep them on board in the first instance, which seemed a sensible move, at least until we had found out exactly what facilities were available on land. Also, at the back of my mind was a realistic, but rather cold-blooded awareness that if any of us were killed in the next few days, we would need to be replaced – by those held in reserve on *Canberra*.

I don't think Erich Bootland was very happy at first with my decision, but it was a case of 'needs must'. The headquarters of Medical Squadron and the Plymouth-based SST 2 were now to get ashore, as soon as possible, and go to Red Beach, the codename for Ajax Bay. There (we thought) we would be meeting up again with Malcolm Hazell and his boys of No. 1 Medical Troop plus their stores from the LSL *Sir Lancelot*, and also the PCT (Parachute Clearing Troop) off the North Sea ferry *Norland*.

Hurriedly, we assembled what kit we could man-pack, mainly surgical instruments, blood and medical replenishment stores. My wet clothing was still hanging up to dry in the cabin. I had no proper military boots, only wellies. In the tearing rush to get down to the loading area on time, we all left little but important things behind.

Then, if that wasn't all complication enough, I was then handed a strange signal on my way down to board the landing craft for our journey ashore. It stated, in contradiction to the previous instructions, that the *Canberra* medical and surgical personnel leaving the ship were not to go to Red Beach at all, but to HMS *Fearless* instead! This signal did not appear to originate from Brigade HQ, and although the custom of the Royal Navy is normally to 'obey the last pipe', I had sufficient doubts about the message's authenticity to question its content.

We had long ago agreed that although she was a splendid ship, HMS *Fearless* was nearly useless as a surgical facility, so the rationale underlying this slightly weird instruction did not make any sense. It was difficult to know what to do, but I decided that it would be better to sort the whole problem out come the next morning. The *Canberra* deck officers were chafing at the bit, anxious to lift the anchor and proceed. We were delaying them.

At 0230, a big LCU (Landing Craft Utility) burbled up to lie alongside the gunport door. In pitch darkness we loaded stores, freight, baggage, weapons and personnel. Everything had happened so quickly that there was no time to make stores lists or to take stock properly. With the last metal bins and gas cylinders loaded, the LCU pulled away from *Canberra's* tall flanks. The liner got under way almost immediately, gathering speed as her pale and ghostly bulk disappeared in the direction of Fanning Head. Under the sparkling and clear night sky, our landing craft now chugged quietly past several darkened ships towards its destination.

About an hour later, at 0330, the ramp went down, and we struggled over the rocks in the darkness, up towards a trackway laid by the Amphibious Beach Unit. All the surgical stores, blood containers, cardboard fluid replenishment boxes, and our bergens were then carried slowly and carefully up to the main entrance of the building. Complete blackout had been enforced because of the very real risk of counter-attack from West Falkland. The Argentine commander there would have had a grandstand view of events in Falkland Sound during D-Day, and if he was worth his pay grade, should have been getting his act together for a riposte.

Entering the darkened building, which was lit only by a couple of Tilley lamps, I found that Malcolm Hazell and his boys had got ashore safely together with all their kit. The Parachute Clearance Troop were also in residence, trying to tamp holes through the thick walls of the building for the exhaust pipes of their small electrical generators. I told them to stop. There were too many people wandering about, exploring their new surroundings and chattering.

I then ordered everyone to get their sleeping mats out and their heads down. First light was due in less than five hours, and we would have to 'stand to' then in case of a dawn attack by the enemy. My military talents in organising fire positions and clearing patrols were about what you'd expect from a Naval obstetrician, albeit a Commando-trained one. Luckily, their Lordships had quite understood this point, and we had Lieutenant Fred Cook and WO2 Terry Moran as part of the team in order to look after that side of the shop.

I took a last look around, rubbing the base of my neck and the muscle that had popped while lifting John Dillon out of the sea that afternoon. It hurt, and my whole shoulder girdle was aching from the muscular effort that had been expended. I hoped that Able Seaman Dillon was well, and wondered if I'd ever see the chap again, or if he would ever know who had rescued him. The words of the Neil Diamond song '*He ain't heavy – he's my brother*' now had a very real and rather personal meaning for me. Eventually, with my mind still racing, but with a body that was totally exhausted, I fell asleep.

Saturday May 22nd

Dawn passed without incident. If the sky had blossomed at first light with Argentine parachutes, heralding a counter-attack from the mainland, it would have been an interesting start to the day. The Royal Marines of the Commando Logistic Regiment were all glad to be ashore in a real soldiering role, even if their first task of every morning at Ajax Bay was a defensive one.

'Standing-to' in allocated defensive positions had always been part of our first and last light routines, drummed into all of us right from the start of training. What was a complete pain in the perineum up on Woodbury Common, or out on Dartmoor, was now a piece of sheer common sense based on many years of British campaigning around the globe. The forefingers that sweated and itched around the trigger guards of many carefully-sited machine guns were highly trained. A rapid response helicopter assault also had to be a serious threat if the Argentine commander on the other side of Falkland Sound had been worth his salt. The British landing force was going to be utterly dependent on its logistic formation for the daily issues of bread and bullets, and a disruptive raid into the Brigade Maintenance Area would have been very valuable to our enemy.

Combat supply was a rather nebulous concept in peacetime thinking, but here it was going to control, perhaps even limit the tactical possibilities, and even if the rumoured Argentine parachute force was not dropped on us to do a destruction job, the 'Loggies' faced a serious and continuing threat from what remained of the Argentine Air Force. There was endless speculation as to how many of the first day's 'air show' participants had been knocked down, or else perforated too badly by machine gun and cannon fire to fly again without downtime for repair.

Our first priorities therefore related to preparing safety trenches outside, with special emphasis on overhead protection.

Stimulated by multiple episodes of heavy adrenaline release yesterday, the boys needed very little encouragement to dig for their lives, because that basic truth was obvious. Wet peat blocks were cut from the rocky soil all around the building, then stacked up to make sangar walls, reinforced by some of the bigger stones. Human ingenuity now appeared unlimited when associated with possible survival. One shelter had a right-angled turn constructed in the entrance porch, while another, built by some of the SST personnel, looked clearly suited for the nuclear age. Then, with somewhere to run out to whenever the air raid warnings were sounded, everyone turned their attention to the business of setting up shop inside the building.

The Ajax Bay slaughterhouse and refrigerated store complex was shaped like a large 'T', with the main spine running from north to south, and longer in length than the 'cross bar', which in turn was a bit wider. At the expanded base of the 'T' there appeared to have been an open slaughterhouse, because an overhead rail system began there, presumably to carry the mutton carcasses along to the adjacent chilling-down and storage areas. There was a set of windows here too, or rather the remains of them; both wind and daylight now had unrestricted passage. Part of the floor was ankle deep in rusting rubbish and tie-on meat labels, swept there by the Quartermaster's staff of 45 Commando RM. They had got into Ajax Bay/*Red Beach* first, and the carefully-stacked pallets of rifle ammunition, anti-tank weapons and mortar bombs bore witness to their industry.

The remainder of the sub-divided areas within the building were cold, airless, and totally devoid of light. Each of the larger adjacent 'rooms' contained refrigeration machinery along one wall, consisting of a complex network of large-calibre pipes and the associated pumping plant. The walls and floors were very dusty and dirty but, thankfully, the spaces generally seemed to be dry and vermin-free. There were some sheep droppings to be found as well, evidence that local shepherds had perhaps taken shelter in the past from some excess in the local weather conditions.

Lighting was an immediate problem to be solved, because No. 1 Medical Troop's diesel-powered electric generator had not taken kindly to repeated immersion in South Atlantic salt spray. For a while, I seriously considered the merits of moving in to the slaughterhouse area, so as to be sure of enough natural daylight to operate by, at least between dawn and dusk. The Quartermaster of 45 Commando could quite understand the black humour of having a field operating theatre positioned within an abandoned slaughterhouse, but the amount of work that would be required to shift his stores to facilitate this request made him rather reluctant. This reluctance hardened into a suggestion that, as our ranks were similar, I should go and 'investigate sex and travel'!

In view of what happened later on, I was glad that my colleague's wishes prevailed. Workshop Squadron then solved our lighting problem by lending us a 6 kVA generator, which began to perform faultlessly. The medical teams thus stayed where we had started, which turned out to be a really lucky break for us.

Although I had sidestepped the rather dubious suggestion of placing all our surgical assets into one of the two assault ships, I now found that pressure was still building to have some kind of surgical presence there. Gerry Wells-Cole was apologetic when he came to see me, especially when I explained my doubts about the signal that we had received at the last moment before leaving *Canberra* in the early hours. However, he said that our old nemesis – the chap we had labelled as 'Not Entitled' – was making life very difficult for him, and couldn't we diversify our resources just a little bit in order to appease the guy and shut him up?

I was not very happy with this compromise, but if that was what Gerry wanted, then I could construe it as a proper and lawful request that had come down the official command chain. I chose HMS *Intrepid*, and sent over Tim Douglas-Riley and Nick Morgan, Commando-trained resuscitation officer and surgeon respectively, along with some staff. The small team was called SST 2 *Alpha*.

Of course, they were almost totally frustrated by the lack of space or suitable facilities on board the big assault ship, but I also planned to extricate them if things got busy in Ajax Bay. Practical common sense had lost out to special interest and wild theory. Our unco-operative senior colleague, 'NE', was still being a nuisance. He *still* didn't appear to have a proper appointment within the Amphibious Task Group, and was just relying on his rank to stir things up. I wondered when he might visit us in Ajax Bay, and what I might end up saying to him when he did. Would he try and get me sacked? I then thought of Julian Thompson's ringing words of endorsement to me, and just got on with my proper duties.

Back on shore, at Ajax Bay, things were much better. With a bit of ingenuity in stacking boxes and then rigging up blanket and scrim net screens, the team had set up a Command Post as well as a casualty flow system. As there were no roads to speak of in this part of the Islands, all the wounded casualties would be arriving by helicopter on a rough little patch of ground outside. They would then be brought through the main door, searched for weapons and ammunition, disarmed, and then passed on into Triage to get priorities for treatment sorted, and documentation initiated.

The weapons would then be made safe, as we did not want any incidents involving our staff encountering grenades and ammunition in personal clothing as they began resuscitating the wounded to get them fit for surgery. Next to the Resus bay were the 'operating theatres'. This was a somewhat grandiose description of a set of rather skeletal McVicar operating tables, plus their surrounding resources. The casualty flow system then looped back on itself, out into the post-operative area and its adjacent high-and-low dependency 'wards'.

Right from the start, we realised that we were going to have very little capacity for holding and nursing any casualties who had survived that far. Whole textbooks had been written on post-operative complications in severely wounded patients of the kind that we would be seeing, so we desperately needed a system of getting them out to the hospital ship as quickly as possible. I had not been given any details to work on as to how we might achieve this, but remained optimistic. I had very few facts or assets to hand, only an expectation that the traditional virtues of flexibility, ingenuity and a grim determination to succeed would get us all through.

Meanwhile, it seemed a sensible idea to position the Evacuation section close to the right-hand side of the door and entrance vestibule; both features were wide enough to accommodate a two-way traffic flow.

The PCT were soon in business with their two operating tables rigged and lit, surrounded by stores boxes. They were certainly an interesting lot, individuals for the most part, of widely differing temperaments and attitudes, but all immensely proud and enthusiastic about the Airborne aspects of military operations.

The CO of the Commando Logistic Regiment had not yet been allowed ashore by Brigade HQ, so his daily 'O' Group was held instead out on the LSL (Logistic Ship Landing) *Sir Galahad*. With the weather deteriorating rapidly, our ride out to the ship was something of a roller-coaster nightmare in the small 'rigid raider' that was sent to collect the Squadron commanders. Conditions then worsened, so I was quite glad later on when we were marooned onboard for the night. There was the chance instead for a glass of beer with some of the other OCs, and an opportunity as well to talk to the Brigade Air Squadron pilots who had yet to hear how Ken Francis and his crewman died on D-Day. My second night's sleep in the Falklands was on a spare mattress, but without a sleeping bag, or 'green slug' to zip into.

Sunday, May 23rd

I returned ashore with Lieutenant Colonel Hellberg. As wind and weather had abated, we were only slightly wet when reaching land once more. I gave a quick brief to the lads about how the battle was going, then a Mk. 4 Sea King arrived as our daily, and dedicated Casevac aircraft. We also addressed ourselves to the problem of whether or not to paint Red Crosses on the roof of the building. The decision turned on the fact that the whole Ajax Bay area of Red Beach was so confined, and the area available for open storage so limited, that we could not honestly separate our medical facilities and personnel from those troops dealing with combat supplies.

There was also a sneaky suspicion about an enemy actually using the Red Cross as a morale-smashing aiming mark. We had noted that while Argentina was a signatory of the Geneva Convention, there were some awful stories in circulation about the military dictatorship that ran the country, and how they had been kidnapping and murdering those who were opposed to them. I took the problem to Brigadier Julian Thompson when he dropped in to see us. The decision was instantaneous. If the legitimate targets were too close to the protected ones, then Red Cross insignia were *not* to be used. I felt at the time, and indeed still do, that this was both a brave call – and the correct one.

I don't know what Julian Thompson really thought about us all, in his heart of hearts, but we must have seemed a rather curious lot, thrown together by the exigencies and circumstance of this war. Obviously, Medical Squadron was the key element of this land-based field hospital team, since we were an integral part of our parent formation, the Commando Logistic Regiment RM, and were actually co-located with them in Ajax Bay.

Our Naval surgical support team members were also old friends, in that we had trained together before the deployment south. The more experienced officers and ratings amongst them had been to Norway with us, and had either dug and spent some time in a snow hole, or 'overnighted' in a snow pit under a 10-man tent sheet. Most of them had also just completed a Chemical Warfare instruction course with us, and had learned just how difficult it was to live and fight in the restrictive clothing and respirators that were key features for survival in this unpleasant but possible complication of a future battlefield.

By contrast, the Royal Army Medical Corps (RAMC) personnel were an unknown entity to us. I had done some courses with them, and also served with Army medics in Northern Ireland, but we were all a bit wary of each other to start with. For their part, the Parachute Clearing Troop, or PCT as the small formation was generally known, seemed rather unsure of the command structure locally. They had come to war in the same ship as 2 Para, but were now separated from them. They regarded themselves (quite rightly) as a semi-independent elite – who could be relied on to jump in with a hostage-rescue parachute assault force, get set up quickly using whatever local resources were available, and then start caring for the wounded within minutes of arriving on the ground.

Inevitably, the odd little squabble broke out. An 'us' and 'them' attitude became apparent, with old tribal prejudices between red and green berets bubbling to the surface. As OC Med I found myself being approached to referee some of these disputes, and as my beret was green, my boys naturally expected me to take *their* side in these arguments. On occasion, however, I felt that I could not.

For instance, a problem resulted when we broke up the bulk of the medical stores that we had brought ashore. These were mainly contained in lightweight, but strong and rigid green plastic containers called Thomas bins. One of Med Squadron's Q (Quartermaster) team had the bright idea of stacking these on their sides, up against a solid, breeze-block wall. This ran the length of a compartment linking the main nursing area and the place where the four operating tables had been set up.

The stores items had been packed tactically to start with, widely dispersed throughout the several dozen Thomas bins, to ensure that the loss of any single bin did not mean the absence of any vital drug, dressing or intravenous solution to accident or enemy action. Under the direction of Scouse Davies, our red-outable Chief MA in charge of stores, the bins were now unpacked onto the dusty concrete floor of Ajax Bay, then repacked into component groups. The narrow compartment suddenly became a self-help dispensary, with everything on view, stacked neatly in these cleverly-designed boxes which became, in effect, the shelves of a hospital pharmacy.

The PCT, quite naturally, took advantage of this Aladdin's cave. Normally, they planned to parachute into action with enough medical stores for around fifty major surgical procedures. They were also always ready, quite instinctively, for a sudden order to change location, because the boundaries of a battlefield can change rather quickly in an airborne operation. As a result, some of their own medical stores remained packed for just such an emergency lift-and-shift, and they were trying to 'borrow' Med Squadron's resupply stores instead of consuming their own ready-use items.

I could understand why, and was not really able to get very upset about these tactics, but at the same time I could also sympathise with the Marines' irritation at such apparent greed. There had to be some form of symbiosis in these new arrangements, and not just straightforward parasitism. I told the PCT commander just that, but the niggles continued. This 'parallel existence' between PCT and Med Squadron had to be stopped somehow. As one of the recruit training team had said to me back at Lympstone ten years previously, it was time for some of that 'leadership stuff' – and a bit of direct action. I called for what the Royal Navy terms a 'Clear Lower Deck', the evolution which occurs when all the hands are summoned to hear their Commanding Officer speak. This is usually done to pass on some important message that has been signalled to the ship. Everyone in Ajax Bay was ordered to fall in outside.

Standing, on my own now, on a large wooden container with the various sub-unit leaders just below and in front of me, I introduced each one of them to the assembled groups. Groups are what they remained in. The Para RAMC boys stood together in a little huddle, with the Marines of Medical Squadron well separated from them; the naval types hung back on their own. As I half-expected, the introductions brought little cheers and hisses from the rival factions, so I got really angry – and let them have both barrels.

I told them that we simply *had* to work together, because there were nearly five thousand potential customers belonging to 3 Commando Brigade out there in front of us. They did not give a damn who was going to look after them if they were wounded, just as long as whoever it was could fix them up properly. For our part, whether the wounded man was a 'Tom', or a 'Royal', or even a 'Jolly Jack' from one of the ships, we now had just one purpose in life – to ensure that they did not die of their wounds. Furthermore, I added, it was an appalling waste of personal energy to continue with this inter-tribal squabbling instead of devoting *all* our attention to the fighting soldiers that we were here to serve.

The PCT looked surprised at this verbal assault, my own Squadron looked a bit hurt, and the Naval SST appeared confused. But the message began to sink in. I finished by saying that anyone who persisted in being difficult would find himself sacked. He would be sent out to the Hospital Ship to be used as they saw fit – working in the galley pot wash for all I cared. Out there he would also find pretty nurses, hot showers and cold beer – but *he would not be with us.* Later on, I noticed that the guys had stopped wearing their different berets, and had taken to conversing with each other instead. We were beginning to become a proper team.

Unknown to all of us, this was the start of a fantastic and hugely fulfilling period in our lives, when the collective efforts of our little group would make military history and be widely admired, not just by the people we had committed ourselves to serve, but also by the enemy that we were on these Islands to defeat.

A little later I received a message from Cdo Log HQ down on the beach. 3 Para had apparently sustained casualties in a fire-fight, and there were eight men wounded, perhaps ten. A helicopter was inbound to us. WO2 Fritz Sterba, one of the two PCT senior theatre technicians, broke out some first-line stores in readiness. There was then a delay, much too long a delay knowing 3 Para's rough position just north of Port San Carlos, so I jogged down to HQ. For some reason, probably interference by 'Not Entitled', the whole load of wounded had been diverted to HMS *Intrepid*! There was no time to work out just how or why this had happened, only a pressing need to get those casualties out from the ship and into the hands of our teams at Ajax Bay. I ran back up to my waiting casevac pilot, and we flashed up the Sea King in a real hurry.

After a very short flight we landed on the LPD's empty deck, and inside the main dining hall I found frantic, but semi-organised chaos. All our direst predictions had come true. *Intrepid* was nowhere near suitable as a primary casualty handling facility. The SST 2 *Alpha* boys were doing their best, working flat out to get drips going and blood transfusions set up on half a dozen paratrooper casualties who had been laid out on the mess hall dining tables. A number of longish-haired gentlemen in military clothing, patrol medics from 22 SAS, were also helping.

Tim Douglas-Riley was concise and despairing in his brief. Two of the wounded had penetrating head wounds and looked unlikely survival prospects. I decided to take the three worst injured ashore, and return later for the rest, while Tim and his boys did what they could. I also thanked all the sailors and Special Forces medics for their skill and help. Nick Morgan and Andy

Yates, his anaesthetist, then operated on one of the few wounded men who was fit enough to be moved along the main passageway and up a steep ladder to the junior wardroom 'operating theatre'.

Ashore, Bill McGregor and Phil Shouler got on with surgery for the remainder of the injured. Later on, Bill removed a bullet from the brain of one of the 'hopeless' cases, and George Rudge put his skills as a jaw surgeon to work by tidying up the other's skull wound beautifully.

It then turned out that this was one of those 'blue-on-blue' incidents, when your own side accidentally engages friendly forces. A map-reading error, accidental penetration of an inter-company boundary by a fighting patrol – and almost before you knew it, two groups from the same unit were trying to tear bits out of each other. The 'defending' GPMG gunner in this incident was a Regimental champion shot. He opened fire at 800 metres or so, and hit half a dozen of his chums. It wasn't until the battalion's mortar fire controller noted a reciprocity in the grid references that he was being asked to engage that the ghastly possibility of fratricidal contact was realised, and 3 Para became the latest military formation to discover the awful truth that 'friendly fire' is a complete misnomer. It really isn't friendly at all.

The CO was now alerted, called for helicopter help, and a Mk. 4 Sea King arrived. They flew to the grid reference, spotted the casualties and ran in to land. The pilot then did a rapid 'fan stop', where the helicopter's nose is pulled up, and the whirling main rotors slow the aircraft down quickly. Unfortunately, he was new to the Sea King, but had many hours in the somewhat smaller Wessex 5. In the excitement of this first 'real' war task, he misjudged his manoeuvre, running the tail rotor along the ground instead, and converting the Sea King into a big, green, semi-portable hut. Misfortune was heaped on adversity, while the wounded watched in despair. Another helicopter was summoned.

Later on, I encountered 3 Para's Quartermaster, Major Norman Menzies, at the daily Logistic brief. He was a former

RSM, and fiercely proud of the Airborne ethos. Like the PCT boys, he also appeared rather embarrassed about this incident, and was reluctant to talk about it. I gripped his arm and made him listen. I told him to spread the good news back at his Unit that *all* the wounded had survived, even the two men with penetrating head injuries, and that they would soon be out on the hospital ship.

Hew Pike thanked me personally for this later on. He had all but sacked one of the company commanders involved, and at the same time, he was able to tell his gallant paratroopers to put this incident behind them, and just get on with the next task. 3 Para's famous long 'tab' across East Falkland, and the nightmare of Mount Longdon were still to come.

Throughout this period air raids were developing with increasing frequency and, for the first time, surgeons, anaesthetists and theatre staff had to face the serious strain of challenged ethics and divided loyalties. Should a man obey his powerful instincts of self-preservation, and run for his slit trench when the six whistle blasts were blown? Or should he stay at his post, looking after a patient on the operating table? The proper traditions persisted and they mostly ignored the whistles. Eventually, we worked out a routine where I would come in and select those who had to stay and those who could leave. Some medical personnel simply had to survive, even if Ajax Bay itself was destroyed. Unfortunately, I was the only one who could not be designated as suitable to go and hide, although I did notice that some absentees had disappeared without my invitation to go. Usually I just stood by the door, visible to those within, but keeping an eye on what was happening outside.

During one alert I suddenly spotted that the figures on the skyline around us had dropped out of sight. I was still somewhat unsure as to why this had happened, when a Dagger flew over the Sussex Ridge behind us. Several of us stood slack-jawed as a Rapier missile sprinted upwards and took it in the tailpipe. Our cheers were loud and long, later confirmed on the radio that a number of Daggers (the Israeli version of the Mirage, which the Argentines flew) had been 'splashed'.

But this score was not achieved without cost to the Royal Navy. Late in the afternoon, the handsome Type 21 frigate HMS *Antelope* steamed into the anchorage, well away from the other ships. She had a big dark hole in her starboard side, and the top of her electronic support measures mast was leaning over at a drunken angle, actually struck by the fuel tank of a low-flying Skyhawk. The frigate anchored opposite Ajax Bay to await the process of defusing and removing the unexploded bomb lodged deep in her hull.

On the far side of San Carlos Water, HMS *Argonaut* was still doing the same thing, with the Clearance Diving Officer Lt Cdr Brian Dutton groping in the darkness of a flooded magazine that contained one live Argentine bomb, several live Seacat missiles, and the body of a dead sailor. Although both ships were out of battle temporarily, they lay under the protective steel umbrella of both fleet and shore anti-aircraft missile batteries.

Then a heavy explosion rattled the walls of Ajax Bay. I ran outside, and in the dusk could see that the unexploded bomb must have detonated inside HMS *Antelope*. The ship's *Lynx* helicopter arrived with an injured colleague of the bomb disposal expert who had actually been tackling the device. Staff Sergeant Jim Prescott of the Royal Engineers had been killed instantly, and a flying steel hatch had all but severed WO2 John Phillips' left arm. I helped Phil Shouler to complete a neat amputation, using one of the PCT tables. The divisions between 'Red and Green' were blurring nicely as time went by.

Bill McGregor watched quietly, assessing and judging, and constantly popping out to see what was happening in Triage as more casualties came in. I realised then how lucky we were to have Bill with us. He was a calming and encouraging influence of huge experience, and no mean wielder of the knife himself. We took six casualties in all that night, and I decided to introduce the PCT to an old Naval Custom – that of issuing a tot of rum to those involved in 'Arduous Duty'.

This was a regulation contained in Chapter 47 of the Queen's Regulations for the Royal Navy (QRRN). The all-important tome was always being updated, and while we were deployed in Norway one time, I had helped with the laborious process of keeping QRRN bang up to date. Chapter 47 was called 'Instructions for Medical Officers', and I had come across a fascinating gem stating that if arduous duty had been undertaken, such as recovery of survivors or bodies by a seaboat crew, and where the commanding officer and medical officer concurred, two-thirds of a gill of commercial spirit could be issued, at public expense, to each of those personnel involved.

Of course, these rules said nothing about the 'commanding officer' and the medical officer being the same person! Our limited stocks would suffice for only two such issues to all the staff, but we exercised this privilege nonetheless. This dark-blue tradition, as well as the tots themselves, went down extremely well.

Outside, the fire took hold of *Antelope* and gradually, like some dreadful cancer eating into the heart of the ship, the flames spread from midships right along her hull. She burned down towards the waterline and then, in a huge shower of sparks, the aft Seacat missile magazine exploded. The lads watched silently in the darkness, standing by the main door. Seeing a ship die like this was agony for anyone who had ever loved the Royal Navy and its way of life. It was all bad, bad news.

Monday, May 24th

Antelope was still on fire, but her outline was glowing rather than burning. As first light turned to dawn, we could see that her main feature now was a huge grey plume of smoke that was drifting and climbing slowly away to the south. As breakfast finished, I noticed that many of the marines and paras were standing together on the track outside the refrigeration plant, sipping their 'wets' of tea or coffee, and just staring out at this unpleasant sight. The ship's superstructure had gone, and there was a distinct notch in the remaining outline, as if the inferno had started to penetrate downwards into her hull.

It was not all doom and gloom inside though. All the 3 Para patients from yesterday were well, especially the two lads with penetrating head injuries whom we had labelled as hopeless cases in the first assessment. They could both sit up, open their eyes, and swallow liquids. One could even give his name and number, which was a huge surprise to us all, and a remarkable tribute to his personal powers of recuperation. I could not yet send them off to the Hospital Ship *Uganda*, because we didn't know where she was, and also had no direct means of communication with her.

Instead, when our daily casevac helicopter arrived, I got a lift out to HMS *Intrepid* before the pilot shut down. I had two aims for this mission, the first to try and ascertain *Uganda's* whereabouts, and the second to repossess our small surgical team. We had spent quite enough time and effort pandering to 'Not Entitled'...

A series of air raids then came in under a blue, blue sky. In the ship's wardroom we all cowered on the carpeted deck as a metallic Tannoy voice called the strikes, ending with the urgent command: *'TAKE COVER – TAKE COVER!'* I was very conscious of not having any anti-flash gear to put on, but the SAS and SBS men in the corner just sat quietly in their cotton hoods and gloves, not bothering to stretch out under the wardroom table, but just ignoring all the fuss and reading the well-worn magazines and newspapers. The upper deck machine guns chattered away, reverberating throughout the ship, echoed by the slower and heavier thudding sound of the Oerlikon cannons.

Once again, General Lami Dozo's airmen did their thing and delivered their loads on target – but the bombs were duff. Two UXBs were positioned in one of the logistic ships, and one UXB in another. Their crews were evacuated to Ajax Bay while the bomb disposal teams were summoned. HMS *Antelope* sank in the middle of all this excitement, her brave back finally penetrated and broken by the smouldering fire. The cold sea rushed in, and a towering pillar of steam and smoke rose up to the sky above the still-surfaced bow and stern sections. These settled slowly beneath the surface too, until the only trace left floating to mark the previous existence of a once living, fighting ship was an emergency life raft. This was still secured to the hull beneath, and its bright Day-Glo canopy contrasted starkly with the grey and fuel-slicked water all around.

Ashore, I found out that the boys had seen the whole attack. One of the A-4 Skyhawks had turned towards them after releasing its bombs. It screamed over the roof of our building so low, and banked over so sharply, that they could actually see the pilot's white helmet. Brave as he was, I fervently hoped that this chap had been caught by our Sea Harriers on his way home.

There was a good reason for my apparent callousness. If that jet had been carrying a photographic camera in its nose, then Ajax Bay's status would certainly alter. Overnight, we would be moved right to the top of the *Fuerza Aerea Argentina*'s hit list.

Some of our chums from the LSL *Sir Galahad* took a look around our facilities while they waited for the UXBs on their ship to be dealt with. They were somewhat taken aback by the primitive conditions in which we were working. Everything seemed so unreal to them after the physical comforts enjoyed in their floating grey hotel. For my part I would much rather have taken my chances ashore, but they disagreed, echoed by another friend who had just come ashore permanently from *Sir Galahad*. Les Short was the REME Major who commanded Workshop Squadron. With a soldier's sixth sense, he had already ordered all his men to get out of any buildings, and move into tented accommodation on the surrounding ground.

He told us some amusing stories about life afloat during the air attacks. One concerned Lieutenant Commander Gervase Coryton, a Fleet Air Arm Gazelle pilot on exchange with the Royal Marines. He was actually on board during one air attack and rushed up to the bridge to get a better look. Grabbing a pair of binoculars he stood out on the starboard bridge wing, focused the instrument and announced: 'Ah, here comes one. An A-4, I think...'

There was a loud crash as the pilot leapt backwards into the wheelhouse, and a strangled cry of 'Bloody *Hell*!', followed by a huge bang as a 30 mm cannon shell passed through the upperworks where he'd just been standing. After that, Gervase stayed airborne whenever he could!

A bit later on that same day, the LSL ship's company and embarked force were listening intently to the broadcast announcements of developing attacks, then playing the serious game of rushing over to the side away from the incoming attack in order to minimise the human cost of a cannonfire strike. *Sir Galahad*, on these occasions, would rock from side to side with the sudden shift of weight. The Second Officer came on main broadcast during one afternoon air raid with: 'Two high speed hostiles to the east, and closing – *plus* another pair to the south west, also approaching fast. Gentlemen – take your pick!'

Tuesday, May 25th

Today was a famous Argentine national holiday, and everyone was secretly hoping that their aircraft carrier – the ARA *Vienticinquo de May*o – would come out to fight, although we also understood the Argentine Navy's reluctance to do so. The loss of their heavy cruiser (and Pearl Harbour survivor from the Japanese attack in 1941) ARA *General Belgrano* must have cooled a few of the more volcanic hotheads, including the naval boss Admiral Anaya. This chap was supposed to have told Galtieri that taking and keeping the 'Malvinas', as the Argentines called these Islands, would be a bit of a doddle. Perhaps, we told ourselves hopefully, Sandy Woodward had a master plan up his sleeve for today, and the first part of the Fleet Air Arm version of the 'Evita' anthem would come true:

> *Don't cry for me Argentina*
> *The truth is we will defeat you*
> *And with our Sea Harrier*
> *We'll sink your carrier…*

But there were also other, much more pressing problems. At last we had a definite booking for Her Majesty's Hospital Ship *Uganda*, and an aircraft allocated for us to reach her. We had asked Northwood if she could perhaps leave the 'Red Cross Box' every day, and close up towards the Islands in order to be nearer to us. They were thinking about this. Otherwise, we would just have to ask them to request her to be in the correct place a day later!

I could foresee that we were going to have problems with this procedure unless we could establish a different but simple routine. Eventually, the promised Mk. 4 Sea King arrived from HMS *Intrepid* at first light, and the aircrewman then asked me where *Uganda* was supposed to be! I sent him back to his parent ship to find out. That aircraft then went unserviceable, so Lieutenant John Miller turned up in another Mk. 4. No problems here. John was an old and really sensible friend from Norway and Salisbury Plain days*. He lifted from Ajax Bay at 1250 with four sitting casualties and five stretchers, plus Bill McGregor acting as escort and liaison.

I suddenly sensed that we really were beginning a unique period in our lives. By the accidents of happenstance and fate, two groups of dedicated doctors and paramedics had come together from quite different backgrounds; we were now a team of medical officers and men who shared their customers' military virtues of being tough, determined, dedicated, tireless – and capable. Our patients were pretty strong and fit too, because they seemed able not just to cope with, but also to survive injuries that would surely have killed lesser men.

Bill McGregor's request to go out as escort to *Uganda* was typical. He had now assessed Phil Shouler as capable of covering a serious emergency, but at the same time he was anxious to establish exactly what *Uganda* could and could not do to support us. Although Bill was not actually in command of the PCT, he was certainly in charge of Ajax Bay's overall surgical standards.

From what I had seen so far, his background of war experience in the Middle East and Northern Ireland had produced a true battle surgeon – a man who was quick to decide priorities, determined when attacking the heart of the operative problem, and generous in the encouragement of his subordinates. Away from the table he was a gentle, rather shy man who spoke with a quiet Scots burr. While the others played cards, Bill read and smoked. Fatigue never seemed to affect his attitude, either to me or to the patients. We were all lucky to have him on strength, and I very much regarded him as my senior surgical adviser.

Charles Batty, the second cutter in the PCT, was different altogether. A big, strong, cheerful fellow, he had had some trouble

*I was devastated to learn of his later death, in 2006, from a brain tumour.

with one of the professional examinations along the surgical road. Quite frankly, I was a bit surprised at this, because although he was less experienced, and (inevitably) a bit slower than Bill, his skill with the knife was definitely there. Perhaps he had held certain opinions a bit too strongly in the eyes of the examiners.

That possibility must certainly have applied in the case of Malcolm Jowitt, the RAMC Major who was Bill McGregor's anaesthetist. A thin, blue-eyed man with a short haircut and strong jawline, Malcolm was obviously a very determined individual. I took to him immediately. He had been at the base of the anaesthetic pyramid for some time, but his style and performance complemented Bill's manner wonderfully, even though their personalities were completely different.

The other anaesthetist was Dick Knight, a cheerful fellow with an impish sense of humour and a quick, darting mind. Every morning he checked on the welfare of the good ship *Elk*, because the P&O freighter's Captain was godfather to one of his children. Like Bill McGregor he was a welcome source of practical consultant-level advice to his younger and less experienced anaesthetic colleagues.

An hour and a half later the Sea King returned. *Uganda* was sitting within her 'Red Cross Box', a hundred square miles or so of sea about 30 miles to the north of us. John Miller then took another load out, and came back some two hours later with Bill McGregor, plus some very welcome blankets and sheets. The medical and nursing staff on *Uganda* had been shocked to see our filthy and exhausted patients, and especially surprised that their bandaged wounds had been left unsutured.

Apparently they had never heard of the concept of *delayed* primary suture, which acknowledged the absolute need in 'high-energy' military wounds to remove all dead material, while at the same time allowing atmospheric oxygen in to kill the gas gangrene and tetanus organisms that were inevitably present.

Bill chuckled as he recounted this story, and I was reminded how military medical history tends to repeat itself. The tale told to me by another well-known Airborne surgeon, Major General Norman Kirby, had been very similar. After the Royal Navy carriers had taken his wounded from the Suez Canal drop zone in 1957 they had requested, at the end of the first day, that he should stitch up all the paratroopers' gunshot wounds!

Because of the ship's 'Geneva-approved' communications fit, no-one had been able to tell *Uganda* about the 'big picture' ashore. One day they had seen some Argentine jets nearby, and then a pair of bombed-up Skyhawks had flown over them, very low, rocking their wings as if in salutation of their neutral status. Suddenly they had realised exactly where they were – deaf, but not quite blind, and right up close to the front line of a vicious and very real conflict.

Outside our front door, the simple slit trenches were being further reinforced. The boys had now had some time to think about design and function, and then apply a form of constructive thinking driven by urgent need. Overhead cover was now very much the 'in thing', and several elaborate roof constructions involving old doors, sandbags and thick clods of peat started to appear. There was a great deal of teasing and humorous banter involved, and I was delighted to note that this general attitude had become contagious, with the 'dark blue' Naval ratings fully involved. It was a subconscious relief to me that here was another potential problem that was solving itself as we went along – one thing less for the Boss to worry about, and that was a very welcome relief...

Throughout the day, the air raid warnings also continued. The information leading to these alerts came from varied sources and was not always reliable. Still, it was some time before the bowels did not turn to ice-water when six short whistle blasts were blown, or when HMS *Intrepid's* mournful whistle echoed around San Carlos Water.

Typically, the only serious air raid that we were involved in that afternoon was preceded by – nothing. A pair of A-4 Skyhawks came screeching in from the south, and one of the Argentine pilots suddenly discovered that a Rapier missile had mated with his port wing. He was running in to attack HMS *Fearless*. His cockpit instrument panel must have suddenly begun to look like Piccadilly Circus on a dark night as the warning captions illuminated, and he ejected just in time.

We watched from shore as his parachute canopy cracked open, but went through only two or three swings before he was in the water. A 'rigid raider' dory rushed across to pick him up, then transferred him to a slightly bigger landing craft, which took him (ironically) to HMS *Fearless*, the ship he had just been lining up to destroy. Here the PMO fiddled about with his broken knee, gave him some morphia, and then sent him ashore to us.

I couldn't help but feel sorry for *Teniente Primero* (1st Lieutenant) Ricardo Lucero when he arrived in Ajax Bay. The pilot was a small, dark man with large, fleshy earlobes, and he was in obvious pain. A quick inspection revealed why. His left kneecap was about four inches away from its customary position. The flying suit had been cut open in HMS *Fearless*, but his orange silk squadron scarf was still tucked around his neck. My boys were now crowding around him, trying to get their first look at a real representative of the enemy, so I shooed them away.

Then, with the help of Corporal Jim Pearson* of the PCT, who was our part-time Spanish interpreter, I told Ricardo that although he was a prisoner-of-war, he was also our guest, and that as far as we were concerned, he was just another of the wounded that we were here to look after. In that sense he was no different from anyone else, and his knee now required an operation under general anaesthetic. We told him that he would wake up afterwards with his leg in a plaster cylinder. I wasn't certain

*Sadly, now deceased.

that I had reassured him totally, and the worry lines on Ricardo's face remained until Malcolm Jowitt slid some of his magic anaesthetic into an arm vein. The 'enemy' pilot relaxed into sleep, and Charles Batty then did a careful and effective manipulation of the fractured knee, restoring the designs of Nature.

Later on I watched as *Teniente* Lucero came round from his anaesthetic. He reached down to his left leg, found that it was still there, and began crossing himself in fervent thanks to the Almighty. Ten years later, I saw Ricardo speaking on Michael Bilton's television documentary for Yorkshire TV, *The Falklands – The Untold Story*. He spoke about his ordeal, and quoted the reassuring words spoken to him in the British Field Hospital by a 'Capitan Holly'! This Spanish pronunciation defeated the translators, who just wrote down instead how 'the doctor' had told him that here he was the same as all the other wounded. He had subsequently found this unlikely promise to be true. This appearance of Ricardo on screen was preceded by the appalling footage of a Royal Marine standing guard over him, a wet, bedraggled heap lying on the tank deck of HMS *Fearless*. It made me feel sick to think that Royal had been pointing a rifle at the chap instead of helping him.

That wasn't all.

Seventeen years later, I spoke to Ricardo on a live radio programme broadcast in Argentina. The dory that had reached him in the water didn't cut its engine in time, and ran right over him. Half-drowned, he also became entangled in his parachute, and suffered damage to one of his ear drums. I'm sorry we missed that detail in our care for him. He then recalled how I had also told him that he would probably not fly fast jets again, because of the degree of disruption in his knee, and how he had used this prediction as a motivating force, because he was determined to prove me wrong!

He did just that (as I had actually hoped) but unfortunately the inner ear damage sustained when he was pushed under by the dory had affected his ability to fly on instruments, and he subsequently had to retire from active duty. This brave and wonderful man became a glider instructor at an airfield near Cordoba, and was responsible for bringing on some of the new generation of *Fuerza Aerea Argentina* aircrew, until his death in an accident.

We then heard a report on the radio about Skyhawks passing to the north but thought no more of it until, suddenly – disaster. HMS *Coventry* had been sunk and, it was rumoured, the big freight ship *Atlantic Conveyor* too. I knew from the daily logistic briefings that this container ship had a lot of 3 Cdo Brigade's specialist resupply items onboard, including hundreds of accommodation tents. The heavy-lift RAF Chinook helicopters were also being ferried on deck. This was a heavy blow to our aspirations. Helicopter hours were getting fewer and more precious as naval aircrew flogged their airframes and engines to the point of collapse.

There was much cause for gloom, and it was time for some leadership and reassurance. While briefing the teams, I reminded everyone that whatever obstacles had to be surmounted, we were going to climb over each and every one of them.

Then came the sound of clattering rotor blades outside, and the arrival of a load of injured *Coventry* survivors. Soaked and burned, they were shivering with cold and pain. There were eight living and one dead – the Chinese second laundryman. Their skin damage had been caused by flash burns as the bombs delivered by two A-4s detonated in and below the warship's operations room. It was interesting to note just how well the cotton anti-flash hoods and gloves had defended the faces and hands of those who were wearing them. We covered their burns with Flamazine, a thick white cream which is both pain-killing and antiseptic, then laid them down on to some of *Uganda's* cool white sheets, their stretchers lowered to floor level.

One of the young *Coventry* stokers, his skinned hands in plastic bags, eyed the sleeping Ricardo Lucero rather aggressively. The fire that had burned his hands now burned in his soul, and he simply could not understand our respect and friendliness for this colleague of the two pilots who killed his ship. Then the morphine took hold, and like the rest of the Flamazine-faced marionettes from HMS *Sheffield's* once proud sister ship, the young stoker fell asleep.

Wednesday, May 26th

There was much cursing as another perfect day dawned. Fred Cook came in for some stick about his pronouncements on Falklands weather. He was always maintaining from his experience down here with Naval Party 8901 that no two days were the same, and that blue skies in early winter were almost unheard of. The lower the cloud base, the less likely that we were going to bear witness to the ground-attack skills of the Argentine aviators, but this year it was evidently all different! Last night's rumours about *Atlantic Conveyor* turned out to be true, but there were something like 450 survivors.

A couple of sporadic air raid warnings were sounded during the early afternoon but, really, things were ominously quiet. Charles Laurence of the *Daily Telegraph* and the Spanish-speaking Kim Sabido from *Independent Radio News* came to interview Ricardo. The pilot seemed much chirpier today, and gabbled away in his native tongue, the worry lines on his face now gone. Like any other soldier who had done his duty and survived, he was concerned about his wife and family back in Cordoba. I arranged for him to write a Red Cross letter, and also sent a signal to Northwood, asking them to contact the International Commission for the Red Cross in Geneva, and have the message relayed to Señora Lucero that her man was alive and recovering well as Her Majesty's guest in the British '*Hospedale del Campo*'.

The Fleet Diving Team also arrived to stay with us, led by an irrepressible character named Bernie Bruen. His affection for proper naval rum and his battered fiddle were combined with semi-professional abilities as a raconteur and musical entertainer, but the eccentricity also disguised his true nature. He was the son of an impressively decorated WW2 Fleet Air Arm fighter pilot, and had become a hard, determined man with a deep knowledge of bombs, mines and improvised explosive devices. The FDT had been tasked to have a crack at a bomb in the LSL *Sir Lancelot* the next day, but after the destruction of HMS *Antelope*, no one envied them one little bit.

Now there was an opportunity to examine the area around us in greater detail. Positioned outside the front wall of our medical facility were the No. 1 Medical Troop chacons which had been brought ashore from *Sir Galahad*. These acted as semi-mobile storage 'huts', strung out along the side of a concreted trackway. This narrow road was approximately 100 metres long, running from east to west and down the slight slope towards the beach. Between the refrigerated storage facility and the foreshore, and parallel with the spine of the T-shaped main building, was a second and smaller construction that was now being used as a storehouse, distribution centre and Field Records Office.

The latter outfit was under the command of Captain Roy Hancock, a genial and cheerful Royal Marines officer who got on famously with us, and who was always a welcome visitor to the Medical Squadron Command Post. This close relationship, born out of a shared affection for Royal, and nurtured by regular practice and rehearsal during peacetime exercises, was to prove priceless in terms of the speed and accuracy during the campaign with which casualty information was transmitted back to England.

The road ended just above the beach, then continued on lengths of special metal trackway down to the left, past the water point and the tents of the Amphibious Beach Unit. Colour Sergeant McDowell was our 'Mr Fixit' here, and proved to be the source of much help to us medics. The rather grubby beach then ran around to the edge of the bay, where rubbish (or 'gash' in

Royal Naval parlance) was stacked and burned whenever conditions permitted. There was some tentage here too, and its residents found and adopted a lost penguin, whose glistening feathers had been soiled by the fuel oil that now slicked the surface of San Carlos Water. '*Marine Galtieri*', as the unfortunate bird was quickly renamed, waddled around cheerfully and soon developed a taste for compo biscuit mixed with a little whisky. The bird was an amusing distraction and outlet for the men's affection, and a welcome change from the harsher realities of war*.

Coming back to the base of the concrete trackway, where the road petered out to the right, a large sandbagged sangar had been built by the Commando Loggies, with two separate compartments contained within it. In one, the Duty Officer and his signaller held court. The other housed the Combat Supplies Cell of Ordnance Squadron whose job it was to identify the whereabouts of any stores demanded by the Units. They also had to co-ordinate the delivery of these items, by whatever means available, up to the front line.

Inside the main Logistic CP, Captain Paddy George, Regimental Adjutant, was usually to be found hunched over the paraffin stove, trying to make sense of the information being passed over the radio. We teased each other gently, well aware of the value of humour under these conditions. My favourite response to the latest of his daily, multiple crises was to ask 'Shall I make out a list?' The line caught on, and raised a laugh every time.

Paddy and the Regiment's Operations Officer, Captain Colin Healey, had the near-impossible job of trying to satisfy everyone's requirements in this new experience of war. Most of the five infantry unit Quartermasters (and the Paras were no exception to this) were used to going on exercises in peacetime with just enough stores and consumables not to have to bother any re-

*I was very pleased to note, when visiting Ajax Bay ten years later, that its home had become the basis of a thriving penguin colony.

supply system. This experience was proving rather different, and the harassed QMs were simply transferring their concerns and demands for priority straight back to the Commando Logistic Regiment. At least Colin and Paddy were deflecting some of the heat from Ivar Hellberg. The CO was living in the back of his long-wheelbase Land Rover, parked between two of the outbuildings.

He was a shy, smiling figure and an expert mountaineer and skier. Even when the logistic pressures were highest, with yet more tasks imposed on his small and inadequate number of specialist troops, Ivar H was never glum. His favourite mental escape route lay in the planning of a 1983 re-enactment of the famous Rjukan 'Heavy Water' raid, by a group known much more widely, thanks to Hollywood and Kirk Douglas, as the 'Heroes of Telemark'. He kept suggesting that I should accompany him as the expedition medical officer. In turn, I kept reminding him that, after one personal descent into the sea from the tailgate of a C-130 Hercules, I was very firmly of the opinion that only fools jumped out of perfectly serviceable aeroplanes, and any jaunt that began with a parachute deployment onto the frozen wastes of the Hardanger Vidda could therefore be labelled as completely daft!

Terry Knott also came into his own here. The Regiment's second-in-command was a long and lean character, who wore a canvas belt around his waist, festooned with high-explosive grenades and extra magazines of SLR ammunition. He was in effect the *gauleiter* and chief defender of Ajax Bay, responsible for the security of the whole logistic area, as well as for the welfare of any prisoners. His flashing smile hid serious capability as a professional soldier, as well as the same instincts and courage which accompanied him down a helicopter abseil rope into a mountain cave above Aden. He still carried the pistol he used that day in winning the Military Cross. The marines on the ground could sense his natural abilities as a tough leader, and a soldier capable of maintaining high wartime personal standards. For my part I was very glad to have Terry around to look after our defence arrangements.

Mail! A letter arrived from Susie, full of news, but long delayed. All around the area men read and re-read their messages from home. If the boys driving the Michigan tractors and Eager Beaver fork-lift trucks up and down the trackway with logistic stores were the key troops in the war as it stood at present, then mail was the single most important factor affecting our morale. I hoped that it would keep coming, and the Royal Engineers from the Courier and Postal Section at Mill Hill moved up several notches in our scales of respect. Their boss was a Captain called Ian Winfield, and I got on very well with him. He even wrote a short but wryly humourous account of the campaign from the 'Postie' perspective afterwards, and some of the stories still make me laugh.

Food was much less of a worry. The Regimental main galley had now been opened inside the much tidier slaughterhouse area. The drainage gullies that used to run with sheep blood, and then became choked with rusting debris for some thirty years, were now carrying away the dirty hot water of a facility feeding nearly 200 men.

The chefs were an extrovert, hard-working bunch who took a pride in being proper 'chefs' and not just 'cooks'. Medical Squadron had to have different feeding arrangements, because when we were operating on our casualties, the surgical teams had to get their food when they could, and could not therefore be sustained on a formal timetable. We had also agreed to feed the PoW guards when they became busier, for much the same reasons. Our chefs were in the true 'bootneck' mould, with a robust sense of humour needed to absorb the old favourites like 'Chef, I'm declaring the result on this bloody scran as a draw – *you* can't cook it, and *I* can't eat it...'

Smoking and spitting in one corner of the galley area was our 'Water Heater, Field Kitchen, Portable'. This US $50 device was 'loaned' to us for trial (on a permanent basis!) by some American Army medics in Germany. The permanence of that loan was underwritten by a crate of British ale. It had been spotted there by my predecessor in Medical Squadron. I had tried every trick in the book to get six more, but had been baulked at each turn. There is a disease that affects many UK and US government purchasing agencies called the 'not-invented-here' syndrome. Time and again I was refused permission to buy these simple, cheap and reliable devices.

The most common reason given was that they had not been approved by the British Army equipment wallahs, which was a real pity, because they used ordinary petrol and could even melt packed snow. Clamped to the side of an ordinary dustbin, a brass tap fitted to the fuel tank dripped petrol down onto a metal baffle plate. This in turn was located above a doughnut-shaped, steel burning chamber. The water or snow surrounding and cooling this chamber then got hot in the process. A long tubular chimney provided the necessary updraught. Unfortunately, if you were unwary in your adjustments, too much petrol could result in an explosion that lifted the exhaust stack up and away, perhaps as much as twenty yards. As a result, the American nickname for this kit was a 'kitchen mortar', but ours was merely old, hard-worked, much-loved and rather carbonized.

A tendency to belch out black smoke had led to its personal label of *The African Queen*, but without it we would have been lost. Our big 'official' British Army water heater and bowser never made it ashore from *Sir Galahad*, so *The African Queen* kept going day and night from the moment we landed, until her sad demise later on. Over a hundred people depended on it, and Chief Petty Officers Scouse Davis and John Smith each kept a paternal and quartermasterly eye on it, not for a sighting of Katharine Hepburn, but to ensure that the communal tea urns were always topped up.

That night saw the last enactment of an important ritual. Jack, the pharmacy dispenser in *Canberra*, had given Bryn Dobbs a large bag of salted peanuts as a going-ashore present. Each night since our landing, we had solemnly celebrated another day survived by dipping into this bag for a handful. Someone joked about the possibility of our luck running out along with the peanuts. There was nervous laughter as the torches were flicked off.

Thursday, May 27th

The young chefs had really got things sorted out now, and produced a hot breakfast at 0800 for the night shift, three hours before dawn. We were working on London time, to make things easier for the Fleet Headquarters at Northwood. Breakfast was invariably the same. Tinned sausages, baked beans and a 'wet' of tea or coffee were doled out to one and all, but it was hot and very welcome for that. That particular morning I surfaced, for once, in time to try it out.

I had a long chat with Marine Neil Blain, a young man with a problem called Osgood-Schlatter's disease. This occurs when the growth centre of the tibia, the main lower leg bone, is delayed in its fusion during the late teenage years. Commando training does not help, obviously, but the right sort of Royal Marine recruit is offered the chance to be a chef instead, with a green beret, and to try and complete the 'full monte' later on, after a couple of year's relative rest. Neil was now pain-free, ran for miles whenever he had a chance to, and was intending to volunteer for SBS selection*.

Our daily Sea King arrived for a trip to the Uganda, and could manage just one round trip with the *Coventry* survivors

---

*He later managed to achieve his ambition, but was then killed before the decade was out in a freefall parachuting accident.

before being diverted to another task. This meant that Ricardo Lucero was still marooned with us, and we apologised to him. There was some concern about the blood circulation in his foot, and we were worried that we might have to bivalve (crack open) the plaster cast because of the swelling in his totally disrupted knee. No more helicopters were forthcoming at this stage, so I went by dory out to Brigade HQ, and spent the morning with various heavies discussing the details of medical support forward after the breakout from the San Carlos bridgehead. London was apparently fretting about the apparent delay in achieving this, but the Northwood desk officers were not present down here to experience the delaying effects caused by the constant threat, and occasional impact, of Argentine air attack. They needed to look up into the skies above their comfort zones, and see some armed aircraft *without* British insignia there!

I remembered that this similar situation had caused a huge rise in battlefield psychiatric casualties during the early days of the 1973 Yom Kippur War. As the Israeli Army struggled to mobilise during the most important national holiday of the Jewish religious calendar, their Air Force was being downed in unusual numbers by modern Soviet bloc anti-aircraft weaponry. It's something that our American friends had no concept of understanding for; they have never lacked air superiority in any conflict since the *kamikaze* attacks in the Pacific during WW2.

Back at Ajax Bay I also discussed future medical plans with Surgeon Lieutenant Commander Phil Shouler, the leader of the Plymouth Naval SST 2. He was a chubby-faced Senior Registrar back home in Stonehouse, but had considerable surgical experience, both in hospitals and at sea. We teased him constantly about the lack of Mars bars affecting his survival prospects, but he was very good-natured and usually failed to rise to the bait.

Andy Yates, his anaesthetist, was still a deep bronze colour from heavy sun worship off Ascension. He seemed quite capable, but then the Naval team had not had that much to do so far. The surgical workload seemed to fall on Ajax Bay whenever it was the PCT's turn on watch, but the stand-by team knew that if and when the load came on, they were required to muster for duty as well. Nick Morgan, the junior surgeon, still looked as though he was losing weight, no mean achievement for a man built like a racing greyhound. He was a former Commando MO, and had just started surgical training.

Outside the building, occasional air raid warnings were blown on the soccer referee's whistle that was now secured to the door. The men were getting more used to this phenomenon, and tended to watch others up on the skyline surrounding them, as well as monitoring the behaviour of the helicopters. As long as the 'paraffin parrots' kept flying in to pick up supplies or land passengers, we felt that we could be sure that enemy aircraft were reasonably far away. When they suddenly lifted off and dived into a nearby gully for shelter, then it was time for our 'battle bowlers'. I had never found a steel helmet to fit my Size 8 head, so had to put my trust in the magical, shrapnel-deflecting powers of the Commando green beret instead.

At about 1900 I went for supper, this time around in the main galley. It was the usual, but nonetheless excellent chicken curry. Tonight's 'choice' lay in what was on offer to accompany this – rice or mashed potatoes! About forty-five minutes later we heard the whistles blowing, with unusual urgency, for Air Raid Warning Red. The galley emptied very quickly as everyone rushed outside to their slit trenches and usual bolt holes. The sun was sinking low in a clear sky as I walked around the outside of the building to the main entrance. Inside, I knew that Bill McGregor and Charles Batty were operating on two Argentine patients. Phil and his team were off watch, but positioned somewhere nearby.

Before I could go back into the building and further check our dispositions, a loud '*kerr-ump*' from the other side of San

Carlos Water heralded an air attack on 40 Commando in and around San Carlos Settlement. I could see what looked like an Argentine Dagger, twisting and weaving as it exited San Carlos Water to the north, then found myself staring, absolutely fascinated, at the large grey mushroom cloud it had left behind. The smoke billowed up vertically in the still air as I watched, wondering if I should get some men and equipment ready to send over there, in order to help 40 Cdo's MO to deal with the inevitable casualties. I was walking back up the track to discuss this, when suddenly there was a rising howl of jet noise and the hoarse cry of 'TAKE COVER!'

HMS *Plymouth*, lying close offshore, began blazing away with all her upper deck guns at a target out of my sight, behind the main building. The adrenaline flowed, and I sprinted to the nearest slit trench, diving into it as a loud '*whoomph!*' blended into the roar of jets passing low overhead.

My arrival in the slit trench had been preceded, by a few milliseconds, by Marines John Nelson and 'Nutsy' Naughton. We were now all three covered with a thick layer of dust, small stones and dirt. Poking my head out and above the edge of the shallow ditch, I could see a San Carlos mushroom cloud again, only this time it was in close-up, and emerging from somewhere in the main galley area. Instinct took over. The marines scrambled out after me and went for stretchers, while I raced into the building for some morphine. I had no time to see if Charles and Bill were OK, but the main medical area looked unchanged. Threading through the linking passages at the back, we emerged into Dante's Inferno. The main galley was completely shattered and broken, and in 45 Commando's storage area, ammunition was starting to explode. Even more strangely, there were men everywhere. From their sangars and foxholes out in the ground all around the building, they had emerged to help their mates and fight the fire.

A pallet of 105 mm artillery ammunition nearby exploded with such a loud bang that I really feared for the health of my

Sergeant Major, whom I knew was in that area somewhere. Then Terry Moran emerged, eyes out on organ stops, his face such a picture that I shouted with laughter and relief. He shared a sangar with Fleet Chief Bryn Dobbs, but for now could only laugh hysterically at the poor man after the latter's scalp had been opened by a piece of shrapnel. Very soon, our own injured were coming in – young Danny Mudge, his forearm shredded; a Royal Marines chef named Callan with a big steel bomb splinter through his belly, and two other marines from Logistics called Burnett and Watt, both with badly mangled legs.

The system swung into gear, and within minutes the worst cases were on the table. Here was Bill McGregor again, deep in tiger country beneath Callan's liver, trying to patch a hole in the inferior *vena cava* and a laceration into his duodenum. Malcolm Jowitt was pouring blood and skill, in equal measures, into the same patient. The Naval team turned to at the rush, and started work on Marine Mudge.

Then an RAF Flight Lieutenant called Alan Swan, a bomb disposal expert who was lodging with us, came up to me and said quietly: 'Excuse me, sir – but will you come and look at this please?' He took me back to one of the refrigeration spaces, two walls away from where the surgical teams were in action. The lights were out, but the strong beam of his torch picked out an incredible sight. Embedded in the grey metal pipework of the refrigeration machinery at the far end of the compartment was a greenish metal cylinder. From one end, a tangled skein of nylon webbing led up to what looked like a parachute, half-pulled through a neat hole in the wall above and behind it. When Alan told me that this was a French 400 kg high-explosive bomb, my first instinct was to turn and run. He grinned at my evident discomfort, and then told me of a second device, lying on the other side of a bulge in the ceiling just above our heads!

There were obviously some big decisions to take now, and we talked over all the options. With his natural caution and understandable desire to cut all risks to the minimum, Alan wanted the building evacuated – prisoners, patients, surgical teams – the lot. My professional instincts opposed this. I felt that, if at all possible, we should try and stay here, because the surrounding ground was absolutely terrible, and we certainly could not get a tented facility erected that would be anywhere near as good as this, bombs or no bombs.

I also knew something else that was still restricted information. The next day would see 2 Para advancing from their present positions close to the settlement of Goose Green. Their assault was bound to be bloody, and there would be a butcher's bill to pay, even if the Paras were both tactically clever – and really lucky.

Fortunately, Ivar Hellberg then joined us and listened in on the conversation. As my direct boss in tactical matters, he made up his mind quickly, and his decision echoed my instincts. Only the immediate area was to be evacuated and placed out of bounds. The ceiling was to be shored up beneath the second bomb, and the intervening walls were to be heavily reinforced, probably with sandbags, by the naval diving team. To compound our worries, Flight Lt Swan then produced an engineering drawing prepared by the French firm *Engins Matra*, showing the various types of fuze that could be fitted to their bombs.

The labelling of these diagrams was all in French, so I sent for Captain Mike von Bertele of the PCT and asked if he would lend us his linguistic skills. Actually, the translation was fairly easy once the right box had been selected, and apparently one of these fuzes was capable of a 37 hour delay! Again, I found myself thinking quite cold-bloodedly, but clearly. We were standing right next to the beast, discussing it as if it was just a lump of metal instead of a lethal device that, with the correct signal to its detonator, could have converted us all into a fine red mist, right there and then. It was quite unlike an episode in Belfast, only eight years previously, when I had shivered with fear watching *'Felix'* (code name for the Ammunition Technical Officer) walk up to a suspected car bomb.

Instinct swayed my final decision. I thought it highly unlikely that if the first bomb in the stick of four had an impact fuze which seemed to have detonated successfully, that the remainder would have been fitted with timing devices instead. This one *must* have had an impact fuze that had failed. Why exactly this had happened, we weren't sure...

We had heard, on the BBC World Service broadcasts we could hear clearly each night, some idiot telling the Argentine High Command that their bombs were hitting British ships but not detonating! Alan Swan also told us that this was the first instance where the French devices had been employed, and I felt sure that the Argentine armourers back at the Rio Gallegos air base on the mainland would have tried to keep things really simple. Fortunately, Ivar Hellberg agreed this point as well.

It was really my call, as my teams were the main occupants of the building, but it was good to have some moral support. We decided to persist with our original plan, but we would also do our very best to find somewhere else to move to in the morning. Malcolm Hazell, the No. 1 Medical Troop OC, left at once to travel across San Carlos Water and look for an alternative site. I then found Brigadier Julian Thompson standing in Reception, quietly surveying the scene, and brought him up to date with our plans. He was grim-faced, and obviously moved by the suffering being endured by the wounded. His tired eyes bored into mine as he took his leave: 'Well done, *all* of you. If there's anything you want, Rick, just ask for it...' I took him at his word, and asked for *Uganda* to come close in, first thing tomorrow morning. Then he was gone, with two of his key staff officers, to continue planning and directing the fighting of this wretched war.

Back in the main theatres, the surgical teams had triumphed once more, and the 100% track record was still intact. It was definitely 'tot time' again and the issue went out – rum for the Navy, whisky for the Army. I discussed some of the news with Phil Shouler and Bill McGregor, and a few of the others who were listening in. We were to shrink into 50% of our previous space, convert the current operating theatres into storage and accommodation areas, then move all the operating tables nearer to the main door.

I did not mention the possibility of time fuzes to them, nor the detailed precautions that we were taking to sandbag the adjacent walls. Outside the back of the building, less than a hundred metres and four intervening walls from us, the stacked ammunition pallets were continuing to detonate in a rather malignant version of Guy Fawkes Night. The blast effects and sheer noise of the explosions shook everything and everyone with the concussion of the shock waves, but we got used to it. When I think about it all now, some thirty years later, I get a little shiver down my spine. What if a really big bang had managed to initiate a sympathetic detonation of our two unwelcome guests in the refrigeration machinery and nearby roof space?

To my utter astonishment, Scouse Davies then appeared from the passageway at the rear that led down into the main galley area. On his back was a rather battered and dusty-looking *African Queen*. He had taken something of a risk by collecting the water heater from the scene of devastation, so close to all the exploding ammunition, but he'd also been having trouble keeping the tea urns topped up. A small group of anxious dependents gathered round as the Chief lovingly re-assembled the components outside, by the main door.

An hour later, the brew was as good as ever, with our trusty, reliable and useful friend back in business despite the attempted Argentine alterations. I mentioned my hot water problem again to Ivar Hellberg, and a sudden gleam appeared in the CO's eye. The plot for an *African Queen* replacement thickened, but he wouldn't tell me what new ingredient he intended to add to this long-running saga!

Ricardo Lucero had behaved very well. The boys equipped him with a tin helmet and laid his stretcher on the floor during the attack. Now in full possession of his faculties, he must have known exactly what was going on, and even now must have been wondering which of his squadron *compañeros* were flying the aircraft that made the attack. One of the Naval Medical Assistants later told me, over his hot chocolate 'tot', that when the Argentine pilot saw the smashed and injured bodies coming in beside him, he had burst into tears. Motioning the MA towards him, he had taken the blankets from his own body and indicated, through his tears, that they should be used for the wounded. This was a good man.

A little later, I certified two Royal Marines of 45 Commando as dead. There were three more bodies visible outside at the back. These had to be left for the morning, to be picked up when or if the ammunition fires died down. The night ended on a high note for me when I discussed the air attack with another of my marines. I was still a bit puzzled by the jet roar that preceded the explosion in the main galley area, and asked him if the two Skyhawks were low.

'*Low?*' came the somewhat incredulous reply, 'Bloody 'ell, Boss, if they'd had their ruddy wheels down, the bastards could have landed!'

Friday May 28th

The day dawned once more, this time (thankfully) shrouded by fog and mist. We had all survived, and even the badly injured Marine Callan was doing well. Out at the back of the building, we could hear some of the ammunition continuing to 'cook off' in a rather desultory way. Detonations of that size and intensity would normally have made us jump out of our skins. Now we were just rather nonchalant about the whole matter.

There were two immediate priorities. The first was to get last night's customers out to the *Uganda* and, second, we had to find out if there was anywhere else we could move to. Malcolm Hazell had already completed a hair-raising trip, through thick fog, over to Port San Carlos. I had tasked him to take a look at the bunkhouse and sheep-shearing sheds there as a possible medical facility, but his report was not encouraging. It gradually dawned on me that the isolated nature of the San Carlos area settlements meant that there were simply no alternatives to our continued existence at Ajax Bay. While the 'Health and Safety at Work' Act of Parliament was not exactly being complied with, because I was asking my teams to continue sharing the facilities with two unexploded bombs, at least we still had a dry floor beneath our feet and an intact roof above our heads.

Bravo November, the sole surviving RAF Chinook helicopter from the *Atlantic Conveyor's* sinking, then helped us out with the first problem of getting the wounded away from Ajax Bay. This wonderful beast had got airborne for a post-storage flight test from the Atlantic Conveyor just before the arrival of the Exocet missile that had sunk the ship. The big heavy-lift machine had then been flown ashore, and joined up with the Naval squadrons scattered on the hillsides around San Carlos Water. With Mike von B. as escort, it now flogged all the way out to the *Uganda* which, inevitably, had not received our 'Flash Priority' message that we had asked Northwood to relay to them by satellite!

Uganda's flight deck was a bit of a Heath Robinson affair bolted on to the back of the former schools cruise liner. The square landing area was supported by metal struts that projected outwards and upwards from the elegantly curved lines of her stern. The structure could never have received clearance to take something as heavy as a *Chinook*, but this was war, and the peacetime rule book had been lost along with the aircraft's maintenance records and tool kit. The pilot, a lovely man called Dick Langworthy, did a super job of landing athwartships, with only inches between the big helicopter's wheels and the heaving deck edge. Because of the potential weight problem, he maintained some of the lift generated by the huge twin rotors, in a bit of flying skill that could not have been very easy. Both the cockpit and tail ramp were stuck well out over the sea on each side, and the patients had to be carried or led out of the big helicopter via its fuselage side door.

Bravo November developed a special place of affection in the hearts of all who saw or flew in her. They just kept her going day and night. She even survived contact with a mountain lake in a white-out, dragging her extended tailgate through the water like a huge surfer's bellyboard, and although bits fell off her at regular intervals, and her appearance and general tidiness deteriorated to an alarming degree, she just kept on flying. The boys of 3 Commando Brigade had an affectionate nickname for her that also reflected just how much out of track her giant rotor blades had deviated. They called her '*The Shuddering Shithouse*', but loved her for all the food and ammunition that she carried forward to them.

We also made an attempt to set up a tented facility on the far side of our clearing, although the ground there was really too rough and wet. It just drove the point home even more that the refrigeration plant was still our best option, despite the two large cuckoos nesting in the middle of it. To reinforce this belief, a sudden gale developed and, despite Norway-proven storm lashings, this wind blew down one of the tents. We doubled the lashings, but a few days later, the formidable down-draught generated by the Chinook as it came in to land at Ajax Bay completed the destruction job, so we abandoned this idea and let the Logistic Regiment's main galley have the tents instead.

The expected assault on Goose Green had gone in. We had been a bit surprised after last night's confusion to hear 2 Para's position given out on the BBC World Service as being 5 kilometres north of Darwin! What idiot of a Press and Information

Officer back in London would have sanctioned the release of tactical information like that? We all hoped that the Argentine *Ejercito* had not taken the hint and, as a result of listening to the same broadcast, then reinforced the garrison at Goose Green with the air-mobile element of their reserves in Stanley. I had sent Steve Hughes a second MO in support – the redoubtable Captain Rory Waggon RAMC, a Resus Officer with the PCT who had once been 2 Para's Regimental MO. He was also backed up by two excellent NCOs from the Parachute Clearing Troop.

The Fleet Diving Team then blew up the unexploded bomb lying down on the beach. The ceiling shook, and the whole building rattled although we were over 150 metres away. A huge crater appeared in the sand and Bernie's No 2, Fleet Chief Trotter, returned with a mega-grin across his face. Those boys loved blowing things up as well as defuzing bombs and mines. To us, they were all completely crazy.

There were also some amusing tales emerging from last night's raid. A Staff Sergeant of Ordnance Squadron was actually standing naked in a washing up bowl, having what the Royal Marines call a 'bird bath', when the A-4s flashed over. A few seconds later he was seen, still naked and soapy, but with his helmet on now, shouting: 'Where's my bloody towel?'

Equally funny was the reaction of two unfortunates down in the area where a small stream met the beach. By common usage this area had become a public toilet, flushed twice a day by the incoming tide. After the first bomb explosion there had been sympathetic detonation of an adjacent stack of mortar ammunition. As huge chunks of red-hot metal began whizzing in their direction, they had no option but to get down flat on their faces, in the cover of dead ground. They may not have smelt very nice, but at least they had managed to achieve survivor status!

My Army 'oppo', Major Les Short, commanding Workshop Squadron, had witnessed the whole attack from *Sir Galahad*. Two Skyhawks ran in low from the south and dropped, he thought, six or eight parachute-retarded bombs between them. At least two of theses, he thought, had detonated. As the aircraft raced away to the north, one was trailing smoke and was reported to have crashed on West Falkland later on. The other was supposed to have been 'splashed' by the CAP Sea Harriers. What was true and what was just optimistic speculation? Who could tell?

As we walked together up the little road in front of the building, I noticed that there was now a large hole in the front of our building, about five metres up and to the left of the main entrance. It looked as if the perforation had been made from the inside, because the wall was bulging outwards slightly, and there were a number of stress cracks running away from it. I wondered if this was evidence of a 2 inch rocket strike, because there was also a shallow crater about two metres long and ankle deep, lined up opposite the hole and on the far side of the roadway. The crater had been freshly made. If so, we had been rather lucky. The crater marked the exact spot where I had been standing, about five metres from the shelter that I had dived into.

Les Short looked at me quizzically when I told him what had happened, and then laughed when I told him my theory about the 'anti-armour' rocket. We had a good relationship, based on mutual respect, but shot through with a ring main of sarcastic humour. I was a kindred spirit, but from the moment I joined the Commando Logistic Regiment, he never stopped teasing me. Eventually, I realised that the only way to deal with my friend was to transmit to him in the same style. We then got on really well.

Back in our Plymouth barracks, the Workshop Squadron that he commanded was always working flat out, maintaining all the mechanical and electrical equipment that the Brigade sent in for repair. By contrast, Medical Squadron could only check their stores and undertake theoretical training courses for the bloody realities of war. He would gleefully sneer at my instinctive assertion that, when war came, our roles would be reversed. I predicted that the frontline troops would throw broken kit away in war, rather than send it back for repair as they did in peacetime. In action, real human casualties would occur, and bloodied wounds would take on an unfamiliar importance. The medics would be flat out while the mechanics looked for things to do...

Already in this conflict, from the reports he was getting and what he had seen with own eyes, Les Short had realised that my predictions were coming true. He then instinctively switched roles, and throughout the war became my sounding board and confidant, someone who I could talk to about personal and operational matters that would be out of place being discussed in the usual circles. In one sense he became something of a soulmate to me, rather than a padre, or chaplain. The real vicars attached to us were not really up to that mark, but that was another story.

Les now gripped my arm, and told me to get up in the roof, if and when I could, and take a look all the holes from the inside. In his opinion, the hole we were inspecting had been made by the bomb that had just been detonated on the beach. Christ Almighty! If Les Short was correct, then we really had been very fortunate indeed...

Meanwhile there were many other things to worry about, and some more dramatic news to ponder. 2 Para had taken the settlement of Darwin, and were now positioned just outside Goose Green. It was a fantastic feat of arms, but one that had cost them dearly because their irrepressible Commanding Officer, Lieutenant Colonel 'H' Jones, had been killed in the run-up to the final assault.

Throughout the afternoon, helicopters began to arrive back from the battlefield, to unload their bleeding human cargoes.

I took my turn as a Resuscitation Officer for these incoming casualties. Our job was to assess the amount of injury and degree of shock in each case, then initiate treatment according to a rough protocol that had been established. Once the casualties were stabilised with regard to blood pressure and circulation, those who were still in need of a surgical procedure were passed on to Triage, where the redoubtable Surgeon Commander George

Rudge, our splendid maxillo-facial surgeon (who had already repaid his fare several times over with his expert use of the bone drill and Gigli saw to open two skulls) would monitor their condition and get their names onto the operating list that was stuck up on a nearby wall.

George was a super human being – thin, fit, completely professional in the way that he deployed his skills, and above all other qualities for me, totally open and honest. Nominally, he and Bill McGregor were senior to me, because they had been in the same rank for longer than I had. However, both Bill and George totally accepted that I was *in command* of Medical Squadron, and that included all the attached ranks, of whatever seniority. In this respect, they had grasped some fundamental truths which had so far eluded 'Not Entitled' – about chains of command and underlying responsibilities.

In his own turn, George was so moved by the conduct of the Commando medics around him that he subsequently volunteered – and completed, aged over 40 – the green beret course! For me, it confirmed just how impressive this wonderful man was. I took an important photograph of him standing by a wall, checking over his hand-written priority list, wondering about its next adjustment.

I now use this image to remind young medical and nursing students that the worst sin that a house surgeon can commit in peacetime is to change the planned operating list that their consultant has decided on the day before. In war however, Triage is a dynamic business, and the priorities for waiting cases can change constantly. The Triage Officer has to be a sharp and totally aware cookie. I've never seen this aspect of reality alluded to in the many textbooks of accident surgery that I've looked at, some of them written by armchair experts who have never been up to their eyeballs in blood, bullet holes and blast injuries while working in the middle of nowhere.

We were criticised later on by some of these same gurus for not observing and recording core temperatures, blood pressure, pulse rate and haemoglobin levels in each of these wounded men at Ajax Bay. One editor even used this fact as justification for rejecting our results for publication! Dear God, if only these self-appointed experts could have been transported from their ivory towers straight to the bloody realities of Teal Inlet, Fitzroy – and Ajax Bay. Our sole concern there was for the preservation of life in a set of terribly wounded friends and colleagues, not the business of data collection for historical purposes.

As soon as the wounded managed to reach us, sometimes after long delays, we started to resuscitate them as energetically as possible. The paperwork could wait. As a result, the unique lessons that we were learning then remained hidden for some time. The medical Establishment back home seemed unable to understand that desperate times required desperate measures – and that by happy accident, Mother Nature was actually helping us to succeed! Only those who had been forward surgeons in the Second World War, Korea, Suez, Aden, Oman, Dien Bien Phu, Vietnam and now Afghanistan and Iraq had or have any real understanding of our situation and its priorities.

So many wounded arrived at various stages that I had to forget my command responsibilities for a while, and remain being one of the 'doctors' instead. Many of the casualties had been lying out on the cold ground for several hours before they reached us. The predominant memory I have of that time is of pale, silent paratroopers with a bluish tinge to their lips and fingernail beds, wearing blood-soaked and raggedly torn items of combat clothing.

One of these patients was a man called 'Chopsy' Gray. He had been hit by the blast and fragments of a mortar bomb that landed beside him. The impact tore his right leg off and perforated the other limb with many metal fragments. Apparently, he had then shouted out: 'I've lost me *fucking* leg!' to which the rather laconic reply from behind a nearby clump of tussock grass was: 'No you haven't, Chopsy – it's landed over here…'

Private Gray was a tribute to 2 Para and all the values that this most gallant battalion stood for. He was breathing hard, as if he had just finished a 400 metres hurdles race, had cyanosed lips and eyeballs, and was talking in between panting breaths at a speed similar to Peter O'Sullevan at the finish of the Epsom Derby. There was no blood pressure to record, no pulse to feel at the wrist, and only a thin and reedy apex beat palpable in his left chest. I got an intravenous line going in his arm, noting how dark and thick the blood was that I managed to withdraw from the half-collapsed vein. There was no time to check his declared blood group, so Chief McKinley returned almost immediately with two bags of Group 'O' whole blood. By that time I'd managed to get a second line up in the other arm, and Stu McKinley stood there, shivering, as he held the two blood bags close against his own armpits, in a desperate attempt to warm their contents as the blood flowed in.

Another two bags went in the same way, then a third pair went up – and suddenly the femoral artery within his leg stump started to bleed. I now had something to clamp off, and Chopsy began to look much better than he had up until now. The brave paratrooper was packed off to Triage, and a bit later on, Bill McGregor completed the formal amputation of his right leg, and also debrided the multiple fragment wounds of his left*.

In the confusion of pale, grimy faces and bleeding bodies that was our blurred collective memory of Goose Green's aftermath, two more names stood out. First, Sergeant Bill Belcher. A Royal Marines Air Gunner, he and his pilot were en route to pick up the seriously wounded 'H' in their Scout helicopter, when it was attacked by a pair of Pucaras. These Argentinian twin turboprops were highly manoeuvrable and also heavily armed. After a des-

---

*Private Gray survived to repatriation, and then worked in Production Control at the Ind Coope brewery in Burton-on-Trent, but sadly died early in the new Millennium.

perate fight, the Scout crashed, somehow throwing Sergeant Belcher clear of the wreckage. Sitting up, he gave himself morphia and then tried to stem the lifeblood flowing from his legs. The other Scout that had been airborne with them picked him up, in heroic circumstances, and raced him to us in Ajax Bay.

What a terrible, bloodied mess. It looked as if a 20 mm cannon shell had pulverised his right leg and, almost as an encore, a machine gun bullet had also traversed his left lower leg and ankle. The doctors in Resus stopped the bleeding, poured fresh O negative into his depleted circulation – and then the surgeons amputated his right leg mid-thigh. Then I discovered the name of his pilot, and a chill feeling enveloped me. Lieutenant Richard Nunn was the brother of Captain Chris Nunn, my son's godfather. But there was no time to mourn or even reflect, because more work was coming through the door.

The second name belonged to a triumph that actually ended the long hard day. The Command Post got a message about another Scout casevac helicopter inbound from Goose Green. Outside, it was blacker than General Leopoldo Galtieri's heart as, under my supervision, the boys set up six torches in the shape of a 'T'. We waited quietly in the darkness for the nasal drone of the Scout's gas turbine engine which suddenly we could hear, but in the wrong place. The pilot had flown down San Carlos Water, stopped in a high hover, and then turned west by dead reckoning.

Slowly, agonisingly slowly, he crept towards Red Beach. We switched on the lighted T for him, and flashed our hand torches along the front of the building, hoping that he would not take his Scout straight into the roof. Suddenly the pilot flicked on his landing lights, then off as he sighted the T, and as if drawn to it by a piece of invisible string, the Army Air Corps pilot brought home the bacon. Even with our limited knowledge, my marines and I realised that we had witnessed an absolutely heroic piece of flying.

The bacon in this case was another 2 Para officer, Captain John Y. The bullet entry hole in his right flank looked ominously close to the liver, and the surrounding belly was rigid beneath Bill McGregor's questing fingers. I could see the anxiety in Bill's eyes, plus the personal pain. This patient was one of the officers with whom he had sailed down from England in the *Norland*. Now the young man was lying on a stretcher, shocked and shivering, with wide staring eyes, his blood-soaked clothing cut from his pale but well-muscled body as the Fenwal blood bags drained into each arm. Chief McKinley, the transfusion technician, had two more bags of the chilled blood warming in his shirt pockets, grimacing as he tried to hide his discomfort.

Four units later, Captain Y was on the table in theatre. Bill McGregor was first knife, with Charles Batty assisting. A bold slash, and Bill was through a right paramedian incision and into the abdominal cavity. Dark red clot flopped into the wound as the surgeon's fingers searched for the bleeding point. 'There it is…', said Bill quietly, and we all craned our necks to see. The right lobe of the liver had been gouged by a bullet. More clots were scooped out as another assistant pulled harder on the retractor that lifted the right edge of the rib cage up and away from Bill's line of sight. Some fancy needlework with deep catgut sutures followed; several folded gauzes made of oxycellulose were then packed in, and the liver laceration was repaired.

But the bleeding continued, and Bill was despairing. He had discovered that there was another hole beneath all this mess, but this one was in the *vena cava*, the wide-bore main vein that carries blood from the limbs and kidneys back to the heart. This was really major league stuff. Malcolm Jowitt whispered his encouragement, and Bill loaded a round-bodied needle with catgut, and tried again.

After a tense moment as he felt his way to the bottom of the deep, dark hole before him, he brought the needle holder out and tied a surgical knot. This time the bleeding stopped. At the head of the table, Major Jowitt looked well pleased with his surgeon as

Bill and Charles packed the recesses of the hole with more oxycellulose, and then closed the belly. His smile persisted as, once again, I distributed the tots for Arduous Duty.

John Y not only survived, but later underwent and passed Special Air Service Selection, and then completed his Army career with 22 SAS in Hereford.

Walking around the now terribly cramped facilities, a bottle of rum in one hand and a bottle of whisky in the other to fill the proferred coffee mugs, I could see that the areas were full of post-operative patients, some now conscious following their anaesthetics, others still drowsy. The boys on night shift, led by WO2 Brian Apperley (another veteran who has since 'crossed the bar' after a long illness), moved quietly from stretcher to stretcher, checking, reassuring, recording and reassuring again.

What a sight! I was even more conscious of the wretched bombs stuck in the ceiling and machinery next door. There was still half a day to go on that possible time fuze, so I asked for some of the patients to be moved out of the theoretical line of flight of a detonating nose cap. It was a bit silly really. Some of the boys looked at me a bit quizzically, unsure of my decision to leave apparently useful space empty down one side of the room. Then I went back into the refrigeration compartment to check that the sandbags were still in place. Bless their old seaboots, Bernie Bruen and his men had doubled the thickness of the sandbag wall at this critical point.

With everyone relaxed and happy, the two operating theatres were scrubbed out, and the staff set up their bedding rolls all round the operating tables. Later on, in the Command Post, we added up the numbers. Nearly 80 casualties had been processed through the dressing station, with 47 actually operated on under general anaesthetic. We were now more than a dressing station or surgical centre, and had become almost a field hospital, but without the appropriate scales of equipment or staff! It was definitely the right way to end the day. Although fifteen paras had been killed in action, plus a Commando sapper – and Richard Nunn – forty-seven major operations had been completed, and every one of those wounded men had survived. If only I could be sure that those bombs really were inert...

Saturday, May 29th

Another bright dawn marked the end of our first full week ashore. If the air attacks continued, how were we going to get our wounded out? Most of the accommodation areas had now been spilled over into by injured bodies, and we were running out of space. A further complication was then provided by Brigade. The reinforcement of *Shelldrake*, a forward airstrip for the ground-attack Harriers, had become such a tactical priority that all available helicopters were being diverted to this task. I told them that I would not argue with this decision, but only if we got our Sea King back later on. Even *our* injured patients could wait a few more hours for this vital escalation of the air war's support.

A Wessex arrived and settled gently onto the sodden peat outside the main door. The aircrewman beckoned me forward, a look of real pain and resignation on his tired face. He was sharing the helicopter's cabin with British dead – the paratroopers from Goose Green. The corpses had been loaded on top of each other, their limbs frozen in *rigor mortis*, and each man's combat smock or poncho cape pulled up over his face.

I gathered some of the marines – I called them my 'steady men' – in to help. Silently, sadly, we unloaded the eleven bodies, placing each corpse on its own stretcher at the side of the refrigeration plant. There was an eight-foot wide level strip of concrete running along the edge here, then a drainage ditch and a five-foot high surrounding bank of earth. The RSM of 2 Para, Warrant

Officer (First Class) Malcolm Simpson, plus one of the lightly injured officers who arrived this morning, Major Roger Jenner, also helped us in this task. The two men then stood back quietly on the bank, near to tears, watching us go about our business.

One by one, we began to strip the bodies, to prepare them for burial. A journalist hovered in the background, obviously thinking about a photograph. I knew the chap well, and liked him, but I think that he had better remain nameless here. Our thunderous looks indicated that production of a camera would result in that device being smashed, and the distinct possibility of his joining our waiting customers. I told the boys to keep him and any other outsiders away.

The cold wet clothing of each dead soldier was deftly cut away. The pockets were examined, and personal possessions sorted, logged and put in a plastic bag. In several cases the spare bright-badged berets which all the Paras seemed to be carrying, in preparation for the moment of victory, were so badly soaked in blood as to be unfit for return to their relatives. With the corpse now stripped naked in the freezing air, under a clear blue sky, I then carefully examined each body to certify both death and its cause. A Field Death Certificate had to be completed for each man. For one thing they had died on British soil. For another, they would all certainly require that sort of detail recorded if any of the bodies were exhumed after the war and shipped back to England. The Paras generally had strongly held views that this ought to happen, but personally I was not so sure. Anyway, to save any later formal examination of the bodies, particularly if a Coroner became involved, I had do the job properly first time.

Gunshot wounds of the heart, multiple gunshot wounds of chest and abdomen, blast injury – some of the names were burned deeply into our memories. Dent, Bingley, Cork, Hardman, Melia, Illingsworth, Mechan, Sullivan, Holman-Smith, and finally, H himself. That same shy, quizzical smile lay on his face as easily in death as it had done in life.

Like his men, the late Commanding Officer of the Second Battalion was stripped of his clothing, then lifted up and turned over. There were only two holes, both on the front of his body, and both made by the same bullet. The entrance wound lay just above his right collarbone, and what was quite obviously a high-energy exit wound was positioned further down in the left lower abdomen. Because his heart had continued to pump blood after he fell, there had been haemorrhage tracking downwards on the skin, both into the waist area of his trousers, and the left shoulder of his battle smock. Under the influence of gravity, probably as he lay on his left side or back, both these areas of his clothing were now severely blood-soaked.

This observed fact was later mis-reported by certain other witnesses at Goose Green, and gave rise to the totally untrue suggestion that H had been shot in the back. I dictated my findings to Bryn Dobbs, who witnessed and recorded them on the Field Death Certificate. When I had finished, we stood for a moment in silence, while I remembered my last conversation with this impressive man on the aft staircase of *Canberra*.

I knelt down beside his body, closed his eyelids very gently, and whispered: 'We didn't let you down, Colonel – we really were good enough, and so were *you* and all your men in 2 Para...'

Then we lifted him up carefully, and placed his naked body into an opaque plastic shroud that had been newly opened. Gently, and reverently, the all-enveloping shroud was lifted up once more, and a thick grey PVC body bag, with its heavy zip opened, slipped in beneath. With everything tucked in neatly, I pulled the zip up, and Scouse Davies wrote H's name on the outside, using a broad felt-tip pen, the matt black capital letters contrasting sharply with the shiny grey plastic of the body bag's material. We all straightened up, our backs aching from an hour's crouching, and our bloodied fingers stiff with cold.

The RSM looked me in the eye, man to man. He then saluted me – before thanking us all. I was confused. It had not been a

pleasant task by any means, but it had also been a significant
honour for us to undertake; we all felt satisfied that a sense of
dignity had been restored to the remains of these gallant men, as
well as honour and respect paid to their memory.

At the back of my mind was the unwelcome knowledge that
Richard Nunn's body had yet to be retrieved from the wreckage
of his crashed Scout helicopter, and that there were another four
paras, and Sapper Melia who died with them, to be examined and
then laid out for burial when they were eventually recovered
from Goose Green.

Back in the hospital, there was still no sign of our promised
casevac helicopter for the hospital ship *Uganda*. Things were
getting a bit serious now, because large numbers of Argentine
wounded had also been brought in from the battlefield. 'Mushroom', the radio title of the duty officer at Brigade HQ, got a
headset full of marginally polite abuse from 'Senior Starlight'
(me!). The effect was magical. Half an hour later, Lt Dermot
Hickey arrived in a Commando Sea King to begin three careful
round trips, in between the air raid warnings and actual attacks
on ships in San Carlos Water. The boys saw another Argentine
A-4 creamed by a Rapier over to the west. A Cup Final shout went
up as the fragments came tumbling down.

The moment that I was dreading finally arrived. Scouse
informed me that the body of the dead pilot had been brought in.
The team formed up again. John Smith and Scouse Davies were
both senior medical ratings, but John Clare, Charlie Cork, Jim
Giles, Tojo Hughes, Peter Pearson and John Thurlow were my
'steady men' – general duties Royal Marines who had volunteered to help me with the task of laying out bodies for burial.
Bryn Dobbs was responsible for the administrative paperwork,
and like the boys, was very much aware both of my friendship
with our latest customer, and my close family links with him.
They must have been talking to some of the others about this,
because two of my medical officers then asked if they could stand

in for me. I was very grateful for their concerns, but declined their offers politely. Then I walked round to the temporary mortuary once more, trying to steel myself.

The sheet was lifted off, and from previous experience in Northern Ireland I knew roughly what to expect, but it is still a severe shock to see the badly injured body of someone you have known well. I sensed that somehow I had to find out whether Richard had died *before* the crash of his helicopter, and not because of it. It took a few minutes of gentle probing, but finally I found what I was, in a way, hoping to find. There was a circular hole in the right cheekbone which just admitted my little finger. I showed each of the interested marines in turn. A ricocheting bullet had penetrated my friend's skull and, an instant later, his brain.

This knowledge helped me to adjust — whatever happened after death, no matter how unpleasant, didn't really matter now. Richard had not suffered in the instant that his life was taken from him. We completed the formalities, and I resolved to write to his parents, friends of long-standing who lived not very far from my home back in Cornwall.

Outside, it was dark. I suddenly felt very weary, and really sad. Richard's death was not prolonged and agonised, although the last few seconds of his life must have been terrifying with the two Pucaras ganging up on him as he twisted and turned, trying to escape. I felt a terrific sense of pride — to have known him, and to have been his friend — but at the same time I was disappointed that we'd been unable to help him. It was illogical really. My young friend had perished, but somehow I was blaming myself.

The 'steady men' came outside too, and asked me if I was OK. That somehow made it all worse, and I mumbled something as I walked away along a line of oil drums, needing to be alone. Eventually I stopped, and looked back at the shaded torches and glowing cigarette tips in the entrance area. Suddenly, I felt overwhelmed and crumpled, my body racked with silent, almost convulsive tears. It's pretty difficult to cry quietly, but I managed, and then just as suddenly as it had all started, I felt much better – and in charge of my emotions once again.

I walked back into the building, and noted that the last neat silver bag had joined the line waiting for tomorrow's funeral. Inside the Command Post, Bryn Dobbs gave me one of those careful looks that indicated he had a fair idea of where I had been; he squeezed my arm and let me borrow his chair, which was a great honour. He'd already prepared the day's formal death certificates, which I signed for him, and we then filled in the Battle Casualty Occurrence Report forms, a painstaking task of great importance.

Now that we had plugged into *Uganda* as a source for medical comforts, including the 'commercial spirit' for our 'Arduous Duty' tots, the cigar supply line was also open and flowing. As a result, my Fleet Chief's concentration was being maintained, albeit at the expense of the air which the rest of us had to breathe...

The forms and certificates then usually went round to Roy Hancock in the Field Records Office, only this time the man himself collected them. We discussed the business of burials and the registration of graves with Roy. This was a subject which never really entered exercise play on Dartmoor or Salisbury Plain, but was really important if the British Army was not to lose the art of campaigning. It was just another aspect of a war which one of my marines had described beautifully: 'Just like a bloody exercise sir, only some of your friends get killed, others get injured, the *Endex* date is unknown – and the bloody umpires don't turn up!'

There now occurred one of the hilarious moments of the conflict that will endure long after other details have faded from memory. A piece of paper arrived which was a signal addressed to the Commando Logistic Regiment, but which was apparently personal for me. We did not have a teleprinter ashore in Ajax Bay, so the thing had had to be sent ashore by messenger, and then delivered to me by hand. The tone was slightly pompous and the contents absurd and unreal. It read:

REQUEST BETTER ASSESSMENT HELICOPTER NEEDS FOR FUTURE CASEVAC IN ORDER TO AVOID THE UNNECESSARY TASKING OF SCARCE ASSETS + DIFFICULTY OF ASSESSMENT UNDERSTOOD BUT MUST IMPROVE + GIVE 24 HOURS NOTICE OF ALL FURTHER CASEVAC REQUIREMENTS.

It was that useless chap 'NE' at work again! I was speechless for a minute, then burst into laughter. The CO's reaction was exactly the same. He had seen us pack wounded survivors carefully into the Sea King and Wessex helicopters that turned up to help. The staff officer who had sent this signal was obviously under some sort of delusion that *he* was actually involved with the treatment and subsequent disposal of our casualties!

'Not Entitled' might have understood our problems if he'd ever come to see us on the ground, but so far he had not bothered himself with such a trivial point. Instead, he was busying himself by getting in the way, and no doubt trying to convince those around him what an important personal role he was playing in the one feature of the war that was going really well. Even if I lost everything else, I decided that I simply *had* to take that piece of paper back to England with me.

The Sea King returned from its third lift and shift, this time with Martyn Ward on board. He was another green-bereted MO who had come to war as Resus Officer and, realistically, a battle casualty replacement if any of the Commando Unit MOs were killed or injured. It was his turn for *Uganda* today, because the surgeons were busy with Argentine wounded from Goose Green, and he had also done much good work around the back of the building immediately after the bombs dropped on Thursday evening.

Martyn bore gifts from *Uganda*, and news. Apparently, they were absolutely dependent on my handwritten briefing notes for any information about how things were going ashore. He also had a letter for me from Surgeon Commander Mike Beeley, a former Commando MO and Alpinist but now a Consultant Physician, to confirm this. They very much appreciated my sentiments that, without *Uganda's* dedication and support, we would all be losing the battle to heal the sick and mend the injured.

Robert Fox, the BBC Radio Reporter, also turned up in the Command Post, looking rather tired and grey; he was immediately 'gripped' by Alan Swan. I didn't think it was Robert's fault that critically important intelligence stuff was leaking out on the BBC World Service news bulletins. What sensible journalist would willingly reveal information, by speculating about incorrect bomb fuzing for instance, when he could himself be killed by the enemy's greater attention to this problem soon after? I took Robert's side in this matter, and later we had a long discussion about 2 Para's action at Goose Green, about their gallant leader, and in particular concerning Steve Hughes' splendid work in the Regimental Aid Post. That young tiger had certainly justified his appointment as RMO, 'big style' as the boys would say.

That evening, I reminded everyone about the bombs at the back – and confirmed the interesting bit of detail that they might have been fitted with thirty-seven hour time delay fuzes! As we were now over forty-eight hours on from the arrival of those unwelcome guests, everything was OK, but I asked them not to touch or tamper with them. There were some muttered remarks like '*kin Hell, Boss!*' but it was mainly grins of relief and pride on show as the boys swigged their 'reinforced' wets of tea, coffee or hot chocolate.

Later on, Phil Shouler saved the Ajax Bay track record in a neat piece of teamwork. Despite the semi-darkness, and while we were doing a sort of post-operative ward round together, one of the marines acting as a medical orderly drew our attention to an Argentinian patient whose face was 'looking a bit too dark Boss, even for a spick...' A quick inspection with a flickering cigarette lighter showed the man to be deeply cyanosed, with complete obstruction of his larynx (or voicebox), and his heart just about slowed to a stop.

By the light of my right-angled torch, Phil then did a perfect emergency tracheotomy, cutting a hole in the man's windpipe to take an oxygen catheter, followed by a flanged, silver tracheostomy tube. The heart rate picked up immediately, pounding back and then settling to a more normal rate as oxygenated blood flooded back into the deprived tissues. Another life saved, this time at the brink of its extinction.

Sunday, May 30th

There was a pleasant start to the day. The personnel of Surgical Support Team One (SST 1) from HMS *Hermes* were dumped by helicopter, with all their kit, on our doorstep. It was the first time that I'd seen them all since their early April trip down to Plymouth on mobilisation. This transfer was in response to a message passed up the chain of command that we were in danger of running out of specialist medical skill and stores, particularly in the discipline of anaesthetics. The established residents of Ajax Bay were mildly amused by the new arrivals' wearing of Red Cross armbands, and there was some light-hearted banter about this wonderful talisman which was supposed to confer immunity from Skyhawks!

I also knew that pressure was building up on the surgeons out in *Uganda*. The techniques of battle surgery demanded that high-velocity bullet and shrapnel-induced wounds should be opened up widely, cleaned out thoroughly, and then left open while the healing process began.

As a result, we were sending explored but open wounds out to the hospital ship, which were needing a second general anaesthetic and DPC (Delayed Primary Closure) about a week or less later. The backlog of work there was becoming severe. *Uganda* had actually asked us for any spare skilled help, but stated that they had plenty of equipment and supplies. For our part we were short of kit, but could also have done with an extra anaesthetist and a few more operating theatre staff at Ajax Bay. If we could somehow acquire those extra personnel, then the existing RN team (SST 2) could man up an additional operating table, giving an expanded total of four.

The elegant solution was irresistible. We split up SST 1, sending Surgeon Commander Neville Scholes and the majority of his team straight out to *Uganda*, keeping the anaesthetist Ian Geraghty and four senior ratings with us. I don't think Neville or his boys were too unhappy with this. By now we had shown them the UXB in the freezer compartment, and the prospect of sleeping on camp beds arranged on a dusty floor had never been mentioned in their holiday brochures.

Ian, a Surgeon Lieutenant Commander based at Haslar, was another of the splendidly extrovert characters that we seemed to be blessed with in the RN Medical Service. He had already acquired an MBE for sterling work in Dominica, following a disastrous hurricane. He and his men were soon happily and totally integrated into the Ajax Bay team.

An air raid was detected as inbound to San Carlos, and the nearby warship sirens and whistles sounded; those staff inside Ajax Bay not engaged on critically important duties came tumbling out of the building to jump into their various air raid shelters. Those that were unsure waited until whoever was on duty in the Command Post refined that decision. The all-important proviso was that the decision-taker (usually me) *always* stayed!

Very often the developing raid was broken up by the Sea Harrier CAP, and the All Clear would be blown soon afterwards, as it was on this occasion. Then the subterranean moles and meerkats would appear on the surface again, and normal duties would resume. There were however three or four people who needed no prompting to disappear into their hidey-holes; at least two of them were never seen during good flying weather, at least until dusk settled on the islands. Mindful of Shakespeare's words from *Henry V*:

> *We would not die in that man's company*
> *That fears his fellowship to die with us,*

I did not interfere except on the few occasions when one of my own guys was being a bit reluctant to 'turn to' for duty when air raid activity was expected.

One older officer in another squadron had been a Regimental Sergeant Major before being commissioned, and wore the history of the Royal Marines in the medal group above the left breast pocket of his uniform jacket. This man had dealt with ambushes in Aden, jungle fighting in Borneo and bombs in Belfast, but found air raids by enemy fast jets in the South Atlantic just a bit beyond his ability to cope. I kept an eye on him from a distance, believing instinctively that, with time, he would gradually improve, adapt – and then be able to cope.

After one air raid, I saw a young marine with a mug of tea heading towards that particular trench, so I made it my business to be nearby – just in case the young marine was disdainful or sneering of the older man's troubles. I need not have worried, because as he crouched on the edge of the hidey-hole, the boy was reassuring, supportive, polite and positive – like a really good professional counsellor. He told his officer 'patient' that the tea would do him good, that the Squadron commander was presenting his compliments, and that there was a discussion meeting due to be held in twenty minutes time.

The whole episode was a perfect example of just how the family feeling in an organisation could sustain and nurture those who were having a tough time, whether they were the newest acolytes unblooded by combat experience, or older warriors who had become a bit set in their ways and felt really threatened by the speed and power of modern weaponry.

We were standing outside, away from the front door when another Wessex helicopter approached, disgorged half-a-dozen passengers, and then lifted off in search of fuel. All the new arrivals put on red berets as the spinning rotor blades moved away, and I recognised the tired figure of Stephen Hughes, 2 Para's Regimental Medical Officer. He seemed very single-minded as he went into the building – without looking in my direction. I finished my mug of coffee, did some other business, and then went in search of my young friend.

When I found Steve, he was looking very distraught. His face was deeply etched with tiredness, and almost grey with fatigue. When he saw me, he began to apologise. At first, I was not sure what he was on about, but then realised that he was blaming himself for the poor condition of many of the wounded that had been sent back from Goose Green during the fighting. I could only imagine the horrors of an open battlefield, without natural cover from tree or bush, trying to deal with dozens of wounded using just the medical supplies that you had brought in on your back. As far as we were concerned at Ajax Bay, the casualty treatment teams of 2 Para had done absolutely brilliantly, but it suddenly dawned on me that Steve had no idea just how much his own efforts had helped in achieving an absolute medical triumph.

I tried to stop him talking by telling him to switch from 'transmit' to 'receive' – and also 'pin his ears back'. Steve looked more than a bit shocked at my abruptness, and then narrowed his eyes in disbelief when I told him that every single one of the 47 wounded paratroopers from Goose Green had survived, and that they were now in the hospital ship. In his disbelief, he tried to dispute this point, saying that he was quite certain they had all died, and were now somewhere else, ready for burial. I held him by both arms and said: 'No, Steve, NO! Thanks to you and your boys, plus what we were able to do here at Ajax Bay, they are *all* still alive…'

He was still unsure quite what to believe, and reached into an outside pocket of his denim trousers for the field notebook in which he had the details. The doubts persisted: 'Oh yeah? Well, what about *this* one then – Private Gray, Dominic Gray?'

I finished the sentence for him: 'That's correct, Steve. *Chopsie* Gray. Traumatic amputation of right leg mid-thigh by a mortar bomb. Virtually exsanguinated when he got to Ajax Bay, with no recordable pulse or blood pressure. I looked after him myself. After two pints of blood, the torn femoral artery started to leak and then spurt a bit, so I could see it and get a clamp on the bugger. After another three pints he was fit for theatre. Chopsie's fine. I saw his name on the *Uganda* list that we got this morning...'

Steve just looked at me, in a state of shock; an impossible dream was coming true. How could I have known Dominic Gray's nickname unless I really *had* looked after him? This superb young doctor, who had done so much before and during the Battle of Goose Green for his beloved 2 Para, was now part of that Battalion's folklore.

He reminded me of one of those compressed and dried paper flowers to which someone had just added water. All of a sudden, he was six inches taller, with vitality and good cheer still flowing back into his face as he went off to spread the good news. 2 Para already knew about their 15 dead, plus the two attached ranks, but were expecting a few more to have died of their wounds. Now he could confirm that 'seventeen' was in fact the final total. There were no more names to be added. All the other wounded had made it through their ordeals, and were *ALIVE*!

The bodies of the five remaining paratroopers from Goose Green arrived by helicopter, and were laid out with the same care and devotion given to their colleagues. The administrative paper-work was also completed with similar attention to the details. Life and work went on all around us as we then carried the seventeen body bags up the gentle slope behind Ajax Bay, and past the stockade beside the refrigeration plant. There'd been some sort of very early construction work done here in the Fifties, but the buildings had later been demolished. The outer margins of the area were now delineated with coils of barbed wire, and it was filling up with nearly a thousand prisoners, all that remained of the Argentine garrison of what, for just under ten weeks, had been called 'Ganso Verde', but was now Goose Green again.

At the summit of the small hill, one of our bulldozers had carved out a broad ditch in the wet earth and peat. This work had been carried out entirely by men of Workshop Squadron and their quite excellent Sergeant Major, WO2 Dave McCalley. There was no specific Graves Unit or burial organisation, only the Royal Marines like us who had volunteered for this noble but unpleasant task.

The funeral itself was a fierce event. About two hundred men stood in silence along the edge of the mass grave, heads uncovered, the majority with hands clasped loosely in prayer. Officers mixed with soldiers, Paras mingled with Royal Marines. Above us was the dome of a perfectly blue sky, while clearly outlined in the middle distance, snow gleamed on the summit of Mount Simon. San Carlos Water was a flat calm, the fleet lying still as the helicopters moved busily from ship to ship with their loads, like bees working an English country flower bed on a sunny summer's day. The snarl of their engines and clatter of rotor blades carried for miles in the crisp cold air. It was a beautiful spot, this carefully chosen, silent hillside.

One by one, the bodies were carried down into the grave. Eleven of the seventeen being buried today were officers or NCOs, showing exactly what the British military still meant by the word 'leadership'. Each body bag had six canvas handles, so the burial party consisted of six men of similar rank to the deceased, plus one more senior escort. Major Chris Keeble, Acting CO of 2 Para, preceded the four dead officers, with RSM Simpson heading each team for the NCOs and private soldiers. Dave Edmunds, another old friend, led the Sapper group bearing Corporal Melia; Major Peter Cameron and several of his brother pilots carried Richard Nunn to his place of rest. Each body bag was covered by the Union Flag which was removed when the bag was in position. With a silent salute, and an about-turn, the burial parties withdrew from the grave. When everyone was back in place, the 2nd Battalion Padre, Major the Reverend David Cooper, began the service.

As his firm voice rolled through the now-familiar words, the emotional pressure wound up to a crescendo. Eyes that were red with tiredness and strain now brimmed over with silent tears that splashed down on the already soggy earth.

'*Ashes to ashes, dust unto dust…*' The sound of handfuls of earth cast by the RSM onto taut plastic body bags echoed like thunder around the grave. Led by Major General Jeremy Moore, we all saluted and slowly turned away.

I had time for a brief chat to the Royal Marines liaison officer with 2 Para, Captain David Constance. He had now taken over as Battalion Intelligence Officer, and had to return at once to Goose Green for the expected Argentine counter-attack. He was also married to Richard Nunn's sister, and gripped my arm tightly when I told him that I would be writing to the family that night. Struggling to control his grief, he whispered a vital message: 'Tell them I was here…'

During that evening I assisted Phil Shouler with his after dusk list. As a general principle I had decided that only really urgent British casualties would be operated on during the day, unless there was an equally serious Argentine case. During enemy air raids, the surgical teams deserved the same chance as anyone else to take cover outside the building. Another bomb in the back, anywhere near the two that we already had, might well have caused a massive and lethal explosion. As soon as night fell, however, we knew that the Daggers and Skyhawks would be unable to attack us, and our work could proceed unhindered.

I heard that a nerdy lecturer at one military academy back in UK actually questioned this attitude afterwards. I just wish that he could have been there with us, staked out as a potential target!

The surgery of battle remains a quite fascinating subject. Pieces of metal moving at high velocity when they strike flesh behave in unusual but totally characteristic ways, as I had seen in Northern Ireland, and as we had found with 'H' Jones. A smooth and symmetrically shaped bullet usually sets up a shock wave which accelerates muscle and other structures away from the bullet's track. It was rather like the bow wave of a ship; as a result, a cavity is formed for a few thousandths of a second. The pressure in this rapidly expanding cavity is below that of the exterior, and so outside contaminants of the atmosphere are drawn in.

In addition, the fine capillary blood vessel network within the organ or muscle is stretched beyond its elastic limit. This network ruptures, and leaks blood into the immediate area. There is no more oxygen being carried in by an intact blood supply, but the real complication occurs when the dying muscle tissue is also infiltrated by the bacteria or bugs that cause gas gangrene and tetanus. These are 'anaerobic' in their nature – germs that simply love the *absence* of oxygen.

Any surgeon foolish enough (or just emotionally upset and unable to remember the training) who tidies up the entrance and exit holes, then closes the wound off with clips or stitches, was simply asking for trouble. Infection would be inevitable, and was present in *all* our Argentine patients who had been treated by their own doctors in the field. Some idiot of a mendicant barber surgeon on their side was putting clips in the wounds and giving his patients a few antibiotic tablets. But how was this blood-borne penicillin supposed to penetrate into a load of dead muscle tissue that had no circulation?

Their small arms wounds and our small arms wounds were much the same, because both sides were using derivatives of the same FN rifle design, which fires a 7.62 mm round. What was different was the way that our surgeons, with the war experience that the Argentine doctors lacked, got on and tackled these wounds. We had laid them all open to the air, then carefully removed the dark purple bits of dead tissue. The work was careful and thorough, demanding intense concentration and a sharp pair of scissors.

Anything that was alive, even a shattered bone or crushed nerve was preserved when possible. We were simply trying to save life and limb at this early stage, so the fancy stuff with fixation bars and operating microscopes could wait until later. When the wound was clean and glistening red, a fluffy gauze dressing got packed into it, then a crepe bandage was applied outside. The wounds had to stay open for a few days more, allowing atmospheric air and its gas gangrene and tetanus-killing oxygen in, until the surgeons in *Uganda* could inspect the wounds again.

No doubt, because of the poor lighting conditions in Ajax Bay, some dead muscle would be overlooked in a proportion of the wounds when first explored. That would not matter at all, providing they removed that dead material later on, under better lighting conditions. When everything was clean and healing, they would be able to close up the wounds formally, but always *after* that all-important and quite deliberate initial delay.

There was also one significant difference in the wound patterns caused by the munitions of both sides. These concerned the fragments associated with exploding artillery rounds. Our 105 mm Light Guns were configured for use in Norway, where snow banks and 'icecrete' shelters could reduce the effectiveness of a bursting shell. Therefore, the Commando gunners employed VT airburst fuze that initiated itself 30 feet above the target, causing clean, albeit rather ragged upper body injuries, especially if the overhead protection was inadequate.

In marked contrast, the 105 mm and 155 mm Argentine ordnance tended to be impact-fuzed, which meant that the shell penetrated the ground before bursting. This reduced and weakened the blast effect, which was excellent news for any involved British troops nearby, but it also meant that any penetrating fragments usually carried a bit of earth or soil in with them. Dealing with the multiple fragment wounds of a British soldier was therefore an unusual form of 'surgical gardening'! Blades of grass and small lumps of peat were being found in some very unusual places.

Private Manuel Caceres was Casualty No. 229, and became the Naval team's 34th patient of the day. He had what looked like a mortar fragment wound of the right calf. After Ian Geraghty had put our customer to sleep, Phil Shouler invited me to explore the wound. I could feel a lump deep beneath the soleus muscle and cut down to it, with my finger lying in the entry wound and associated missile track. Surprise, surprise! A 7.62 mm bullet popped out. I wondered if it was one of theirs – or one of ours?

The operation took 20 minutes, and I got my name into the operating theatre casebook, then Nick Morgan donned his gloves to debride a nasty gunshot wound of a young Argentine's forearm and thumb. It would be his seventh operation of the day as the lead surgeon, and there was one more to do before the team could clean out the area, cover the tables with a couple of sheets, unroll their bedding, and get their heads down until the next morning.

Monday May 31st

It was the Spring Bank Holiday half a world away, in England. Down here, the war went on.

The Royal Marines Mountain and Arctic Warfare Cadre took out an Argentine Special Forces lying-up position near Top Malo House. There was a brisk and vicious firefight, and three of the marines were injured in achieving total success against their opponents. I recognised two of them immediately, 'Touche' Groves and Taff Doyle, who were both colleagues from ski-ing and rugby days. Touche's 'magic lantern show' was a Sod's Opera highlight whenever he performed it, but now he was fighting for breath with a nasty gunshot wound of the chest. Taff Doyle came round from his anaesthetic wanting to know if he would still be able to 'slip his shoulder' (illegally) as a rugby hooker, as I had seen him do so often from my position just behind him in the second row. Judging by his bullet-smashed upper arm I thought it was unlikely, but could not bring myself to say so.

Our boys were followed into Ajax Bay by their opponents. The three officers and four Senior NCOs represented an unusual rank mix of the kind found in Argentine Special Forces. We prepared them for operations on their gunshot wounds, but remained wary, with their stretcher trestles placed together in one corner of the post-op area. For the first and only time during our tenure of Ajax Bay, we also posted an armed guard close by.

Another unlikely encounter then took place. Two SAS men had been flown in with gunshot wounds that were quite obviously more than 24 hours old. We knew better than to ask them about the circumstances of their injuries, and instead simply operated on them. The anaesthetist, Malcolm Jowitt, used Ketalar, an injectable and steroid-based general anaesthetic that had some occasional and highly interesting side effects. One of the SAS men, a big ex-Sapper, came round from his op and started singing bawdy rugby songs, quite tunefully, at the top of his voice!

The cabaret act was much appreciated, but when I wandered over to check that everything was going well, the other SAS soldier half rose off the stretcher, looked at me strangely – and then reached up and and grabbed my camouflage jacket. With his long hair and scruffy beard it was some seconds before I recognised him. What a strange place for a re-union! As a teenage Royal Marine trainee, Dick P was in No. 14 Recruit Troop when I had joined, over ten years before, to complete the Commando course at Lympstone. He had helped me greatly, especially on the day that I gave up, while trying to complete the Endurance Course pass-out test.

We were running back to camp, against the clock, as a syndicate of three. I'd decided that enough was enough, and that being a doctor in a Polaris submarine had suddenly become much more attractive than this wet and muddy existence with the Royal Marines. I could (and can) still shut my eyes and recall Dick P's upturned face, pleading with me: 'Come on, sir! If you don't get to the line with us, we'll have to do this bastard again tomorrow..' followed by: '*Doc*! PLEASE don't let us down...'

Those simple words summoned a huge tidal wave of shame that washed over me, dissolved all the fatigue, and enabled me to beat my two companions to the line – in time. From him I had learned a very simple, but life-long lesson. When you think you are beaten, and have nothing more to offer, you've only just scratched the surface of what you are really capable of...

I had heard on the grapevine that he had subsequently left the Corps, possibly to join the French Foreign Legion, or become a mercenary. Now here we were, in the middle of nowhere, clutching each other's hands like long-lost brothers, which in a sense is exactly what we were. I explained this to a group of marines who were watching my strange behaviour; they understood instantly. The sufferings endured on Woodbury Common and on the Tarzan Course were severe enough to bind together forever any men who had shared this experience. What a fantastic privilege I had been granted this day, in that I was able to repay him for his devotion and concern some ten years earlier! Dick made a good recovery, and later on went back to complete his time at Hereford, after a stint as a weapons instructor.

The television and radio crews turned up, and asked if they could film and record us. I agreed, because I knew them. Mike Nicholson and Brian Hanrahan did brief interviews with me, the contents of which I could not even recall a few minutes afterwards. The BBC pool cameraman, a nice chap called Ken Hesketh, lingered for some time on a shot of Charles Batty in theatre, carving dead meat from the large bullet exit wound of an Argen-

1. **Loaded for bear and looking for trouble** A pair of the superb, match-winning
Royal Navy Sea Harrier FRS.1 interceptors on their way out to a designated CAP station.
In fast-jet combat, the score was 27-0 in the Fleet Air Arm's favour. Six aircraft (from a
total of twenty-eight) and four pilots were lost in a collision, deck handling accident or
to defensive ground fire. (*MoD Navy*)

2. **Role change**
Canberra lies alongside in Southampton as she undergoes conversion into a fast troopship. *(pp 13-19)*

3. **Heath Robinson at work!** The ingenious flight deck stretcher lift constructed from a porter's trolley. *(pp 17-18)*

4. **The importance of a robust sense of humour** This Southampton 'dockie' is grinning at the camera because he is getting ready to load *Canberra* for her war duties with a pallet load of corned beef – from Argentina!

5. **Fitness training** (for 3 Para here) The Promenade Deck was a vitally important 400-metre continuous running track. *(p 29)*

6. **Helicopter training drills at Ascension** *Canberra*'s two Sea King Mk 4s conduct a simultaneous approach. *(p 30)*

7. **Sunset ceremony** Naval tradition with the RM Band plus 3 Para's drum team; the P&O freighter *Elk* steams along in company.

8. **A view from space** courtesy of NASA. Note the long curve of Argentina's eastern seaboard in the mid-upper section.

9. **Load lifting** and repositioning of combat supplies from *Canberra* to other ships as she closes with the Falkland Islands.

10. **Investment with potential** Over nine hundred units of blood were donated by embarked troops a week before landing. *(p 46)*

11. **D-Day Dawn** The RFA stores ship *Stromness* moves quietly past *Canberra* as dawn breaks in the eastern sky. *(p 53)*

12. **First casualty** A paratrooper with a twisted back awaits evacuation by the author's Wessex 5 helicopter. *(p 55)*

13. **Enemy injured** With their gunshot wounds dressed by the SBS, two Argentine soldiers await lifting from Fanning Head. *(p 58)*

14. **'Like ducks on a duckpond'** Looking south from Fanning Head into San Carlos Water, early on Friday May 21st 1982. *(p 59)*

15. **'He ain't heavy...'** A superb painting by David Hardstaff of the rescue, by the crew of a Naval Wessex 5 helicopter, of two survivors from HMS *Ardent*. The aircraft was on other duties at the time, but diverted to the scene, and performed a rather unorthodox extraction of the two men from the bitterly cold water of Falkland Sound. *(pp 66-70)*

16. **'Vengeance is ours...'** David Hardstaff shows two SHARs rolling in on the trio of Armada A-4s that finished HMS *Ardent*.

17. **'Time to go, amigo!'** Another Hardstaff original showing the moment of '*Martin-Baker departure*' by a gallant Pucara pilot, the victim of an admiring Cdr Sharkey Ward's Sea Harrier's 30 mm cannons.

18. **The abandoned slaughterhouse and refrigeration plant at Ajax Bay** This building and its surrounding ground became the Commando Brigade's logistic support area. Red Cross insignia could not be used for the medical facilities because of the close proximity of 'legal' targets such as food, water and ammunition. *(p 75 onwards)*

19. **Ajax Bay exterior** The windowless mutton storage area lies at right angles to the refrigeration rooms and slaughterhouse.

20. **Ajax Bay interior** Major Malcolm Jowitt anaesthetises a chest injury patient for John Williams (centre) and Nick Morgan.

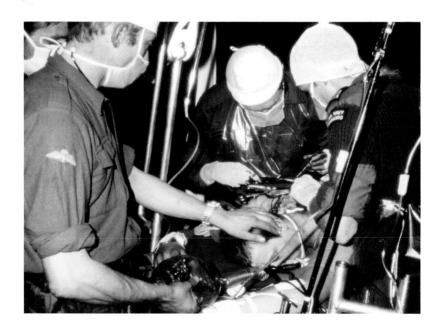

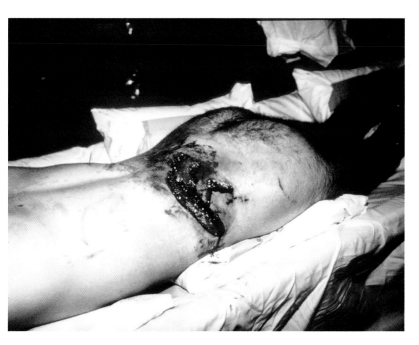

21. **High energy gunshot wound, left loin** Opened along its track to show the damage beneath – which must all be excised. *(p 140)*

22. **The 'come as you were' party** Phil Shouler (centre, white mask) and RN SST members, two weeks into life at Ajax Bay.

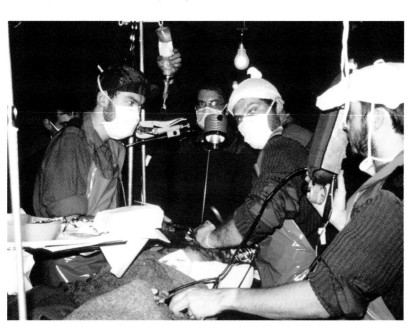

23. **Preparing the dead** Seventeen body bags lie ready after the battle for Goose Green; each man was examined and certified by the author, who can be seen making final adjustments. *(pp 125-127)*

24. **The steady men** A quartet who helped with this difficult task; Marines Jock Ewing, John Clare, John Thurlow and Jim Giles were also known as '*The Awesome Foursome*'. *(p 125)*

25. **The bomb that detonated** A huge ammunition fire burns in the remains of the Ajax Bay slaughterhouse/galley area. The air was filled with flying metal splinters; five men died. *(pp 107-109)*

26. **The bomb that failed 'safe'** Something nasty lurking in the fridge – a parachute-retarded 400 kg UXB of French manufacture that behaved correctly when Argentine armourers tampered with it. *(p 109)*

27. **UXB No. 2** lying in the roof space; its retarding parachute has been ripped off. The SLR rifle gives an idea of scale. *(p 109)*

27a. **'The African Queen'** *(right)* This American field heater unit was the sole source of hot water for nearly 100 men for three weeks before it expired, to be replaced by six more units parachuted in to the Falklands as the war ended. *(p 103)*

28. **Bomb happy** Extract from the author's televised interview with Jeremy Hands at Ajax Bay: *'We've got two unexploded bombs at the back of the building – but the less said about them, the better!'* *(p 145)*

29. **Casualty outload** After surgery at Ajax Bay, the wounded of both sides were back-loaded, whenever a helicopter became available, to the British hospital ship *Uganda*. *(p 149)*

30. **HMHS *Uganda*** The converted schools cruise ship operated under protection of the Red Cross symbol; she was a brilliant success.

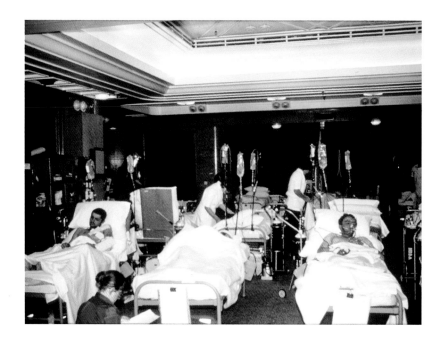

31. **Intensive Care Unit** This dealt with all our post-operative problems, and was the
golden link in a long casevac chain. *(p 150)*

32. **Ambulance Ship** Three hydrographic survey vessels carried 580 British patients up
to Montevideo, in Uruguay.

33. **VC10 Air ambulance I** Yesterday's newspapers are made available to the casualties, secured in their stretcher racks as they fly from Montevideo back to RAF Brize Norton, near Swindon.

34. **VC10 Air ambulance II** Only three 'official' in-flight photos were taken of this wonderful service to the wounded!

35. **Welcome sign** The author and a famous piece of *graffito* that told the world of the Field Hospital's success. *(p 159)*

36. **Taking a break** Ian Geraghty *(left)* and Nick Morgan *(right)* read about the Pope visiting a place called England. Note the bomb exit hole at left edge of the image, and the sign above the door, in colour!

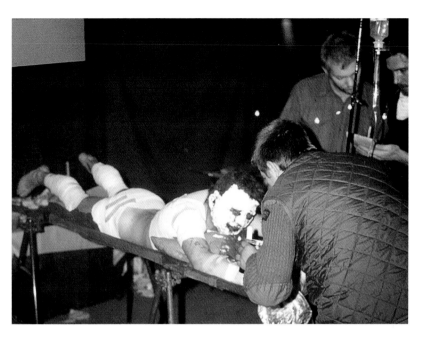

37. **Galahad Night I** One of our chefs applies Flamazine to a burned Welsh
Guardsman; his medical colleagues confer. *(pp 180-185)*

38. **Galahad Night II** The scene at 0430 the next morning. All the casualties have had
their burns dressed, lost fluid replaced, and their pain relieved. Most are asleep, and away
from their nightmares.

39. **Nearing the end** Ajax Bay presents a tranquil face as the front-line moves closer to Stanley. Only the wrecked slaughterhouse roof *(right)* and PoW compound *(left)* give any clue about war and action.

40. **Humanity in victory** An Argentine medic and casualty are helped by a Royal Marine guard after the battle of Mount Harriet; a British casevac helicopter subsequently landed on the track. *(Holgate)*

41. **Field burial** Men of the Special Boat Squadron stride out from the settlement at Teal Inlet, carrying the body of Sgt Kiwi Hunt to its final resting place. *(p 172)*

42. **Stanley and inner harbour** The Argentine Hospital was located in the Community Centre (foreground). Poor field hygiene in the immediate area gave rise to the descriptive nickname of *'A Close Encounter of the Turd Kind'. (p 214)*

43. **Having a smashing time** A bearded author and one of the boys smash boxes of unusable Argentine morphine ampoules. *(p 215)*

44. **Time to go home I** Bronzing Royal Marines enjoy the Sunday afternoon sunlight and applaud the final ceremonies of the *Canberra Medical Society. (p 237)*

45. **Time to go home II** P&O Nursing Sister Angela Devine, Ross Adley, Phil Shouler, George Rudge and a clean-shaven author take wine in the mid-day sunlight. *(p 237)*
46. **Southampton – and busts!** A cheerful and spontaneous welcome home from two lovely ladies. *(pp 240-241)*

47. **Southampton again** The very crowded quayside. *(p 241)*
48. **With President Menem at St Paul's** A quintet of veterans after a fine night out: *(left to right)* Denzil Connick; Major Gustavo Aguirre Faget; author; Cdr Alvaro Lonzieme; Major Eduardo Elmiger. *(p 253)*

49. **HRH in Buenos Aires** The author accompanies The Prince of Wales and interpreter as they move along a line of veterans. *(p 258)*

50. **A sunlit asado** The crew of the Argentine submarine *Santa Fe* toast enduring Anglo-Argentine friendship at a superb BBQ. *(p 266)*

51. **Gonged by both sides** The author, with insignia of *Orden de Majo*, is embraced by Dagger pilot Gustavo Aguirre Faget. *(pp 271-272)*

52. **Paying respects** A *SAMA82* chaplet of poppies about to be laid by the author on the Monument to the Fallen in Buenos Aires. *(p 273)*

53. **The 'Super E' command team** Captain Jorge Colombo was CO of the Argentine Navy's 2nd Attack Squadron, flying the Super Etendard/Exocet combination. His wingmen are the author *(left)* and Rear Adm. Roberto Agotegoray, his Operations Officer in 1982. *(p 269)*

54. **'Permission to Wear'** The author's OBE takes precedence, on the left, but the Argentine insignia is displayed and worn with the personal approval of Her Majesty the Queen. *(p 272-73)*

55. *(above)*
Pilgrimage I A
visit to Ajax Bay
shows how more
demolition with
high explosive was
needed to make
the 'slaughter-
house' area a bit
safer. *(p 275)*

56. *(right)*
Pilgrimage II
Rick Jolly, the
author, in the
freezer again! This
machinery once
stopped and held a
400 kg unexploded
bomb moving at
over 200 mph.
The device was
only made safe and
removed after hos-
tilities ceased.

57. **The SAMA82 pilgrims** at Mount Pleasant Airport, Falkland Islands on 13th November 2002, before their return to Gatwick. *(p 276) (Nigel Hawks)*

58. **SAMA82 presentation to Her Majesty The Queen at Buckingham Palace** (*left to right*) Sukey Cameron MBE (Falkland Islands Govt. Rep.); Denzil Connick (Founding Secretary); Tony Davies MBE (Founding Treasurer, now Chairman) and Dr Rick Jolly OBE (Founding Chairman) present Her Majesty with two gold replicas of the South Atlantic Medal. *(p 279) (Press Association)*

tine Special Forces officer's leg. It seemed possible that it might become an image to go around the world. I sincerely hoped so.

Then, before I could do a special piece to camera for Jeremy Hands, who unlike the other two had been with us in the *Canberra*, one of my senior NCOs suddenly asked to see me, in private. This was a request that I instantly agreed to. Sgt S then told me, in no uncertain terms, that he totally disagreed with my decision to let the media people into Ajax Bay!

This was his privilege of course; I listened to his reasoning, which was full of the usual bias and prejudice, then pointed out two things to him. The interviewers had received nothing but the truth from me, and I also wanted the word to get back to all the wives and mothers in UK that the medical teams at Ajax Bay were doing well. We had become an effective team, and were happy in our work, but just as anxious as anyone else to finish this war and return home. We were also very proud of our track record – everyone who had made it to Ajax Bay alive had also left alive. After 107 major operations, and even in defiance of the awful wounding power of modern munitions, that was no mean achievement.

My subordinate started to bluster again, but I exercised my powers inherent in the Naval Discipline Act, and told him to *'face aft and salute'* – and get back to work. Most interestingly, the same NCO asked to see me privately again while we were on the way home. I told him he was already forgiven for what he thought he might have done! He grinned cheerfully, but still apologised for his attitude. His wife had apparently written to say how much my cheerful and optimistic words had meant to everyone back home, and how from her standpoint, if the Boss of Medical Squadron seemed to be on good form, then her husband was undoubtedly OK too!

When I got back to Jeremy Hands, I mentioned to him, almost as an afterthought, the bombs next door. The 37 hours for the time fuzes had been exceeded, and we regarded them as part of the furniture now. Jeremy was rather nervous at first, but then reassured when I told him that I was happy to stand next to the UXB in the refrigeration machinery. Ken Hesketh was not so keen, and politely declined my invitation to film the beast. That was a pity, because it would have been one of the enduring images of the war to have J. Hands Esq. telling the world that he was standing in front of an unexploded Argentine bomb that had come to rest in the British field hospital!

Sadly, Jeremy Hands died before the new Millennium was in, but I often teased him at our reunions about his missed stellar opportunity. The cameraman, Ken Hesketh also died early, in ill-health − possibly because of an incident in the Iran/Iraq war when he filmed too close to a unexploded chemical warfare munition that was being dealt with. The other Jeremy, Major General Jeremy Moore, had no inhibitions about seeing the UXB. A wiry and tough man who was once my Unit CO, it was all we could do to restrain him from taking a piece of the thing as a souvenir. Some of our other VIP visitors also professed interest in an inspection, but had usually seen enough from the door of the compartment, fifteen yards away. Perhaps we were all becoming slightly 'bomb-happy'. For our part, we had almost forgotten about the two devices next door.

A remarkable Argentine casualty arrived, the very last one from the Battle of Goose Green. Private Donato Baez had just been found, barely alive, in a water-logged trench some distance from the airfield. Like the other occupants of the trench, he had been left for dead. He had a penetrating wound of the right eye, and fractures of the right hand and left thigh as well as a rigid belly and a very low body temperature of 32 degrees Celsius. Young Donato should not really have been alive.

Poor, dumb peasant soldier. All my marines and medics, now refreshed by some decent sleep, felt very sorry for him and proceeded to lavish fantastic care on the helpless Argentine conscript. He was surrounded with hot water bottles and foil blankets, given fresh blood, and received a warm Savlon wash for his filthy hands and feet – followed by the best surgeon in this sector of the South Atlantic for his wounds. His low temperature played havoc with the anaesthetic drugs, and Malcolm Jowitt had to ventilate him by hand for two hours after Bill's operations were successfully completed, until Donato's body warmed up and the muscle-relaxing agents could be successfully reversed.

Later on in the evening, during the daily brief to all hands, I mentioned the bombs again, plus the possibility (now passed) of their time-delayed detonation! Everyone looked a bit shocked, then highly relieved. Good fortune still flew in tandem with us. I felt sure that the *Fuerza Aerea Argentina* planning staff would have put a big red '*destrozado*' mark through our map location, and that they would not want to waste further airstrike efforts on us.

But might we run out of ships and missiles before the enemy ran out of planes? It all promised, as the Duke of Wellington once remarked about a completely different battle, to be a rather close-run thing.

Tuesday, June 1st

For some unknown reason we were told this morning that Ajax Bay could not link up with the *Uganda* as our hospital ship was 'unavailable'. The duty casevac Sea King also failed to turn up as usual. My subsequent discussion with Brigade HQ as to the reason why not, indicated that medium to heavy-lift helicopters in this category had now become so precious that they could no longer allocate one to me. My cold anger concerning operational planners who failed to take battlefield medicine seriously must have had some impact. My chums in Brigade then stated that, from now on, I could definitely have a daily Wessex 5 instead!

In its reliable and robust way, the venerable Wessex was more versatile, although it could carry fewer casualties. The important point was that I would still have a utility helicopter under command. Brigade trusted me to use it wisely, and also gave me full authority for its tasking; they also reassured me that *Uganda* was most definitely in her 'Red Cross Box' (RCB) to the north of the Islands, although they were not sure of her exact location within this artificially designated area of the chart, and admitted that with twenty mile long sides, the RCB represented about four hundred square miles of Southern Atlantic Ocean.

The Argentine Special Forces guys were not yet ready to move on, but were being truculent and unco-operative as their wounds were tended. I stood next to the armed Royal Marine on sentry duty and 'picturised' them in stentorian tones. At first, they pretended not to speak any English, so I then got really wound up in my very finest tourist Spanish: '*No habla Ingles senors? Es mierde, amigos*! We *know* that you are Special Forces, and we know that you have been to Fort Bragg to be trained with the Americans, so don't bloody well try to *lie* to us...'

That was all a bluff, really, but I then told them some real home truths – that they had done their proud duty well, in the same way that we had done ours, and that they would soon be moving out to the British hospital ship, and then on to the Argentine *buque de hospital*. However, I warned them, although we had operated on the holes in their bodies that had been made yesterday, we would not hesitate to make a new set for anyone stupid enough to put their escape and evasion training into practice...

One of the officers looked at me and said: 'Thank you sir, we understand what you are saying...' The Spanish-speaking 'secret squirrel' who was located with us then confirmed that this message was properly translated to the others. Calm and good order were thus restored.

Uganda suddenly became 'available', and when the Wessex finally arrived later on, I decided on a liaison run out to Her

Majesty's Hospital Ship. With Malcolm Jowitt in the back, along with us for the ride as well as for the task of seeking out some anaesthetic resupply, we lifted off and headed out to the north of East Falkland, past Fanning Head. The pilot bent a few peacetime rules by allowing me, without helmet, up into the left-hand seat.

He was soon enjoying the scenery as his co-pilot, the frustrated aviator dressed as a Commando doctor, took charge of the controls. There was a rugged beauty to the Falklands coastline, and it was easy to understand why so many of the Royal Marines who had served with Naval Party 8901 had come to love the place so much during their year's service in the Islands. Some of them had even left the Corps and settled here.

We'd also all heard of a nasty piece of work named Major Patricio Dowling, an Intelligence expert and 'hero' of *La Guerra Sucia*, the 'Dirty War' conducted against some of its younger citizens by the Argentine military *Junta*. This chap had personally interrogated a number of the Royal Marines who were captured in Stanley after the invasion of April 2nd. His professional technique included placing a hood over the subject's head and then cocking a pistol close to his ear. How was he sleeping at the moment? Was he aware that all the marines in Naval Party 8901 had volunteered to come south again, and had expressed their keenness to 'interview' Major Dowling – but under their own terms this time?

From the cockpit of our helicopter, nose down at 100 knots as we hurtled along about sixty feet above the sea, the air smelled clean – and the beaches looked fresh and perfect as they flicked past. We even saw some penguins, scattering in panic as the unfamiliar and threatening clamour of a helicopter entered their lives. Call sign '*Nurse Uganda*' eventually answered our open channel radio calls about a quarter of an hour after we had left the coastline behind, and she then transmitted a long message for our direction-finding radio receiver. The needle on the panel indicator swung to the right, so I added ten degrees to our heading and settled on the new course. Another fifteen minutes flying, now well out of sight of land, and there she was...

A tiny speck on the horizon split into three – *Uganda* was transferring patients to two of her attendant Hospital Ambulance ships, which were converted Hydrographic Service survey vessels. I climbed gradually to 500 feet as the details became clearer. We were, hopefully, out of threat range from the enemy airstrip at Pebble Island, or the '*Isla de Borbon*' as the invaders now called it. However, when the attack did come in, it was from a totally unexpected quarter – ahead of us! HM Ships *Hecla* and *Hydra's* Wasp helicopters broke off from their transfer tasks and headed out towards us. The Fleet Air Arm had decided to play. My pilot's instructions in the headset were brief: 'Thank you sir, I have control...'

The light of battle glinted in his eyes as, watching the pair of approaching Wasps, he timed the break perfectly and cut underneath them, rocketing back down to sea level. The small helicopters were shaken off, left well behind. Still, I was very glad that the little black dots in our cockpit windscreen had not turned out to be Pucaras. The SAS had done an excellent job the previous month when they raided the Pebble Island airstrip, and had apparently wrecked nearly a dozen of the armed aircraft that were based there, but reinforcement by the Argentine Air Force was always a worrying possibility.

After settling on *Uganda's* helicopter deck we unstrapped and climbed down. Surgeon Captain Andrew Rintoul, the Medical Officer in Charge, was there to greet us, and if he was surprised at the grubby (and in my case unshaven) creatures that saluted him and then shook his hand, he showed no sign of it.

In charge of the Reception/Resuscitation area, at the base of the ramp leading down from the flight deck to the medical facilities, was another friend of long acquaintance named Jean Kidd, normally Sister in charge of the Accident and Emergency Department of the Royal Naval Hospital back in Plymouth. She had also worked in the medical department at the Royal Marines Commando Training Centre at Lympstone, and was particularly fond of Surgeon Lieutenant Ross Adley, a young colleague who was now up front with the other medics of 42 Commando, on Mount Kent. Jean looked really fresh and pretty, in marked contrast to us. She still greeted us warmly and I took a letter for Ross ashore with me later on.

What a cool, beautiful haven that lovely ship was! From the moment that a wounded man had been stretchered down the ramp by the attendant Royal Marines Bandsmen, there was a definite feeling that *Uganda's* staff and organisation had been designed to help him heal just as quickly and smoothly as possible. The wards were spotless, the staff wearing white plimsolls as they padded silently along the carpeted decks. Best of all, there were female nurses! The girls looked divine and smelled impossibly fragrant as they tended our customers of the previous week. With their faces now cleaned of camouflage cream, those patients who were not asleep grinned cheerfully at us as we walked past their beds, and some even gave us a 'thumbs up' sign.

Most impressive of all was the Intensive Care Unit, which had been created from the ship's Durbar Room. In an atmosphere of quiet calm and purposefulness, all the post-operative problems and complications that we would not have been able to treat back in Ajax Bay were being coped with by Jane Marshall and her team.

It was a statement of the obvious that no chain can be stronger than its weakest link, but this ICU was definitely the golden feature of our 8,000 mile long casualty evacuation linkage that reached back to the UK.

In the wardroom anteroom, with its beautifully figured panelling and bar, I met some of the other key medical and surgical personnel for the first time. Mike Beeley was the physician specialising in respiratory problems; Peter Bull and David Baker were the anaesthetists, while Roger Leicester and Charles Chapman were surgeons, the latter trained in plastics work that

151

was already proving of inestimable value in tidying up the ugly wounds that we were sending out to the hospital ship. We swapped my stories of our life ashore for their accounts of the clinical problems they were facing at sea. Some of their other colleagues then turned up for a curry 'tiffin' served by the Goanese stewards. It all seemed totally unreal.

A brief conversation with the MOIC and Andy Gough, the RN Commander who was also the ship's executive Senior Naval Officer, revealed a few more problems. Tomorrow, *Uganda* was due to pass her numerous Argentine patients across to the ARA *Bahia Paraiso*, her Argentine Navy equivalent. This vessel had a strengthened hull and was an Antarctic supply vessel in normal times. She had also been 'declared' to Geneva, and was sharing the Red Cross Box with *Uganda* on occasion. I explained in turn that we no longer had our high-capacity, longer-range Sea Kings, and were hoping that *Uganda* would soon be able to close the Islands on a daily basis, thus minimising casualty flying times.

However, I also reported to them that *Canberra* was due back in San Carlos Water with the Guards and Gurkhas from *QE2's* call into South Georgia. This might solve one mutual problem, as we would be able to take wounded cases to her while *Uganda* was otherwise engaged tomorrow. Andy, a Fleet Air Arm Observer by specialist qualification, promised to try for Northwood's permission to get *Uganda* in much closer to Ajax Bay every morning after that.

If he could achieve this concession, it was going to be very helpful, because it would knock our second difficulty concerning range and transit times completely into touch. No more long haul flights out to *Uganda*; instead, our Wessex could be employed on short hops, of high frequency from field hospital to hospital ship.

I took the opportunity for a quick face and neck wash, as time was limited. At the time, I also recorded in my diary the twin wonders of cold beer from one chrome-plated tap, in the anteroom, and hot water, from another, in the MOIC's cabin!

We lifted off, burdened with fruit and other supplies, including a bottle of Black Label whisky, the gift of Lieutenant Commander David Porteous, *Uganda's* RN Supply Officer, who was acting as Deputy Purser. He and I had shared a superb run ashore in London following an Army/Navy game at Twickenham a few years before. Not only that, he lent me his 35 mm Canon camera and some slide film, to replace my little Olympus that had been ruined by immersion during the rescue off HMS *Ardent.* How marvellous it was, in the small and splendid club that they call the Royal Navy, to be able to rely on people who were true friends.

Back at Ajax Bay – disaster. An explosion at Goose Green in a pile of captured Argentine ammunition had killed two prisoners and injured many more. Phil Shouler looked up, despondent, from the fresh and legless corpse he had been working on in Triage: 'Sorry Boss, but we've lost him. Pulse was about thirty when he came in, picked up after four units of blood, but then collapsed again. That's the Ajax Bay track record gone...'

I was initially a bit despondent too, then cheered him up by re-phrasing our proud claim. Every *British* soldier who had made it to us alive had also gone out alive. That really would be something if we could still say it truthfully at the end of this war.

Some of the other casualties were ghastly, and Phil then asked me to help with another victim of the explosion. It seemed likely that the incident was caused by a booby trap both set and (ironically) triggered off by Argentine soldiers. They were prisoners of war, and were quite legitimately, within the rules of the Geneva Convention, being used to move some artillery shells away from a dump positioned next to the schoolhouse. Our next customer had lost most of one leg and suffered major damage to the other one as well.

Phil supervised my amputation of the left leg mid-thigh, after the preparation of muscle and skin flaps to create a reasonable stump. The right leg took much more time as we teased the lumps of melted plastic and dirt, blades of grass, and small pieces of jagged shrapnel away from the charred and bleeding muscle. It was a real horror show, and I could appreciate even more the sustained quality of the surgical team's efforts.

During our earlier flight back from *Uganda*, Malcolm Jowitt had discussed with me the possibility of getting some of the fitter Argentine prisoners to donate their blood. His idea now became a critically important one, because apparently we were running very short of fresh red cells. There was a problem however. The senior Army Officer in their PoW compound had refused point blank to allow any of his men to co-operate. I asked for Colonel Pioggi to be brought to the operating facility as soon as possible; Malcolm acted as his escort.

With typical Argentine bravado, the former *Jefe* of the '*Ganso Verde*' garrison swaggered into the small space available behind the blanket which acted as a dividing curtain. He was behaving as if he was the landlord, rather than the guest of British forces. I turned to face him, looked him in the eye, and saluted him. He was a full Colonel, after all, and therefore senior to me. The message to him via our interpreter was clear, and succinct: 'Sir, some *bastardo* booby-trapped an ammunition dump beside the schoolhouse. This is one of your men who we are trying to save, and there are two others. We need more fresh blood – and with urgency…' I paused, and then stepped to one side and gave him the full-on, Technicolour visual impact of Patient 275's dreadful wounds.

The bald-headed senior officer averted his gaze from the shocking diorama, narrowed his eyes in apparent disbelief, and then tilted his head down to one side, in order to look at our patient's face! He obviously suspected a trick, in which Argentine boys were going to be conned into giving their blood for the benefit of British wounded. When he saw instead the olive skin, flattened nose and Amerindian features of the unconscious patient attached to the anaesthetic machine, he straightened up, his own face now registering surprise and disbelief. He stared at the operating field, then began swaying on his feet, unable to look any longer at all the blackened meat and gore laid out before him.

Colonel Pioggi then turned away, muttering in Spanish: '*Cuanto – cual tipo?*' He was asking how much blood we needed, and which blood group in particular. Malcolm and his team then set to again. The corridor that acted as their transfusion clinic was narrow, dusty and poorly lit, but two hours later Chief McKinley returned with much better news. There were 60 pints of fresh red stuff cooling down in their bags now, with as much again available 'on the hoof' if necessary. The blood shortage crisis was over, at least for the moment.

Coronel Italo Pioggi had been so badly shaken by his visit to the operating theatre, and so moved by our obvious efforts for his men, that he now lost all his previous surliness and haughty attitude. He asked to see me again, and told me that he wanted very much to give some of his own blood, but felt unable to do so because he had suffered from hepatitis in the past. In truth, he was absolutely correct to declare this, and I found myself warming to the man. He had also told his own explosives experts to have a little talk with Flt Lt Alan Swan, our resident bomb disposal expert. Some surprising facts emerged later from this technical *tête-à-tête*, including the position of a large explosives cache, all ready to be detonated by remote control, beneath the runway threshold at Goose Green. Alan was able to tackle this personally, and with complete success, a day later. On balance, it was a good way to end another bad day in the meat market.

Wednesday, June 2nd

Missed breakfast after oversleeping. There was a thick mist lying on San Carlos Water. The helicopters were totally unable to fly this morning, at least until the sun got up high enough to burn off some of the low-lying clag. The absence of clattering rotor blades and whining engines had allowed me extended time in the arms of Morpheus. Still, I had the persistent feeling throughout the day that I had actually been dreaming about being asleep, before waking up to find that it wasn't true.

The Amphibious Beach Unit confirmed the rumours that *Canberra* was back in, lying about a mile in front of HMS *Fearless*, and out of sight·to us in the sheltered and fogged-in recess of Ajax Bay. One of the theatre Petty Officers, Fleet Chief Bryn Dobbs and I hijacked a cheerful and willing Royal Marines coxswain and his dory for a brief ride out to the liner. She looked even more weatherbeaten than last week following her journey to South Georgia. There would certainly be no cruising brochure photography today.

It was wonderful to see the familiar face of Surgeon Captain Roger Wilkes again. A short private chat with him confirmed some details, and I also unburdened myself about some of the difficulties I'd had with 'Not Entitled'. None of the team at Ajax Bay knew just how much extra baggage had been placed on me by this chap's nasty attitude, but FRW listened quietly and then gave me some good advice. He also wondered if the nickname '*Proctalgia*' might have been more appropriate for my nemesis – it's the Latin medical term for a 'pain in the rectum'!

His counselling preceded a much longer brief to all the *Canberra* medical staff, in his cabin, about events since we'd parted company on D-Day. There was much to tell on both sides. FRW also insisted that I should use his bath facilities, probably because I was no pleasure to be downwind of. The bath water looked like black railway coffee by the time I'd finished, but the feeling of cleanliness was most uplifting.

Culinary standards were as high as ever in the Pacific Restaurant, and the staff still as cheerful. Up in the Bonito Room, our Argentine Special Forces wounded had been admitted, as well as the victims of the Goose Green booby-trap incident. Everything looked busy and efficient, so I returned ashore with FRW to show him around Ajax Bay. His reaction to the guided tour of the set-up was quite different to that of another senior officer who, having been cocooned in *QE2* and remote from the medical action for the first ten days of our war, looked around, came back to Reception and, in all seriousness, said: 'Well, this isn't how we *planned* it...'

I also felt very guilty when Bryn Dobbs wrinkled his nose at me and said that I stank of perfumed soap! I had of course exercised a privilege that was unavailable to my boys, and decided to take immediate steps to correct this particular failure of leadership.

Now that 45 Commando and 3 Para had passed through Teal Inlet on a long 'yomp' and 'tab' (respectively) across the northern part of the island, it would soon be time to move some of our medical assets forward, along with other logistic bits and pieces. Malcolm Hazell would be leading an advance party around there that night on one of the LSLs. They would be reinforced later on by Charles Batty's Field Surgical Team. We were not due to get any extra operating capability to replace them for the moment, but at least Erich Bootland's Troop could now come ashore from *Canberra*. It was like a complicated game of musical hospital beds, with limited facilities being spread thinly in order to keep some kind of service going in two different locations.

Another Argentine soldier nearly croaked on us. A *Cabo* (Corporal) slipped into a deep coma following an operation to remove some shell splinters from his leg. Nothing seemed capable of waking him, and his snoring respirations got more and more shallow, and less and less frequent. Although his eye pupillary reflexes appeared normal, we began to wonder about some kind of exotic brain damage.

For the patient's sake, as well as trying for one of Father Mulcahy's 4077th *M*A*S*H*-type miracles, we called for a cleric. Without a Roman Catholic padre of our own, we had to rely instead on one of the Argentine priests captured at Goose Green. On inspecting our patient, he saw the need immediately, and performed the Last Rites of the Roman Catholic Church. By now, our man was pretty far gone, his mouth forming an enlarged 'O', death apparently only a matter of hours away. I certainly didn't expect him to be around in the morning.

Thursday, June 3rd

Not only was the Argentine NCO alive, he was also well! It was an incredible transformation from the previous night. The man was sleeping quietly on his side, and easily rousable. *Muchas gracias*, Don Mulcahy! We were left reflecting that it wasn't only in television and film scripts that miracles came true. Like the others, our Argentine Lazarus went out to *Uganda*, along with some fresh blood which we had landed the previous day from *Canberra's* replenishment stocks.

The P&O medical and nursing staff from *Canberra* also came ashore to look around, take photographs, and be amazed by the guided tour, which started with the unexploded bombs at the back. With his characteristic and instinctive generosity, Peter Mayner very kindly left a case of beer for the lads. Later on it was rationed out at one can per three men, but never were a few mouthfuls of cold Australian lager more gratefully accepted.

In the afternoon I felt like doing some painting to celebrate Ajax Bay's success, so I climbed up above the entrance doorway with a pot of red gloss. For some obscure reason, Marine Fraz Coates had a small paint-brush in his personal kit, which I now borrowed. The bold, foot-high letters were blocked in for all to see:

WELCOME TO THE
RED AND GREEN LIFE MACHINE

The first of a new type of casualty also came in, a young Royal Marine of 42 Commando who had stepped on the edge of a buried anti-personnel mine during offensive patrolling in the area of Mount Kent. Apparently, the ground over this device had been frozen for most of the morning, and could bear the weight of several passers-by. Then the soil had softened as the air temperature rose, and the Italian-made device detonated with a loud bang. The company medic crawled in to his position and then carried him out (of what was now a suspected minefield) via the same route. The front half of the marine's boot was completely shredded, with the mangled remains of his forefoot attached only by a bridge of skin that had flapped back on itself.

This nineteen year old young man had a really positive mental attitude as I took a pre-operative photograph and apologised to him that we were going to have to remove his foot, above the ankle:

'Lucky really, sir, because I didn't get it quite right...'

'What on earth do you mean?' was my reply.

'Well, those bloody things are designed to blow your leg and your balls off. If I'd stood on the bugger properly, instead of just at the edge, I'd have lost much more than my foot...'

I stood there, simply astounded at the moral courage of such a remark. Well done, Royal. Without any help from the medics, he'd already taken the first and biggest step back on the road to recovery.

There was more encouragement too from *Uganda*, with a message written by four of the Logistic Regiment casualties from our bomb attack. Their letter was taped up on the Reception area wall for all the boys to see, for them to feel just as proud of the men who sent it as they could of their own efforts that night:

From: Mne Watt, Mne Burnett, Mne Cragg and Mne Mudge

To: Surg Cdr Jolly and all the officers and men of the medical team ashore at Ajax Bay.

Dear Sir, on behalf of the lads injured in the attack on Ajax Bay on the evening of 27th May and now onboard the SS UGANDA I'd like to thank you and your fantastic team for saving our lives and limbs. You cannot ever know how much we appreciate it, you were all great. Please pass on our gratitude to all the staff for doing such a marvellous job. Thanks a million, and take care.

Yours sincerely, Gerry Watt

(Royal Marines Ordnance Squadron)

Friday, June 4th

Dreadful day, with heavy rain. Spent much of the afternoon with General Jeremy Moore's newly-arrived medical adviser, Surgeon Captain Barry Blackstone, bringing him up to date on events so far. For some reason it appeared to be raining inside the Triage area as well as outdoors. Beads of rainwater formed on the ceiling and fell in muddy puddles on the floor. We had to get up into the roof space somehow, and stop this leak. Corporal John Clare and I found a trapdoor in the dimly-lit main corridor, and levered ourselves up. There was a loud drumming sound above us as the sheets of rain struck the galvanized tin roof, but we soon found the cause of the problem. Because of the wind's direction, some of the rainwater was now coming straight in through a hole in the upper part of the front wall, the one made on May 27th when we had that dusk visit from the Argentine Air Force. The loosely shredded cork insulating material lying on the ceiling joists and beneath the hole had absorbed a proportion of this influx, but the soggy pool was now overflowing.

At the base of the hole I also found a piece of twisted, shining metal. Peering through the hole, and aligning my gaze with an oval split in the roof behind me, I found that I was staring at the shallow crater outside that had also appeared on May 27th, as I dived into the nearby sangar! Les Short had been absolutely right. That depression in the ground really had been fashioned by a bomb, moving at high speed as it passed through the front wall and bounced on the ground outside. '2 inch rocket' be damned!!

I had been reluctant to believe another of my marines who had witnessed the whole incident, and who had later commented wryly: 'Lucky you moved a bit sharpish there, Boss. If you hadn't, you might have been legless again…' I'd only had one bad dream about the incident as a result, partly because of my wilful ignorance, and partly because of the undoubted therapeutic value of such classic black humour.

We plugged the hole with cork blocks, stopped the leak and descended to ground level again. Flight Lieutenant Swan confirmed my worst fears. The piece of twisted metal was part of the tail fin of an *Engins Matra* 'SAMP' parachute-retarded 450 kg bomb.

That was bomb number four, therefore. It had struck the tin roof, crossed the space above the main Reception and operating area on a descending track, parallel to and about three feet away from a main joist; impacted with the front wall, nose cap on; passed through the breeze blocks without detonating; bounced on the ground outside, still travelling at a couple of hundred miles an hour, and then finally ended up about three hundred yards away on the foreshore. If it had gone off as advertised in the maker's brochure, it would have killed us all, patients, staff – the whole lot. Who would have tended the injured then? The war would have gone on, of course, but what a price to pay in damaged morale, as well as destroyed medical assets…

The whole incident did not really bear thinking about in depth. It was merely time to breathe a silent and heartfelt prayer, praising the Almighty for small mercies – and then just get on with the job. Humour, of course, continued to play an important part within our range of coping strategies. I showed the piece of crumpled bomb fin to Bernie Bruen and the Naval divers, now successful conquerors of UXBs in both *Sir Galahad* and *Sir Lancelot*. They suggested that I should mount the thing on a wooden plinth, and then lend it to the Tate Gallery as a piece of abstract sculpture entitled *Adrenalin is Brown*...

Saturday, June 5th

I found that I had been affected by the PCT virus, and their wretched Airborne disease had finally cracked me! That morning, I climbed out of my sleeping bag and, without thinking, started to clean my boots. The Para medics all laughed heartily at my unthinking adoption of the first of their reflex morning routines – but I drew the line at wasting water by shaving.

It was basically another quiet day, with not much happening. We tidied out the whole building as best we could, but the choking clouds of dust which rose in response to the use of our new *Canberra*-donated brooms made cleaning the floor very difficult.

The *Fuerza Aerea* Medical Officer who had been helping us to look after some of the wounded prisoners then revealed an interesting side of his character. It also highlighted the way in which some Argentine officers tended to regard their soldiers, and the cultural and attitude differences which existed between the officer corps of the two nations. We had been allowing Lt Miranda free access from the PoW compound to our medical areas, providing that he had an escort to take him there and back each time.

Tonight, I had asked him to stay and help us at the time when he and the other PoW officers were normally fed. Quite naturally, I then asked him to go to supper with me, and gave him my second mess tin to use. We joined the galley queue, as usual; several of the theatre technicians went past us in the line, to the head of the queue, also something that was entirely normal. I suddenly became aware of a change of attitude in our young colleague. On asking him what was wrong, in halting English he explained that he could not understand why the '*Jefe*' of the hospital should have to stand in line for his food. In a funny way, I sensed that he had been a bit insulted by this queue-jumping, but on my behalf!

Despite our language difficulty, I tried to explain to him that the operating staff could only take their meals when there was a lull in the surgical load, so it made sense for them to have some sort of priority. He looked at me a bit blankly. I then also mentioned that no British officer would ever take his meal in the field until he was sure that his men had eaten too. Once again, this was a concept of operations quite beyond his understanding. I was to recall this incident again about ten days later, in Stanley.

Sunday, June 6th

Another rubbish day from the meteorological point of view. We started the traditional day of rest with an 'Air Raid Red' warning long before dawn, followed by the sound of an Argentine Canberra jet dropping bombs somewhere in the distance, but then the clag and rain set in again and we were spared any further attention. Later on, the rain clouds cleared, to be replaced by high winds which made flying very difficult for the casevac Wessex helicopter, and severely tested our pilot. He rose to the occasion however, and *Uganda* got her customers without any additional injuries sustained in transit.

At one point during the morning, I met Ivar Hellberg wandering up the track from the satellite communication facility, looking slightly dazed. He asked me what day it was, which was a surprising question from our normally switched-on Regimental CO. When I confirmed to him that it was indeed Sunday, he suddenly roared with laughter and explained what had just happened.

Apparently, Ivar was in the habit of calling up a senior Royal Marines logistician, based in Northwood, by satellite telephone whenever the occasion demanded. This system was backed up by typed signals of course, but voice contact had an immediacy and urgency that could be very useful. Some acute and specific shortage had occurred, so Ivar had just dialled up the usual Northwood number, and was surprised when a woman's voice answered. He thought he had a wrong number, apologised, and then ended the call.

His second attempt produced the same responding voice, who identified herself as the duty Wren clerk in the section! Ivar, a bit shocked, asked where his colleague was, or when he was expected to be there:

'The Colonel's not due to be in today, sir..'

'Really? Why ever not? It's after nine in the morning, isn't it? I need to speak to him, and urgently...'

'Well sir,' came the sweet reply, undistorted by the miracles of modern signal technology bouncing off the Skynet satellite, 'we aren't really expecting him to be here today – because you see, it's *Sunday!*

We were both roaring with laughter now, at the simple concept of a day back in England where everything stopped just because of the standard conventions and rules of society. We had already started to formulate a definition of the difference between war and peace, and this new twist simply begged to be fed in. War was like an exercise in which 'the umpires didn't turn up, the injuries were real, the *Endex* date was unknown – and some of your friends were killed, *even on a Sunday...*'

But the Lord's Day was still observed by the military in the field, even though this was not a day of rest as such. We had to have a Church Parade, and Father John Ryan of HMS *Intrepid* came ashore to hold an inter-denominational service in the main treatment area, which was well attended. Bernie Bruen's fiddle doubled as church organ for the occasion, and his proper (and talented) musical accompaniment made a great difference to the standard of our hymn singing.

We then heard that an Army Gazelle helicopter had crashed over to the east during the previous evening, apparently having flown into high ground during bad weather. By now, I was merely listening to such rumours, but only believing (and reporting) whatever I saw with my own eyes. I knew that all the bodies would eventually come back to us for certification of death and burial.

My 'doubting Thomas' attitude was just as well in this particular instance. When the four corpses were brought in to our makeshift mortuary, I had them laid out in the relative positions that they would have occupied inside the aircraft. The two aircrew, a Staff Sergeant pilot and his Lance Corporal air gunner were relatively intact, although their flying suits were punctured and torn in many places – the pilot (who would have been on the right) displayed more of this damage than his companion, and I also had the distinct impression that the fragments had been sprayed at them from below and the right. The cockpit seats had absorbed some of this shrapnel storm.

Exactly how their two passengers had been positioned behind them was a mystery at first, particularly as these bodies were much more seriously distorted, again worse on the right than the left. Their names were Sergeant B and Major F. The latter was a Royal Signals officer, and a tough chap to judge from his parachute wings and the loaded .44 Magnum pistol in a close-fitting shoulder holster. It quickly became apparent that their cause of death was certainly not ground impact. Something like a military warhead had exploded just below and behind the aircraft. Their deaths had been instantaneous, and had come long before the helicopter fell to the Falklands peat.

To aid the inevitable later forensic investigation (which I was not equipped to pursue myself) I then removed several of the little twisted curlicues of sharp metal fragments embedded in each body, rinsed them off, and placed these in four labelled envelopes.

They had been killed by some kind of surface-to-air, or even air-to-air missile. We stopped our work for a short period of silence and respect. Then, as we placed these friends and former colleagues, whom we had never known in life, into their body bags, I began to think. Had they been shot down by our own side? By a ship – or a night-patrolling Sea Harrier perhaps? Did the Argentines even have a night fighter capability? I didn't know of one, and I was an aviation enthusiast. Did the Gazelle have prior permission to be where they were at that hour, in one of the protected air-defence corridors that our Special Forces helicopters operated in? Still, this was all a bit beyond my pay grade, as the saying went, although I decided to report my findings to General Moore's HQ the next day.

The team did the messy job quietly and reverently. Again, we drew satisfaction from the thought that we had restored dignity and respectability to four brave men who had, in one blinding flash, become part of British military history. The forms and certificates were filled in, collated and sorted, and the details beamed back to London by satellite. Curtains would be twitching on the married patch at Middle Wallop. There were three widow's doors for someone to knock on, and a mother to be informed that her son was now on the Roll of Honour.

Still, it could have happened to any one of us. For my part, I was even more determined that the Brits should redouble their efforts to roll the Argies up and get back home, before there were too many more of our friends to examine and bury. Little did I know then how the saga of this shot-down Gazelle would run and run, how misunderstanding would be piled upon misrepresentation, and how later on it would take the determination of a brave mother – and the committed support of a decent and honest Labour Minister – to bring truth to the surface.

Monday, June 7th

There was not a cloud in sight as the sun came up in a clear, cold sky over San Carlos Water. As I wrote up my diary, I saw from the day's only entry so far that I had been booked for a speaking engagement that morning in the Training Division at the Royal Naval Hospital, Plymouth! It was too late to send my apologies – but then most of my potential audience were probably down here anyway.

One occasional feature of those cloudless days was that we could see, from the ground, the long white condensation vapour trails of high-flying aircraft. These were just like the contrails over my house back in Cornwall, left in the track of big passenger jets heading out over the Atlantic towards the New World. This morning, something was rather different, because HMS *Exeter*, lying out in San Carlos Water, sprang into life. With a bang that was clearly audible inside the buildings at Ajax Bay, she launched a Sea Dart missile at a fast-moving contrail passing from east to west above us.

I raced outside to find out what was happening, and was met by a group of chortling, rather sarcastic Royal Marines. The missile had begun to climb, then went 'rogue' and either fell with toppled gyros into the Sussex ridge behind us, or else was steered there under limited control: 'Useful bit of matelot kit, eh Boss? Sea Dart? We'll give you Sea Dart. More like Sea Fart we reckon!'

There were more roars of laughter directed at me as the boys tried to stop their steaming mugs of tea spilling on the ground. As the plume of the missile's rocket smoke drifted away, I could still see a steady white line moving across the sky above us. In San Carlos Water the sunlit scene looked peaceful, the destroyer lying quietly out in the middle of a glassy, calm anchorage. I was about to say something about Type 42 destroyers having a twin Sea Dart mounting when, with a *whoosh* and bang that echoed around the hills, a second missile leapt upwards from its launch rail.

With an awesome, irresistible grace it climbed fiercely, sprinting up towards a target which was now obliterated from us by the exhaust plume. The booster motors fell away. We stood in silence beneath the steadily decreasing roar, until suddenly someone said: 'Jesus Christ – the poor bastards...'

As the white cloud of the second missile's trail drifted away in the wind, we could now see that the thin line of its target's contrail had stopped abruptly. The tumbling fragments of wing and fuselage were invisible to us as they fell against the velvet-blue backdrop of the sky. Had it been a Canberra bomber? Or a photo-recce Learjet? Who knows – but the crew must have seen their deaths coming for ten or fifteen seconds. What a way to die – a Learjet would not have had ejector seats. Well done HMS *Exeter*, anyway. If the Argentine aircrew were taking photos of San Carlos for target assessment, then they had been involved in a warlike action, which fully justified a warlike response.

Once again we were up against the paradox of war. We could admire our enemies, even respect their courage and skill, but also cheer when they were removed, violently, from the battlefield...

I was only to learn the complete story many years later. The Learjet pilot was the squadron CO, Lt Col Rodolfo de la Colina. There were two aircraft, taking stereo pair photographs. The Sea Dart missile was fitted with a proximity fuse, and it detonated below and behind the leading sleek executive jet in the same way that (as we also later discovered) another had brought down the Army Air Corps Gazelle two nights before. This time, the whole tail empennage was blown off, leaving the pressure cabin (and its five passengers) intact. The totally uncontrollable aircraft spiralled down from eight miles up, twisting like a sycamore leaf in the strong westerly wind. It hit the ground nearly fifteen miles away, next to the grass airstrip of Pebble Island.

The sound of its impact startled the occupants of a SBS hide concealed very close by. An Argentine retrieval party which then came out to extract the bodies almost stumbled over them, and because of the danger of having been compromised, the Royal Marines were lifted out by helicopter later on that night. De La Colina, Major Falconier, Captain Lutufo and the NCOs Luna and Marizza all now lie in the Argentine cemetery at Fitzroy.

Back at Ajax Bay, the daily Wessex arrived as promised. We had no customers for *Uganda* that day, but there were some replenishment stores awaiting delivery to the medics of 2 Para. With everything quiet in the shop, and Tim Hughes, today's pilot, keen to keep his hand in, we indulged in a spot of contour flying down to Goose Green. The intercom was unserviceable so, in the back, I relaxed initially as we tore along, close to the bleak terrain. The sheep scattered in all directions as we flashed past. What war? Mount Simon had a close covering of snow and looked deceptively close in the middle distance.

But then we came out from the gun and missile zone of San Carlos, where the air defence systems were interlocked for mutual protection. I dragged my eyes back to acquisition range in the immediate vicinity of the Wessex, trying to be serious about the threat of Pucara. These Argentine-made turbo-prop aircraft hunted in pairs and were well armed; we knew that there were still some left in Stanley. Our helicopter would have been a nice target for them, a fat little Wessex operating on its own. I fingered the cocking handle of our port window-mounted General

Purpose Machine Gun rather uneasily, trying not to think about Richard Nunn's last, desperate fight.

The main purpose of today's trip was for me, as the Brigade Medical Adviser, to check that all was well with Goose Green's military garrison, which was now transferring from 2 Para to 1/7 Gurkhas.

That task was certainly important, but it did not take long. On the way back, we landed on the airfield to look at the two derelict Pucaras that were sitting there. Further on, we then photographed the grave of Lieutenant Nick Taylor, the Sea Harrier pilot who was shot down and had lost his life while attacking the airstrip in early May. The cross was wooden and beautifully made, his grave tucked in behind a fence at the far edge of the field.

Then, while we were hover-taxying along at about thirty feet, I spotted a large but manageable-looking piece of an Argentine Navy jet as well, part of a pile of wreckage that had been strewn around in the grass runway's undershoot. The downwash of our rotor blades flicked this piece of fuselage over, to show the black letters '*A-R-M-A-D-*' of *Armada* (Navy) on its green camouflaged outer surface. This souvenir was quickly acquired and flown to Ajax Bay. As will be described later, I then brought it back to England – and passed it on to the Fleet Air Arm Museum at Yeovilton.

In the interim, and during my absence, we had been sent a young British casualty with a bad bullet wound of the chest. Unfortunately, this was a 'negligent discharge' originating from one of the most dangerous weapons in the British military inventory, the 9 mm sub-machine gun. He was rather unwell as Nick Morgan, John Williams and Malcolm Jowitt got to work. Later, this patient would complain about the three tubes inserted into his chest, but those drainage routes did a vital job in carrying away the blood leaking from the bullet's long track. He was a rather lucky boy – another survivor, and very much against the odds.

The mail arrived. There was nothing for me, so a temporary gloom set in while the duty staff in the Command Post tore into their news from home. We also had some medical stores to go forward to Teal Inlet, the harbour on the northern flank that was acting as logistics base for the assaults on Mounts Kent and Longdon, as well as the attack on a feature called Two Sisters. We loaded the helicopter again, this time with Chief Petty Officer Jethro Young and one of the PCT Corporals along for the ride. They accompanied the boxes of dressings, various drugs, a sack of mail, and a morale-boosting pair of whisky bottles.

The push forward of men and equipment from San Carlos continued. The Gurkhas had managed to march overland from San Carlos to Goose Green, but this task was beyond either of the two Guards battalions which, to be fair, had only just completed a spell of 'public duties' in London.

So, each night, either of the two assault ships *Fearless* or *Intrepid* disappeared around to Fitzroy, to the south, with their tank decks full of men and supplies. The off-loading process could have been very tricky if the weather turned unpleasant, but there simply did not seem to be any real alternative. The overland route from Fitzroy to Bluff Cove, the next settlement up the line, was along nine miles of difficult track.

Up on the northern flank, HQ LFFI had kept a couple of the smaller LSLs moving around into Teal Inlet, and one was busy unloading there as we arrived over the bunkhouse after a twenty minute flight. Tim settled the Wessex down on the Day-Glo landing panels secured to the wet ground in the near corner of an adjoining field. Inside the Forward Dressing Station, as the bunkhouse was now called, Malcolm Hazell and his men seemed both cheerful and comfortable. With running hot water they had every reason to be, but conditions were still very cramped – and they had been forced to rig two large tents outside, blistered on to the main building, in order to provide extra space.

Charles Batty and Dick Knight had also brought their Forward Surgical element of the PCT up to Teal Inlet and, supported by the resuscitative skills of Tim Douglas Riley, Howard Oakley and the other members of the RN team, they looked ready to tackle anything. Most important of all, the senior ratings were in good heart, especially CPOMA 'Nutty' Edwards. It was usually pretty easy to pull his leg or, as Royal Marines would say, 'get a bite' out of him, and the unfortunate Chief did not let us down. Jethro Young said it wasn't even sport any more! In fact, secretly, we all cared desperately for him. Back in Plymouth, his lovely wife Landy had been born and raised in the Falkland Islands, and was a true 'kelper'. Her mother and father were still in Stanley, which was under the Argentine yoke. We were on our way to free them. It was a great relief for me to discover that I did not need to have any worries about this bunch of senior NCOs.

As we boarded the Wessex again for our flight back to San Carlos, I noticed a small, sad procession moving out from the hamlet. At its head was a padre, striding out. Just behind him was a flag-draped body bag containing the mortal remains of Sergeant 'Kiwi' Hunt. The Special Boat Squadron were burying their dead, in the weak sunlight of a Falklands winter afternoon. Cradling their Ingram sub-machine pistols, long-haired, wild-eyed and wearing a variety of outdoor and Alpine clothing, their general appearance was somewhat bizarre to those onlookers totally ignorant of their methods and skills. Today, they had stopped the war for an hour to pay their respects to a dead Royal Marines colleague. From over 400 metres away I took a photograph (later presented to his widow), saluted – without embarrassment – and then climbed back up into the cockpit.

Flogging back at low level to San Carlos, there was time to notice how different the terrain was here. Layers and layers of long white tussock grass flicked backwards and forwards in the wind and pale yellow light. Tim diverted the aircraft slightly towards the coast, and then tightened upwards into a 360-degree turn so that we could see a colony of penguins on a clean spit of sand below. We stayed high enough not to frighten them too much, then coasted back down towards San Carlos Water and a landing at Ajax Bay.

We then held another funeral, this time of the two Gazelle crewmen and their pair of passengers who had all been killed two days previously. Once again, Workshop Squadron did their highly honourable thing, and dug a beautiful grave for the officer, staff sergeant and two junior NCOs to lie in, united by death.

Later on in the evening the CO called his Squadron Commanders in and outlined Division's battle plan to us. The final attacks would commence on the nights of June 10/11 and 11/12. By then, 5 Infantry Brigade would be in their designated positions on the southern flank, ready to assault Mount Tumbledown and Mount William, and thus help to draw a steel noose even tighter around the defences of Stanley. Tonight, he told us, the remainder of the Welsh Guards were journeying around to Fitzroy in one of the LSLs, having being unable to make any rendezvous with the landing craft last night when they made the trip in HMS *Fearless*. The Scots Guards, he said, were already ashore having been carried in HMS *Intrepid*.

The troops of 3 Commando Brigade were mainly up on the northern flank. 3 Para were still under 3 Cdo Brigade's command, and were due soon onto the slopes of Mount Longdon; 42 Commando were harboured and patrolling aggressively near Mount Kent. They were lined up with Mount Harriet as their final objective. 45 Commando, after their epic 'yomp' that paralleled 3 Para's 'tab' across East Falkland, had been given Two Sisters as their destination.

Another new clinical problem started to manifest itself. Some of the marines and paratroopers were starting to suffer from the effects of their continued exposure to the cold and wet. At Ajax Bay, we were now seeing men with 'trench foot', an insidious

World War I-vintage problem that we were reasonably familiar with, at least in theory.

The proper description for this condition was 'non-freezing cold injury', but that was also a heartless accountant's way of describing the myriad changes brought on by night after night in the open, at sub-zero temperatures, with boots that never dried out properly, and socks that were never warm, even when stuffed into armpits and groins at night. Men who had got their feet seawater-wet to start with, on landing in the Islands, were suffering even more. The residual salt crystals in the leather of their boots had acted rather like hygroscopic magnets and attracted further moisture. Furthermore, their cheaply-manufactured DMS (Direct Moulded Sole) boots, so adaptable and smart in normal daily use back in UK barracks and training areas, were now falling apart under operational conditions that were considerably tougher.

We had already passed our comments up the command chain to General Moore's HQ staff. Later on, General Jeremy was to describe an infantryman's boots in this war with the memorable and excellent term 'leather personnel carriers'. It was a scandal that the standard-issue Army (and Royal Marines) boot had been designed to an inadequate specification, then built to a low price by different contractors, who cared not a whit as to how these items subsequently performed under arduous conditions.

Out in the commercial world, there were some excellent boots for walking and climbing which, while expensive, embodied the very best of new materials and design experience. Why was the military procurement system unable to get an unglamorous but absolutely critical item like infantry boots right, in this modern era of microprocessor technology and satellite communications?

With the plentiful supply of high-quality leather from their huge beef industry, each set of Argentine conscript's footwear was far superior than the supposedly 'professional' boots worn by their British opponents. It was all so stupid, and matters did not really improve in the aftermath of the Conflict either, as the British Army clothing procurement system tried to remedy matters.

A small number of men were broken by the pain in their feet and were then casevaced to Ajax Bay. We attempted to give them the dryness and warmth that their damaged limbs needed. Our standard tactics were not always successful, and every morning John Williams had the heartbreaking task of selecting those in Evac who had not improved, and had now got to be passed on to the *Uganda*. Some of the young marines and paras were almost in tears, because they knew that *Uganda* was Red Cross territory and that as a result of this rearward progress, they would be considered as out of the final battles, unable to return.

Later on, one of the doctors in the hospital ship (another chap who had better remain nameless) was to suggest to me that trench foot was just the latest way for marines and paras to get out of the war! He might have said this because of the speed with which their signs and symptoms improved under the ideal conditions aboard *Uganda*, but my reaction to this slur on the integrity of the Parachute Regiment and Royal Marine Commandos, as well as the slight on John Williams' clinical judgement, was rather vehement. This individual's later apology was much more graceful when he had been given an opportunity to understand the background to the story.

If only we had been able to have *Canberra* back in as a 'rest and recreation' facility in San Carlos, we could have prolonged this campaign almost indefinitely. The men with serious symptoms would have been treatable, and those who were about to become serious could have had this deterioration forestalled. Judging from the condition of some of the troops evacuated from the forward areas with trench foot, and on hearing their stories, it was obvious to us that there were many others in the hills with exactly the same problem.

Up front, men were suffering silently in the certain knowledge that other members of the section or platoon were similarly afflicted. In their mutual discomfort, they were all equally reticent about declaring their problem. If it was true last week to wonder whether we would run out of ships before the Argies ran out of aircraft, then this week's theme had to be the possibility that we would run out of capable feet up forward, before the order was given to cross the final start line. I made my feelings known to Ivar Hellberg, a hugely experienced climber and expedition leader who knew all about frostbite from his time in the Alps and Himalayas; he then came to visit the men in our Evacuation Section, and went away looking very thoughtful. The sooner we got going on the final assault against Stanley, the better it would be for all of us.

Tuesday, June 8th

30 minutes after first light, the daily Wessex launched from Ajax Bay with a load of post-treatment injured. Our HQ LFFI (Land Forces Falkland Islands), or Divisional HQ as it was sometimes called, had told us, quite categorically, that *Uganda* would be in close this morning to make up for her absence yesterday. Foolishly, I believed them – without checking first.

With its fuel almost exhausted from inspecting Grantham and Falkland Sounds, our Wessex returned and landed outside the door for the second time. The wounded tried to hide their disappointment and pain from me, but I was really upset. Div HQ replied to my ill-concealed fury with a '*Wait – Out*' on the radio.

An hour later, there was still no explanation, but a different voice came on the net as the watch-keeping officers changed over. Perhaps they had been too busy to discuss my 'minor' problem of *Uganda's* whereabouts? Once again, the word from on high was '*Wait – Out*'. I was feeling very frustrated and irritated by their apparent indifference.

The time had now come to investigate HMS *Intrepid's* potential as a large-scale forward hospital for the final battles, possibly by using the flight deck, ramp and tank decks for medical purposes, instead of just the wardroom and adjacent compartments up forward as had been previously proposed. This time, the order for a recce and report came down from Brigade, so Bill McGregor, Erich Bootland, Ian Geraghty and I took a ride out to the LPD, where we were met by a very frosty RM Major, the Amphibious Operations Officer. He must have thought this was all a fantastic plot to undermine him, because apparently this was the first time that he had even heard of a 'floating hospital' concept for his ship!

I was very surprised by this news and said so to Captain Peter Dingemans, the model of courtesy and hospitality up in his cabin. Was this another of the wretched NE's intrigues to get himself established on the operational map? I had no real way of finding out. Besides, there were a lot of far more important things to worry about.

After our brief inspection of *Intrepid*, we returned to report to the Captain, and found that our analysis very much concurred with his. His ship could certainly be made into an emergency medico-surgical facility and parked in Barclay Sound, to the north of Port Stanley, but she would be a very poor choice. No seafarer likes to remain static and anchored while at war. Equally worrying were the large quantities of field engineer stores tucked away down below. These would obviously be needed for the rebuilding of Stanley. So, why should anyone think of ditching them, in order to make room for emergency hospital facilities that might not be required for anything other than the short term?

After a quick lunch we then went over to the *Atlantic Causeway* by landing craft. The big container-ship, sister of the ill-fated *Atlantic Conveyor*, was a far better bet. The vesseel had three large but empty vehicle decks, a lift, and a helicopter platform. There was only one key unknown in the profile of her potential – just how close could she get into Stanley Harbour?

The rest of the party flew back to Ajax Bay, thanks to a friendly passing Wessex crew, while I journeyed to HMS *Fearless* by dory, in order to find some answers to my questions. The responsible staff officer, one of Gerry Wells-Cole's team there, was most apologetic. Apparently, the new concept of using HMS *Intrepid* as a 'forward floating hospital' had just gone out of fashion, although it had not been dismissed entirely. He asked me instead to look at Goose Green as a more suitable location for this 'forward' facility, because here we would be just a little closer to the front lines around Stanley. There was no serious objection to this plan, apart from the overcrowding already extant at Goose Green. Bombs, or no bombs, I argued that Ajax Bay still looked like good value, operating as a back-up in support of the Teal Inlet and Fitzroy forward surgical facilities.

Further discussion was interrupted by an 'Air Raid Red' warning. I finished my coffee at carpet level, and was then distressed to hear the bridge's Tannoy information about HMS *Plymouth* having been hit by enemy aircraft out in Falkland Sound. For the next ten or fifteen minutes the Executive Officer's voice kept his ships' company silent at their duties with a description of the battered Rothesay Class frigate limping into the San Carlos anchorage under a cloud of smoke and steam, listing to starboard but apparently refusing help because they could cope on their own. Then the tone changed. *Plymouth* had reported that they were short of fire fighters and breathing apparatus, so Captain Larken began to muster his available resources and prepared to get them across.

Back aft in Flyco, I chatted to Lt Cdr Ed Featherstone, *Fearless's* Aviation Officer. My suggestion that the frigate's request for fire fighters would probably mean they also had casualties, in need of evacuation, was accepted gratefully by the Command team on the bridge. Within minutes I was on my way to the stricken frigate, in a commandeered Wessex that had been passing by.

Shades of *Ardent*! It was just like May 21st and D-Day all over again, only this time there were no fires apparent, only smoke pouring from the mortar well, flight deck hangar and funnel. Fire-fighting hoses snaked across the flight deck as HMS *Avenger* pulled up along her starboard side, to play cooling streams of sea water onto the hottest danger areas. Our only access point was up on the foredeck, in front of the gun turret, so I was winched down here.

On the slippery deck surface, the main rotor downwash threatened to push me over the side. I had time, as I struggled to regain balance, to notice a pile of empty shell cases beneath the twin 4.5 inch mountings. HMS *Plymouth* had been in a stiff fight. The bridge staff looked pale and dazed beneath their anti-flash hoods as they wrestled with their various damage control problems. It took me a minute to manoeuvre the stretcher up through the starboard wing, then down and aft into the main passageway below. There was just time for a cheerful salute, in transit, to Captain David Pentreath, then the acrid smoke engulfed my face. I was soon choking, with fiercely watering eyes, and only managed to continue by tying a towel scarf around my face.

In the main passageway, or 'Burma Road', the fire fighters were briefing carefully in their fire-resistant 'Fearnought' suits, all wearing compressed-air breathing apparatus. There was a clear layer of air next to the actual deck, along which a man could crawl in comfort. The fire fighters were quite cool and collected – the whole thing could almost have been just another Portland damage control exercise generated by Flag Officer Sea Training. That was probably the best way to play it, too.

In the wardroom, the ship's medical staff were very busy. The young MO was Surgeon Lieutenant Alasdair Walker, and he was here as well. They were tending to one man with severe smoke inhalation, another with a fractured arm, and a third with a broken lower leg. Lying against a bulkhead was the most severely injured member of the ship's company, a stoker named

Warner, with a depressed fracture to his skull. Sticking out of the top of his head was a piece of metal support bracket, embedded in the bone. This chap needed Bill McGregor, and soon.

Very carefully, I led MEM Warner up on to the main deck level, having passed the empty stretcher up to the deck via another companionway. One of the First Aid Party then helped me to strap our patient in, and we carried him aft to the listing Flight Deck. The tilt to starboard appeared much greater now — perhaps they were having trouble with their counter-flooding. It was no problem for the Sea King that arrived. The big helicopter came and hovered right in over the deck, until we could practically hand the stretcher up to the waiting crewman.

Five minutes later we were round the corner, and once again walking into the 'Red and Green Life Machine'. So concerned was I about HMS *Plymouth* — and my chance involvement with her problems — that it took me a little while to realise that nobody really wanted to know about what was happening just outside our door in San Carlos Water.

Instead, some terrible event had occurred down on the southern flank, with rumours of fifty or sixty men from 45 Commando killed! I remembered thinking that this made no sense, because 'Four Five' were 'yomping' towards their final objective via a northern route.

Gradually the true picture emerged. It turned out that the LSL *Sir Galahad* had been bombed by a gaggle of A-4 Skyhawks while anchored near Fitzroy; her sister ship, the LSL *Sir Tristram* had been attacked too. There were apparently large numbers of casualties, including some from our own sister organisation, 16 Field Ambulance of the Royal Army Medical Corps.

A Gazelle aircrewman then rushed into the Command Post with a scribbled note to me from the CO of 16 Field Ambulance. John Roberts' message was terse and direct:

RICK, GALAHAD HIT BEFORE SURGICAL TEAMS UNLOADED. MANY (NOT YET COUNTED) BURNS

CASUALTIES NEED FLUIDS / MORPHIA PLUS PLUS.
THANKS JOHN

We responded to this *cri-de-coeur* as best we could. John Williams grabbed some kit and flew off immediately in the waiting Gazelle. Mike von Bertele followed soon after in a Scout, with a couple of intravenous fluid resupply boxes. Very gradually, the scene around us degenerated into a complete and utter nightmare.

As darkness crept in over the horizon, load after load of helicopter casualties began to arrive at Ajax Bay. Each new patient seemed worse than the last; eventually the Triage and Resuscitation areas were completely choked. Helicopters continued to clatter in, and stretcher-borne casualties kept appearing in the main door. No one knew for certain how many more were coming, only that we had received about a hundred and twenty victims of the bombing, mostly with burns. The phrase '*Mass Casualty Situation*' flicked into the forefront of my memory.

By NATO definitions, this was said to have occurred when an overwhelming number of incapacitated or injured people arrived in a limited medical facility which, as a result, could not cope. Hell, we could certainly deal with *some* of them, but we were duty-bound to try and bring the greatest benefit to the biggest number. After a quick discussion with Erich Bootland, on the ball as ever, I raced down to Log HQ and got on the radio to Division HQ. I asked them, urgently, to prepare a list of ships that could take about a hundred of the lightly burned or injured. The total number we had received (150 and rising) rather staggered the duty officer, but by the time he had recovered enough to query it, I was back up in the hospital. Our ever-reliable Regimental Adjutant, Paddy George, then took over those negotiations.

Mercifully, at around 160, the numbers began to slow. With around ten wounded from HMS *Plymouth*, that meant we now had around 170 injured, standing or lying around in the building. The medical teams got to work on the more severely afflicted as Paddy's runner came up from the beach with a new message.

HMS *Fearless*, HMS *Intrepid* and MV *Atlantic Causeway* were standing by, each ship willing, and getting ready to receive around three dozen injured each when we could get them over.

Down at the Beach Unit, Colour Sergeant McDowell then produced the necessary landing craft from somewhere, and suddenly, we really were coping reasonably well. It was the old human nature bit of helping out your mates. People turned up from the most unexpected quarters and offered their services. The RN Clearance divers came to help, as did some boys from 40 Commando who had come over earlier from Port San Carlos for some rest and relaxation in relative warmth, under a tin roof.

The main question now was how we were going to decide which of our patients would stay, and who would be passed on. In the demanding circumstances of a Mass Casualty Situation, the normal principles of priority for medical treatment get completely inverted. With normal casualty loadings, you tackle the most severely injured first, while the least injured have to wait. That instinctive reaction had to be suppressed now.

Instead, we had to do the best we could for the largest number, and recognise that some of our potential customers might be too badly injured for us to treat – because they would take up too much in the way of time and resources, and thereby reduce the chances of many others. At the opposite end of this spectrum was another sub-group which might be classified as too lightly injured to deserve any effort from us, and for the very same reason. So, exactly who was going to determine the entrance fee to Ajax Bay? There was only one answer, of course. It had to be me.

The responsibility was huge, and I knew that I had to get it right first time. Luckily, my instincts proved correct. About half of the waiting Welsh Guardsmen had flash burns to face and hands only – about 10% of the total body surface. I decided that these men would constitute the 'too lightly injured' category, but at the same time felt very guilty about the dismissive aspects of this judgement. We also had to tell them, as individuals, why we could not take them in, and where we proposed sending them to.

I expected some ranting and raving, perhaps even accusations of betrayal or flint-heartedness, and prepared myself mentally to apologise for my personal decision which, even as I made it, felt absolutely right.

However, the young Welsh Guardsmen were stoical and cheery as we broke the news of another move to them. Fred Cook and I moved amongst them, each holding a lit cigarette cupped and shielded in one hand so that they could have a smoke without getting a stinging pain in their cheeks from the glowing red tip. Standing near the doorway, blowing on their tattered and painful hands to keep them cool, many of them were totally pathetic sights. Strips of skin hung from their fingers like thin, wet muslin, and their faces were blistered and raw, the hair singed short. But by God, they were *brave*.

The bad news of another half hour in a landing craft before they could be treated was simply accepted without demur. Each man seemed to know of someone else in the building more seriously injured than himself, and all of them would rather have had him treated first. The sing-song accents of the Welsh valleys repeated the same sentiment to us, again and again: 'Don't worry about me, sir. What about Evans 36/ Williams 49/ Jones 27? 'Ave you seen him? He's the one that needs you, not me...'

It was simply heartbreaking to turn nearly ninety young men away from what was the Accident & Emergency Department door that they had paid so much to reach, but there was no other way. I shall never forget the magnificent moral courage of these splendid young men, whose instinctive response did so much to ease my own moral burden in dealing with the collective problem. We only knew how many there were because each man had a field treatment card attached to his clothing, and these had been pre-numbered. There was no time to record any other details, and we never knew or learned their names.

I watched them as they marched away into the night, still blowing on their hands as they went, still maintaining good order and discipline, and with not a single word or gesture of dissent. With the serious overcrowding problem solved now, it was time for an all-out effort directed at the other burned and wounded.

A simple treatment plan was developed for each individual; this was assessed and written down by a medical officer, and then carried out by either a medical assistant, or more frequently, one of the marines. Bernie's divers had turned to as well, to lend their capable and willing hands. For each patient there was one attendant, sometimes two. It was a heartening sight as order was imposed on chaos, and calm returned to a rather frenzied scene.

The fused and charred clothing was cut away, and the total percentage of burned skin area assessed and recorded on the treatment card. When necessary, an intravenous infusion was set up, with the flow rates and volumes calculated individually depending on the burns percentage. Careful titration of intravenous morphine was then embarked on, to control the pain. Then, carefully and lovingly, Flamazine was spread thickly over the affected areas. The cool white cream contained a silver and sulpha drug mixture which was pain-killing, antiseptic and promoted healing. Hands and fingers were enclosed in sterile plastic bags to avoid the risks of bandaging.

If a scar formed under a hand dressing it would probably have remained undetected until too late, and a claw-like contracture might well have been the severe and unwelcome penalty. In the worst cases, Phil Shouler and the other surgeons now performed escharotomies, deliberately slitting the sides of each bloated finger to allow tissue fluid to leak out, and thus prevent strangulation of the digital circulation. He showed me how to do the procedure, as there were dozens to be done. This technique was surprisingly painless, even for the patients! It was a night of 'see one, do one under supervision, plus a few more without a mentor – and then start teaching others to do the same'...

The concrete floor of Ajax Bay was soon ankle deep in rubbish, littered with torn paper dressing packets and cellophane wrappings. We ran out of Flamazine on the last patient, a Guardsman with flash-burned forearms. Bryn Dobbs then remembered that he had a tube of the stuff secreted in his First Aid kit, so he retrieved it. There was now less than an ounce left for any further casualties, so we could only hope that we had finished for the night. Bill McGregor had earlier completed an unpleasant surgical case, revising the traumatic amputation of a lower leg that had been, surprisingly, the most serious item in our workload – that was, apart from Guardsman Simon Weston.

This young man had a terrifying appearance, with his face and scalp reddened, blistered and swollen, and some of his hair charred. The whole thing must have been a complete horror show for him. Ironically, some of the least burned areas of his upper body were the most painful, because the flash burning caused by the bomb detonations had lifted the superficial layers of the dermis (skin) and exposed the nerve endings beneath. His pain was severe, and although we did our best with intravenous morphine, the poor chap was still suffering terribly.

It was Malcolm Jowitt who solved the problem for him, using intramuscular Ketamine, a steroid-based anaesthetic that he had particular experience with. Prior to relaxing into a pain-free and trance-like state, Simon had actually been begging me to put an end to his overwhelming pain and misery.

Afterwards, he became a media star thanks to his autobiography and a couple of television films about his recovery, and he put this to good use by creating *The Weston Spirit*, a benevolent trust that works to help youngsters who have to face the consequences of crippling accidents or deforming injury when they are young. Simon is a shining example of how extraordinary such 'ordinary' people can be.

Within us all there are deep and powerful resources that don't usually get tapped into, because we lead comparatively safe and predictable lives. Hooray for him, although in Simon's subsequent 'autobiography', the ghost writer did not get the description of his time in Ajax Bay quite right. There was a description of Simon joking and laughing as we looked after him that night, but the reality was in fact *very* different...

When I reported our situation to Divisional HQ, I found that they were being a bit obtuse again. They were unable to grasp the sheer magnitude of our problem, and even tried to query our need for *Uganda* to get in close the next morning! A one-syllable word picture to the poor duty officer brought him up to date at the rush, and suddenly all was understood. Someone had told him that *Uganda* had been just over the hill from us, in Middle Bay, throughout the day, but without any business! An hour later he was back on net with welcome news from London. *Uganda* would indeed be close in, at first light, although there was an embargo on telling them exactly why.

I thanked him gratefully and told him to forget our differences, although at the back of my mind was an even more important, but unanswered question. Why had neither of the two senior medical officers – either Barrie Blackstone or the chap we had labelled as 'NE' not come ashore to see for themselves what was happening? I never got an answer to that particular query...

One of the RM officers in charge of prisoners of war then started to behave like an idiot, and needed some '*Rembrandting*', or 'picturising' in the superb vernacular of the Corps. Apparently ignorant of events on our side of the building, he had demanded to know why our galley was not serving hot meals to his staff at the usual time! He was shown the galley chefs all helping us to spread Flamazine on burned faces rather than margarine on dry biscuits, but continued to grumble. I came very close to losing my temper completely, but one of the HQ team, sensing the impending explosion, whispered a splendid alternative suggestion in my ear. As a result, the selfish idiot was invited as an individual, from now on, to use the main

Regimental galley some 200 muddy metres away, rather than our facilities.

John Williams was very worried about a lad from HMS *Plymouth* with smoke inhalation damage to his lungs. Steroids and bottled oxygen via a mask seemed to be holding the problem at bay, but even in the dim light of our 60 watt light bulbs, it was easy to see the cyanotic, bluish tinge of the young sailor's lips. Captain Terry McCabe and WO2 Brian Apperley led the nursing effort. Once again, there was a constant round of soothing, checking, adjusting, recording and checking again.

The marines had been simply magnificent throughout the night. One little group containing Jan Mills and Jock Inglis were secretly very pleased to have survived the test and done so well. As I poured out another 'Arduous Duty' tot, whisky for the Army, rum for Jack and Royal, their delight was expressed in a slightly oblique fashion, tinged as usual with Corps humour.

One of the boys – it was John Thurlow I think – took a long pull from his somewhat strengthened mug of hot chocolate, and looked at me with an innocent expression on his face: 'Cheers, Boss! Bloody good wet that – and now we've done the practical, any chance of getting the theory some time?'

How could we lose, with men like that on our side?

Wednesday, June 9th

An hour before dawn I got up and stepped outside the main door of Ajax Bay. The boys were tucking into breakfast, whispering quietly to each other over their baked beans and tinned sausages. At first light, the galley hydro burners would be doused, and all the surrounding stand-to positions manned and made ready. Yesterday's effort by the *Fuerza Aerea Argentina* might not have been just a final fling, but a prelude to much worse. Either way, the clear pre-dawn sky promised more fast jet activity, or perhaps a parachute assault from the mainland. The Argentines certainly had the capability, even though some authorities on our side doubted if they still had the willpower.

The old joke about the three lies that every sailor will hear at some time in a career had been given a new twist. '*The Portland Sea Training Teams are here to help you…*' and '*This appointment will be a boost to your career…*' had now been supplemented with: '*WE will have achieved air superiority by the time YOU get there…*' Whilst none of us had actually seen a Sea Harrier, their mounting tally made good reading at the 'Clear Lower Deck' held each evening. We had been forced to put our trust in them rather than Red Crosses on the roof; the two 400 kg unexploded bombs in the back of Ajax Bay were a constant reminder of our luck.

Now there were over seventy burned and helpless men to move out from our overcrowded refrigeration plant, and eighty-five more in three of the ships lying out in San Carlos Water. Most of our patients appeared to have had a comfortable night, although some of the Chinese crew were beginning to suffer badly. Their faces seemed to have swollen more with the flash-burning than their European counterparts. Perhaps they were closer to the bombs or had received the detonation in a different way. Two of the worst affected had blackened, Buddha-like visages.

My problems were now getting serious, and I suspected that I was going to have to find some ingenious solution of my own manufacture. But how? HMHS *Uganda* had no casevac assets of her own, and without a military radio set in her communications fit, her staff probably didn't even know about yesterday's events – either at Fitzroy Cove, or out in Falkland Sound where HMS *Plymouth* had been attacked by that gaggle of five Daggers. I also knew that with the final push on Stanley imminent, every airframe that could engage its rotors was now being tasked for re-stocking the front line with combat supplies and artillery ammunition. Some ignoramus – 'Not Entitled', I think – had already sent me a signal requesting 24 hours' notice of my helicopter casevac requirements!

So, how would HQ LFFI now react to my urgent bid concerning one hundred and sixty-plus mostly stretcher-borne casualties for immediate evacuation? It was probably going to be yet another invitation for Rick Jolly to investigate 'sex and travel' – adding a further dent to his already parlous career prospects! I thought about using landing craft too, but as one of *Fearless'* LCMs had recently been sunk in an air attack, those assets were now limited – and only offered a long, bumpy and clinically dangerous ride.

It was a worrying time, the pressure on me increased by looking at the ghostly, Flamazine-covered faces of the young Welsh Guardsmen. Hair and eyebrows had been singed short or replaced by reddened skin and oozing crust. Their fingers looked like those pale tinned sausages of our breakfast compo, swollen and damaged beneath the plastic bags which kept the dirt out, but allowed some form of movement. As our eyes met, some of the cracked and blistered lips parted in a vain attempt to smile. They were all so young – and brave. Somehow I simply had to get them out, before the next Air Raid Warning Red, away to the cool comfort, the clean sea air, and the devoted nursing of our hospital ship.

My secure call to HQ LFFI got the expected response. No helicopters were available for medical tasking today, but they would
do their best to find something for me tomorrow. I shook my head
in disbelief, torn between my understanding of the need to get
this war finished quickly – and the more immediate needs of
these tough and courageous young Welsh Guardsmen who were
my charges.

I began to wonder whether the *Galahad* incident was such
bad news that nobody wanted to know about any subsequent
problems related to it. I could understand that Lt Col Johnny
Ricketts, the CO of the Welsh Guards, was right up against it as he
tried to re-organise his shattered battalion, but it would have been
nice to have had a visit from one of his subordinates. 5 Brigade's
Commander, a chap called Wilson, was also notable by his
absence, and HQLFFI's Assistant Director of Medical Services,
Surgeon Captain Blackstone, was not exactly knocking on the
door at any stage. We'd never seen 'NE' ashore of course, so at Ajax
Bay we seemed to be all on our own in caring for the wounded!

About thirty minutes later, one of the good guys from Divisional HQ did in fact turn up to have a look around. Alan Piggford
was a Medical Services officer, and a much liked former colleague. He was actually working for Barrie Blackstone, and
unlike his boss, had a green beret. He was also trying to help us,
although there was still a note of slight disbelief in his early
questioning about the number of injured that we claimed to be
caring for. That attitude evaporated instantly when I showed him
the serried ranks of burned and semi-naked casualties inside the
main building, all looking at him with the quiet optimism and
expectation that here, at last, was the person who would arrange
their 'escape' to the safety of the hospital ship.

Alan looked rather shaken when we re-emerged into the
light. He promised that he would go straight back to his ship,
convey to certain key staff officers the sense of urgent priority
that our situation now warranted – and then call in a number of

favours that he was owed. He was going to get us some helicopters, by hook or by crook. I thanked my old friend, saw him down to the beach, and then returned inside.

A familiar sound now penetrated the gloom. Our faithful, but sometimes occasional casevac Wessex had actually turned up! I let the crew shut their aircraft down, then invited them to help themselves to tea while I briefed them on the day's flying plan. After that I took them both into the main treatment area to see the size and nature of our problem. The pilot was a young Sub-Lieutenant who had absolutely no idea that we had taken all the wounded from the *Galahad* incident. He had spent the previous day up in the northern part of East Falkland, flying stores ashore. Now he just stood there, looking rather shocked.

He then did something totally unexpected. Putting his tea down on a nearby table, he reached into the side pocket of his flying suit, and pulled out his flying gloves. I asked him why, and was told, quite matter-of-factly, that as there was a lot of work to do, it would be a good idea to get started as soon as possible! I wanted to hug the lad, but told him to drink his tea instead. I was his tasking authority for the day, and his mission was not going to be quite as simple as he thought.

We went outside again, and I explained that none of us had any idea whether the hospital ship was actually in Falkland Sound that morning. Furthermore, it was almost certain that none of her staff would know about the disaster that had befallen *Sir Galahad*. So, he was to get airborne now and go and find the hospital ship, and no, they couldn't have any casualties until I was sure that 'Mother Hen' was actually there!

Also, I asked my pilot and his crewman to tell any Naval helicopter on the radio net that, if they had any spare capacity, time or fuel, I was looking for volunteers to help with the casualty evacuation task...

We watched as the aircraft climbed up the dark mass of the Sussex Mountains behind us, then flew along the ridge line to the south. Curses! They could obviously see over into Falkland Sound, and the hospital ship wasn't there! Suddenly, the Wessex banked over sharply, circled round, came straight back down the hill to us, and then executed a glorious fan stop, using the main rotors to come to a spectacular halt before settling onto the ground. Thumbs up! The crewman showed me the hospital ship's location on the map. She was in Grantham Sound, near the southern end of Falkland Sound, and the scene of HMS *Ardent*'s gallant last fight.

I scribbled a quick note to the Medical Officer-In-Charge, Surgeon Captain Andrew Rintoul. I warned him to expect up to 170 casualties throughout the day, a total that would ultimately depend on how many helicopters we could manage to recruit for the evacuation task. As I did this, the first patient was carried out from the freezer plant. It was Simon Weston on a stretcher, with John Williams as his escorting medical officer, plus two walking wounded, both wrapped in blankets. John took the note from me. Three down, 165 to go – and when would the Argentine Sky-hawks return?

The Wessex departed once more, disappeared over the skyline, and then returned. We reloaded it, and then I suddenly heard another familiar but completely different sound – the buzz-saw noise of a Sea King's tail rotor.

To my complete astonishment, I then saw a Culdrose anti-submarine Sea King appear from behind the building, and then hover, looking for somewhere to land. Even though its fuselage side number had been hurriedly painted over, I could still see its white '95' serial beneath the dark blue paint. It was one of the training aircraft that I had flown in on Search and Rescue missions during my tour of duty at the Cornish Fleet Air Arm base in the late seventies. I had absolutely no idea that these helicopters had also been mobilised and deployed down South.

Its pilot saw me, brought the aircraft over towards the main door, landed, and was now grinning down at me from the cockpit side window. I plugged my helmet in, and heard these never-to-be-forgotten words: 'Hello sir, nice to see you again. I hear you've got a problem. If you can load us quickly, I think we can take one load of casualties to the *Uganda* for you, before we have to go for fuel and carry on with our other tasks...'

Of course we could load him quickly, and we did. The boys turned to with all the enthusiasm and vigour that the Royal Marines are famous for. Then there was another Sea King behind that one, then another, and another. Anti-submarine versions, Mk. 4 Commando variants – the whole morning passed in a blur, interrupted by several air raid warnings which the helicopters simply ignored. Each time, I received the same sort of message, the same willing and affectionate support, some from distantly remembered faces and others from aircrew I had never met before.

By midday, the job was done. We diverted the next lot of our volunteer aerial helpers to the three ships that had taken our overspill casualties. Ajax Bay was suddenly empty of suffering, the stretchers all cleaned and stacked, the ready-use stores replenished, the drips run-through and hung up, the whole organisation ready for the next intake of casualties. Our young Wessex pilot and his crewman came back too, and stayed for lunch. They both deserved their precious egg each, awarded only to our very best friends. It was a fine effort by everyone concerned, not least being HMHS *Uganda* herself. According to John Williams they were all a bit shaken by the suddenness of the news, and silent at some of the sights as the burned guardsmen were brought to them, but they had responded well and were determined to do their best.

Thank God they were there for us...

Alan Piggford also returned, disappointment etched deeply in his bearded face. He had done his very best, and had visited all the key staff officers and told them of our desperate plight. Each time, their answers had been the same – no helos available today, but maybe tomorrow? I told my old chum not to worry, and asked him to come inside for a wet of tea. Alan cringed at the idea – he didn't want to see those burned faces again, and declined. I practically gave him a direct order to accompany me, which he eventually did, although somewhat reluctantly.

Lieutenant Commander Alan Piggford's anguished expression was now replaced by one of total astonishment. The medical assistants and marines, who also knew him reasonably well, acknowledged him in their cheerful way as they sat around drinking tea and playing cards. It was a scenario that he did not expect, and he simply could not believe that, apparently without any 'official' helicopters being made available, we had somehow moved all the casualties out by air. Furthermore, we had achieved this feat without a single formal casevac request being routed through his Headquarters!

I liked Alan a lot, and as Royal Navy men with green berets we had a shared and deep affection for the Corps. But, he had forgotten that I also had a Fleet Air Arm background. Now, as I showed him around, I tried not to display my feelings too obviously, but as OC of the Ajax Bay medical facility I was a very proud and well-contented man. In the hour of our greatest need, my Fleet Air Arm family had not let me down.

One of the returning helicopters then brought the Red Cross inspection team ashore. They were from the headquarters of their International Commission in Geneva, and were supposed to be concerned with prisoners' welfare and conditions. Although well-versed on points of International Law, the civilian team of three men and one woman annoyed us by speaking amongst themselves in Swiss-German when it suited them. What they didn't know was that one of our officers could speak this language as well; he now slipped off his rank epaulettes and pretended to be an ordinary foot soldier as he helped to show the group around. At one point on the guided tour he also whispered to me that I should watch them very carefully. They were reminding each other to get the tall

British doctor's name for their records, because any complaint would be made against him (me!) personally!

I changed my opinion about these rather arrogant Swiss chappies on the spot. They were nice enough when they spoke English, but seemed to have a rather strange grip on the realities of life in the Falklands. Their leader, and for some reason the name Antoine Bouvier sticks in my mind, enquired politely where they could now hire a car to drive on to Stanley, and then seemed rather non-plussed when he was shown the trackway outside as being the only road for many miles! I also told him that the nearest Hertz or Avis auto rental facility was probably in mainland Argentina.

Then it turned out that our dusty accommodation was not much to their liking either. I'd offered them the hospitality of a set of stretcher racks in our admission area, but they declined, asking instead if I knew of any hotels locally that took American Express...

At that point, they decided to fly back to *Uganda* and then visit the Argentine hospital ship, the *Bahia Paraiso*. So, off they went in their three-piece suits, tailored wellies and big white ski anoraks decorated with the Red Cross, but not before the Argentine prisoners had managed to have a go at them. A couple of *Ejercito* (Army) Huey helicopter pilots had complained that they had to sleep in the same building as an unexploded bomb! I informed our Swiss colleagues that this complaint was technically incorrect, as there were actually two such devices in the building, and we Brits were not very happy with the Argentine Air Force for putting them there in the first place.

The whole episode had been a little surreal, and we never saw or heard from the International Commission for the Red Cross again – until the Gulf War some nine years later, when they got very upset that the British deployed a part-medical ship called *Argus* into the combat zone which did great work, but was not marked or declared according to the Geneva Convention, because no 'Red Cross' protection was required.

Some 16 Field Ambulance RAMC officers and men then arrived, to be accommodated with us. I took an instant shine to Major Jim Ryan, a quick-thinking and cheerful Irishman who wore parachute wings, and who was full of energy and enthusiasm. He had lost practically all of his kit in the *Galahad*, including his precious pipe. I'm still not quite sure how, but a replacement was found. Jim would stay with us in Ajax Bay as a surgeon, along with Lt Col Jim Anderson, the bluff and hearty Scot who was his anaesthetist, and who had wrenched his shoulder badly during the disaster. He and Bill McGregor now greeted each other like the old friends that they were.

The others would eventually be moving forward to Fitzroy again, to re-establish the Forward Dressing Station there. The majority of them were still badly shaken by the unpleasant events on *Sir Galahad* and we could well understand their reactions. One medic (another individual who had better remain nameless) got very aggressive. He stated bluntly that he did not accept my authority to give him orders, that he was a survivor of an abandoned ship, and that just like all the 'Navy guys' who were going home, he felt that he had a right to be repatriated to England too.

It was no use pointing out to him that as a specialist, and an undamaged one at that, he was still needed up near the front line, whereas the sailors and stokers were surplus to requirements — with their gallant ship still on fire.

For this individual, whom I judged to be salvageable, I now made a real effort. I drafted a one-paragraph order for Barrie Blackstone to authorise in Major General Jeremy Moore's name, and then got him to sign it. When I returned to Ajax Bay, I found that my reluctant colleague had now actually thought matters through — and changed his mind. Some of the other 16 Field Ambulance survivors also implied their reluctance to continue soldiering, but did so in a less aggressive way. They all benefited from a quiet talking to, plus a little walk around to the back of

Ajax Bay. The bomb in the refrigeration machinery, although now surrounded by white tape barriers, was still easily visible.

We explained that we knew exactly how they were feeling, because we had been along and down the same emotional route ourselves. Thankfully, a measure of optimism was restored, and we told our new but temporary visitors that once we had found some spare kit and supplies for them from our own resources, they were going to have an opportunity to end this war on a high note, with their pride intact, and a sense of duty fulfilled.

They did just that, and hooray for them too. It was amusing however to see the banner that some of them slung along the passenger rails of the *Uganda*, when the 'Mother Hen' finally returned to Portsmouth later on that year. Paraphrasing Julius Caesar's *'Veni, vidi, vici'* summary of his triumphs in Britain, the wording read *'16 Fd Amb RAMC – We came, we saw – and we treated'*. It was proud stuff, but I couldn't help wondering whether the word *'were'* should have been inserted before *'treated'*!

During a quiet spell later in the afternoon two Navy helicopters paused at Ajax Bay for a tea break in between their load lifting tasks, and I spoke to the pilots and crewmen. They'd all been involved in moving the casualties of the *Sir Galahad* incident to the *Uganda* on the following morning, and I thanked them profusely for helping us out of a tight spot, promising a friendly annual medical next time we met back at Culdrose!

The lads all looked a bit embarrassed, and started mumbling. I asked them why – because surely it had been their instinctive desire to help when they heard that we were in trouble? One of the pilots decided to come clean: 'Well not *exactly*, sir – the real reason that we were so keen to take the casualties was a buzz that went round between us all that if you arrived on the back of the hospital ship with a load of wounded, one of the chefs came out with bacon butties and cups of coffee while the aircraft was being unloaded!'

I was stunned to learn of this fantastic thoughtfulness. You could have had a diamond-encrusted, platinum credit card as evidence of your wealth, but the one thing you could not have bought for yourself down in this remote terrain was a bacon sandwich! Twenty-three years later I found that same junior assistant chef again; Roger Cheney had long since been promoted, and was Executive Chef of the P&O superliner *Aurora*. I was on board as a guest lecturer at the time. It was a real pleasure to tell him of the huge effect that his positive thinking and kindness had had, and for me to thank him, in person, for all that he'd done to help us...

Thursday, June 10th

Today was to be a very sad day in the history of 'The Red and Green Life Machine'. For all sorts of very good reasons, the original organisation that had worked so well for just twenty days was going to be broken up. With Charles Batty and his support group supporting the northern flank, up in Teal Inlet with Malcolm Hazell's Troop, we had now decided that Bill McGregor and his surgical team should move forward to support the southern aspect of the investment of Stanley, at Fitzroy. There they would join the re-grouped and re-organised 16 Field Ambulance. The loss of 16 Fd Amb's excellent 2ic, Major Roger Nutbeem, had severely affected that organisation's command and control arrangements. They also needed serious beefing up in the confidence stakes.

It wasn't just their key leader that had been lost. Most of their equipment had also been destroyed in the bombing of the *Sir Galahad*. By dint of careful stock-taking, and then division of our resources at Ajax Bay, we managed to provide them with a scale of replacement medical stores, including some surgical instruments that were landed from HMS *Hermes*. What thanks did we get in return? Not very much. One officer's gratitude was expressed with a personal raid on some of the Logistic Regiment's other storage facilities, where he was caught thieving and handed over to our Regimental HQ police. This toad was threatened with Field Court Martial, and reminded of the possibility of enhanced penalties for any offences that were committed in wartime, including summary execution...

For his part too, Bill McGregor was not a happy camper, and felt far more comfortable and useful in the positive atmosphere of Ajax Bay, but he was also a hard soldier. Bill could understand the point I made to him, that by being in Fitzroy, in conjunction with the totally inexperienced Major David Jackson's surgical team, he would provide the right blend of reinforcing skill and reassurance for them all, and be even closer to the new front line.

Major Jim Ryan was staying back with us at Ajax Bay, where we had also been joined by the members of another Naval surgical team, Surgeon Lieutenant Commander Tony Mugridge and Surgeon Lieutenant Sean Tighe, his anaesthetist. These operators had been somewhere up in the Persian Gulf when the Falklands caper started. They were diverted south in their RFA stores ship, and having fixed the wounded from the retaking of South Georgia, had now ended up in Ajax Bay. After nearly twenty moves between a dozen ships, they were rather pleased to be somewhere that they could call 'home' and, furthermore, to be in the company of old friends.

There was more interesting news from Ivar Hellberg. Earlier on, he had asked me if there was anything that I needed and which the Americans might be able to supply. I had reminded him of the running battle that we had been conducting since the summer of 1980 with the British Army supply system, in order to acquire some examples of the excellent American Army field kitchen water heater. Our requests had always been rejected for some reason or other, but all the refusals were basically of the 'not invented here in UK' variety. We had managed to acquire one of them in 1981, during an exercise in Germany, when the purchasing power of a crate of British beer suddenly became apparent.

I had shown him the American stock number engraved on the ID plate of our hard-working water heater, and wondered if we could have a few more of these. There was a delightful gleam in Ivar's eye. I'm not sure how he had made the contact, but suspected that his being 'Landlord' of the Brigade Maintenance Area had meant some form of rental payment in the shape of a few minutes' chat to London and America on the Satcom telephone system!

Ever since she had survived our bombing on May 26th, our '*African Queen*' had been pumping out a bit more black smoke than usual, and one of the welded joints in her fuel supply was looking dodgy. Ivar was now brandishing a signal in which we were being promised several replacements which would be delivered 'as soon as possible'. I was absolutely delighted by this news. All things come to those who sit and wait...

Having had a planning discussion with Brigadier Julian Thompson and his staff, I could now also go firm on our medical support plans for the final attack. Together we had also managed to forestall a crazy proposal to place *all* our forward surgical assets at Fitzroy. I never did find out exactly who or what was behind this item of especial lunacy – but had my suspicions. Anyone who had experienced the vagaries of Falklands weather as winter approached would have known better than to expect unrestricted helicopter flying operations in a place like Fitzroy. There simply had to be an alternative destination if the weather suddenly clamped, and that was Teal Inlet.

A Wessex helicopter crewman then gave me an envelope containing three or four bits of paper which had been written on in ballpoint pen. A brief inspection showed it to be a despatch from one of the correspondents up in the front line. Apparently, these were being auto-censored by the aircrew in that, if they thought the text was rubbish, the piece got torn up and ditched from the cabin door! I took this journalistic effort down to the Satcom terminal and asked them to deal with it. It seemed to be a reasonable 'dit', and devoid of the usual hysterical exaggeration.

The only correspondent who seemed to have a real grip on all this was Max Hastings. He was entitled to the Airborne camouflage smock and para wings that he wore, having served as a parachutist with the Territorial Army. He wrote beautifully, and apparently knew which one of the LSLs was equipped with a satellite terminal. As a result, his pieces tended to get back to England – while the other hacks fumed with irritation and jealousy as the Press 'minders' debated whether the punctuation in their creations was good enough to merit onward transmission!

Another brief on HMS *Fearless* with the Divisional Staff, including Surgeon Captain Blackstone, enabled me to integrate all these arrangements with those in hand for 5 Brigade. My counterpart in 16 Field Ambulance was still badly affected by the *Galahad* experience, and took no part in this planning process, but what we decided was both solid and sensible. All he had to do was turn up on the day – and just *be* there!

I also relayed these plans to Ivar Hellberg back in Ajax Bay. Although Ivar was always interested in what was happening medically within the Brigade, he left me very much to sort these specialised matters out within my own lines of authority. As we were still in the process of ferrying customers to the *Uganda*, I then hitch-hiked a ride out to the hospital ship, and kept her command structure in the picture about the forthcoming investment and final assault on Stanley.

There was a sad little ceremony to conduct just before we returned, less than twenty minutes later. Paul Callan, the young 45 Commando chef who was so grievously injured on the night of May 27th when we were bombed in Ajax Bay, had finally died of his wounds. Following up on the skilled efforts of Bill McGregor and Malcolm Jowitt, Roger Leicester had done his very, very best. Despite three operations and over 30 pints of blood, the young marine's exhausted and badly injured body had finally given up the ghost.

Slow marching with their usual fine precision, a detachment of *Uganda*'s Royal Marines bandsmen ascended the ramp. The body bag was loaded into the Wessex cabin, and the flight deck party snapped off a sad salute that showed on their faces. We then started the engines, engaged rotors, and lifted off to deliver Paul Callan back to Ajax Bay once more, for burial alongside his friends.

Friday, June 11th

Tonight was the night for the final assault, but today was also the day that 'The Red and Green Life Machine' went 'Green and Brown' instead. All the remaining red-bereted elements moved forward to Fitzroy that morning, and we were sorry to see them go. There was still much to do of course, and a war to finish off, but we all had the feeling that an important episode in our lives had drawn to a close.

If I was sad about that, there were plenty of other distractions as we tried to distribute equipment and personnel evenly between the various types of helicopters which turned up to help the move. There was also some mail, which included my April Mess bill from the Royal Marines Barracks in Plymouth! Another rather tatty brown paper parcel, addressed personally to me and also kindly mended by the Royal Mail, contained soap, toothbrushes, and toothpaste '*with love from the Wives Club of HMS Drake, Plymouth*'. How kind those good ladies were, and how stunning their generosity – but how on earth had they heard of us?

It had to be an early turn-in tonight, for all of us. H Hour was at 0200, so we were bound to be in business before first light.

Saturday, June 12th

45 Commando and 3 Para had gone in against their respective objectives, Two Sisters and Mount Longdon. Their attacks were on time and progressing well. As we had predicted and prepared for, first light brought Sea King and Wessex helos in profusion to our door. They were carrying the overspill of casualties from the Advanced Dressing Stations at Teal Inlet and Fitzroy, close up to the front lines. I had time to hope, out loud, that whoever had tried to close Teal Inlet was now consumed with embarrassment. This facility was full, with everyone working flat out. Fitzroy was also very busy.

At Ajax Bay, we were getting the overflow, mainly those wounded who had been assessed and selected as being fit for travel for about 30 minutes longer before they could receive surgical care. Freed of their human loads, the helicopters soared upwards from the boggy landing site, moved across to the concrete hardstanding behind the main building, and hooked up to yet more pallets of netted artillery ammunition. We could clearly hear their rotor blades changing in pitch as they bit the air fiercely, taking the strain as the aircraft struggled into the sky with their vital loads. This was logistics for real — broken bodies back for repair, and combat supplies forward to win the war — with scarcely a pause in between.

Our three operating tables were soon in full flow, with Phil Shouler now acting the part of Ajax Bay's surgical ringmaster. What a change there had been in him three weeks on! Like Nick Morgan, his confidence and judgement had come on in leaps and bounds. At this moment there could not be many other senior registrars in the western world with such practical experience of war surgery.

A Royal Marine friend arrived from Two Sisters, injured by fragments from an Argentine artillery or mortar round. Lieutenant Chris Whiteley was the son of Jersey's Governor and himself a former Commandant General of the Royal Marines. The shrapnel wounds of both thighs and one hand were nasty but not life-threatening at this stage, so it was nice for Major General Jeremy Moore to have someone familiar to talk to when he visited shortly afterwards.

My admiration and respect for JJ Moore was total. Despite his huge personal combat record (with a Military Cross and Bar) he was still a soldier's soldier, and high command had not altered this. He was a leader who suffered agonies to think that the casualties might somehow be his own fault, caused by some oversight in his planning and preparation. For that very reason, the major general did not exactly relish the prospect of going inside the medical facilities at Ajax Bay to say hello, but also knew that he had to. I was aware of his discomfort, and shepherded him straight to Chris's stretcher. When we got outside again, Jeremy looked at me, gripped my arm, and made his genuine gratitude palpable. Nearly twenty years later he had to have a liver transplant for cancer, and celebrated the operation's success by attempting to repeat the 30-mile 'yomp' of his 1951 Commando course on Dartmoor!

Later on I recognised another of the casualties as a fellow-traveller from *Canberra*. Corporal Jerry Phillips was a compact, muscular sniper from 3 Para. He had played the 'man-dressed-as-tree' act for journalists on the way down, and then went ashore to prove his skills in no uncertain terms. Now he had been exceptionally lucky to have taken a high-velocity bullet in his left arm instead of his heart. We debrided the wound carefully in anticipation of his eventual return to duty.

Our second Argentine to die in Ajax Bay then slipped out of reach. A nasty, sucking chest wound had been deftly sorted out but the patient suddenly collapsed as his blood pressure rose. Resuscitation was to no avail. The bullet probably damaged the main vessels of the lung, which then tore open as his systolic pressure came up again.

At around 2200 the line of customers in pre-op had dwindled to one, an Argentine officer with multiple shrapnel wounds. He got fixed up in the proper manner, and business closed for the day. There had been a total of 32 major operations carried out in Ajax Bay, and our 'Red and Green Life Machine' track record for British casualties was still intact.

Forward, at Teal Inlet, Charles Batty had not stopped either, in an all-day session of some 16 major surgical procedures. Fitzroy had been a bit quieter with eight, but their turn would come tomorrow, when the other units went for the southern objectives.

3 Para's losses had been especially heavy, because they had to endure an all-day Argentine artillery stonking of their newly-captured objective. It must have been awful to lose men in the frenzy and chaos of a night assault – and then have as many more die in the daylight – due to long-range 155 mm artillery fire that your own artillery batteries could not counter. Talk about help-lessness! We also heard that some of the Argentine guns were positioned among the houses and buildings of Stanley, which pre-cluded taking them out with the laser-guided munitions that the RAF Harriers flying from HMS *Hermes* were becoming much more skilled in delivering.

On Two Sisters, 45 Commando had lost four men, while 'Four-Two' had lost one NCO killed as they seized Mount Harriet. We heard on the grapevine that 42's attack had been an absolute military classic, with the leading company going right behind the enemy in its approach march before joining battle. The route had been marked by a resourceful RM patrol commander who had bumped into his Argentine counterparts one night, but then held his fire in the silence and darkness until the Argies got fed up and returned to their base. Little did they know that Sergeant 'Jumper' Collins was following, and marking out the trail just behind them.

So, careful patrolling to identify some of the minefields had certainly paid dividends in low casualties, but overall the losses were surprisingly small when considering normal offensive doctrine. Attacking units, according to the textbooks, should have a numerical superiority of three to one, not the other way around. And as for the business of assaulting well dug-in units uphill, on foot – that was a really big no-no indeed!

If we Brits had been defending those mountain tops, there would have been barbed wire entanglements, pre-registered artillery targets, and machine guns firing on fixed lines into those same 'killing zones'. What had the Argies been doing during the ten weeks that they had been preparing for the British arrival? Their failure in this respect had certainly reduced our surgical workload, but it was now hooray for the 'Red and Green MEAN Machine' and all that the Toms and Royals of 3 Commando Brigade had achieved that day.

Later on, as we listened to the BBC World Service News in Ajax Bay, we also heard that today, on Horse Guards, Her Majesty the Queen had celebrated her Official Birthday in the usual manner – with a Trooping of the Colour. Eight thousand miles to the south, her Naval subjects and some of their Guards guests celebrated too, in a rather different way, but with just as much pride and enthusiasm. The boys had earned an 'Arduous Duty' tot anyway, so there was a bit of finger trouble as Fred Cook and I poured out the rum and the whisky into waiting mugs of coffee, tea and cocoa.

Since he would normally have been at Horse Guards and on parade, we invited Major Charles Bremner of the First Battalion Welsh Guards to celebrate his Colonel-in-Chief's birthday too. He had carried the Colour at a previous Trooping. Our new friend was somewhat confused by my traditional toast in front of the assembled ranks of Medical Squadron: 'Gentlemen, let's drink to the health of The Lord High Admiral of the Royal Navy – *Her Majesty the Queen*!'

Sunday, June 13th

Terry Moran's wicked sense of humour had been at it again. The area around Port Stanley was marked on our large-scale wall map with cross-hatching and the bold letters 'SSZ'. We'd all heard of the TEZ (Total Exclusion Zone) and SSTs (Surgical Support Teams), but what exactly was the SSZ? Visitors who asked this question were given an explanation by our irrepressible Sergeant Major that implied official truth within its earnest, but deadpan delivery: 'It stands for *Spick Splattering Zone*, sir – an area designated for bringing as much artillery fire down on the Argies' pointed heads as we possibly can...'

The visiting personages would then be led away, most of them muttering about our collective sanity, but still not quite sure whether the crazy jargon of war hadn't come up with another completely unintentional winner!

The southern assault on Tumbledown and Mount William was delayed for 24 hours while 5 Brigade's HQ struggled to get their rather weak act together. The gallant men of 2 Para, now supplemented with a new Commanding Officer who had parachuted into the South Atlantic after being sent out from UK, moved forward to push through 3 Para's position on Mount Longdon – in order to go for the adjacent Wireless Ridge. I remember thinking how tough it would be for 2 Para to have to fight a second battle in this campaign. They were the only land unit to do so, and it must have been heart-breaking for the Royal Marines of 40 Commando, held in reserve back at San Carlos settlement.

Not a day passed when our boys at Ajax Bay didn't wake up in the morning, go outside and look across San Carlos Water – and then give a silent prayer of thanks that 40 Cdo were still there to defend us if the Argies ever counter-attacked the beach head. I was also well aware of the hard-learned lesson in the British experience of war that every military group – whether Battalion, Brigade or Division in size – must have good reserves positioned to move up in reinforcement if required. 40 Commando were now fulfilling that historic role, by bolstering the damaged and reduced resources of the Welsh Guards. Two companies of the skilled Royal Marines infantry were being flown forward for the planned operations on and around Sapper Hill.

It was a relatively quiet day for new casualties therefore, while we moved our most recent customers back to the *Uganda*, but our business was then made much more interesting by the arrival of two very welcome visitors. For the first time since the war started, Surgeon Captain Andrew Rintoul and Commander Andy Gough of HMHS *Uganda* were able to come ashore and see for themselves exactly what their Hospital Ship was supporting.

Now they were able to understand why their patients were arriving out at sea dirty and almost naked – but with reasonably healthy-looking, open wounds. Our cramped conditions, the cardboard field latrines, the dust and dirt, and the general shortage of water were all baseline features of a system in which we were struggling to provide life and limb-saving medical care. A thousand words of description by me had meant very little until today. Now, half-an-hour of personal inspection revealed everything. They were shocked, quite frankly, and a bit embarrassed that they had assumed our conditions were much better than they actually were.

These two were good men – and sympathetic. Andrew Rintoul was, in truth, a bit out of his depth; he was a hospital-based consultant opthalmologist whose specialist opinion I had come to value during my Fleet Air Arm service. However, unlike 'Not Entitled', he was always the model of supportive courtesy throughout the Conflict, and I trusted him. Andy Gough had been trained and then commanded as a Fleet Air Arm Observer, and possessed all the sharp awareness typical of his branch of Naval aviation. It was no surprise when he later achieved Flag rank. I could be open and honest with him, and know that my trust was reciprocated. I brought them both up to date on the battle picture before they flew back onboard with the last load of our wounded from Mount Longdon and Two Sisters.

Uganda would be out from Falkland Sound that night, then back in before dawn. I warned them that she might even have to take patients straight from the battlefields if all three of the British ground surgical units became too crowded. They had been clearing the wards all day in anticipation, transferring any lightly wounded and recovering patients into the ambulance ships for delivery up to Montevideo. There, despite Uruguyan support for the Argentine cause, the Geneva Convention was being strictly observed in the name of humanity. The RAF's VC10 air ambulances were being turned around and refuelled very efficiently. Apparently, that aspect of the casualty evacuation chain back to RAF Brize Norton and the Service hospitals at Haslar (RN and RM) and Woolwich (Army) had been working extremely well.

An Air Raid Warning Red spoiled the later afternoon – twelve enemy aircraft in three waves which attacked Brigade Headquarters up near Estancia House. Again, some of the bombs that were dropped didn't go off, and those that did had any blast effect weakened by the thick, wet peat. One man was injured but nobody was killed. This fact simply reinforced the widely-held belief that the Almighty also had a green beret. All the boys were laughing again, imagining plump staff officers abandoning their map cases and notebooks to dive under the nearest bit of cover.

It was somehow rather reassuring to think that the chaps who were directing your lives had also been able to discover, for themselves, that adrenalin was brown and tended to run down your legs! If only some of those clever people back at Northwood could have had the same experience...

There was something very different to celebrate that night. Some almost unbelievable news had come through about the preliminary rounds of the World Cup, in Spain. The scoreline read 'Argentina *nil*, Belgium – *ONE*!' Our morale was about as high as it could be when we turned in, early once more. It was to be the Scots Guards, the Gurkhas and 2 Para's turn (once more), and there would be another butcher's bill to pay come the morning.

Monday, June 14th

There was about half an hour between dawn and the arrival of the first casualties, mainly Scots Guardsmen from Tumbledown. Fitzroy was saturated, and Teal Inlet very busy with 3 Para casualties from the continuing and all-night stonking of Mount Longdon by Argentine long-range artillery. In between helicopter loads of bandaged bodies, the picture began to emerge of 2 Para being 'shot in' to Wireless Ridge by the light armour of the Blues and Royals, positioned on each flank in close support. In a classic display of firepower and manoeuvre, akin to the demonstrations given at Warminster Army School of Infantry, 2 Para had lost just two killed and twelve wounded in taking their objective.

The Second Battalion of the Scots Guards had also had a famous night, adding the name of Tumbledown to the many others on their Regimental Colours. It had not been easy, because they were up against the Fifth Regiment of Argentine Marines. Some desperate hand-to-hand fighting and the cold steel of unsheathed bayonets had been required, in a wake-up call to those Staff and doctrine planners back in the UK who had confidently predicted that the bayonet would soon be outdated as an infantry weapon.

The Argentine defenders of Mount William were also defeated, with many of them falling victim to some subtle psychological warfare. They had been persuaded that their opposing Gurkhas were stoked up on cannabis, and equipped with personal

Sony Walkmans that played Nepalese war chants! Johnny Gurkha was and is a fierce chap – of that there was certainly no doubt – but their reputation (and their sharp *kukri* fighting knives) allowed them to knock off Mount William without loss, although there were many injured. We took those all in, and saved them too.

Then came the All Stations and quite electrifying order: '*Weapons are not to be fired except in self-defence*' followed by a situation report which stated that there were white flags in profusion around Stanley! There was much to be cheerful about, but a big operating list still to complete. Surgery continued. *Uganda* was now taking some casualties direct from the front line but, as she was the real lynchpin to our war's medical effort, I felt that her people should be among the first to know about the Conflict's likely end. I jumped on a Wessex and flew out to her. The BBC World Service had not yet released the news, so I soon confirmed that the ship had not yet received the glad tidings.

We had a hurried conference in the Master's cabin, and Captain Clark ordered two bottles of chilled champagne to be uncorked immediately. He then piped for all available crew and embarked officers to assemble in the ship's cinema, where I repeated the breaking information to a sea of relieved and smiling faces. With three cheers for Her Majesty the Queen, it was then back to managing the bloody consequences of war.

The moment that we lifted off from *Uganda's* deck and began to fly back towards East Falkland again is now engraved for ever in my mind. The champagne's absorption by my empty stomach simply accentuated the colours and detail of the scene. *Uganda* was steaming along quietly, her white upperworks glowing in the afternoon sun. Behind her, Fanning Head stood out blue and clear in the distance, mute witness to much bravery as well as the savagery and destruction of over three weeks' fighting. As the Wessex picked up speed and climbed away from the liner, there was another memorable moment. One of the stewards had pressed a paper bag into my hand as I went up the ramp to the flight deck. In that bag, and now consumed with greater enthusiasm than any gourmet dish from the Savoy Grill, was a fried egg and bacon roll! No ambrosia was ever sweeter.

We cleared most of the casualties out to *Uganda* by nightfall, and then took stock. There had been over 50 admissions and 32 operations, much the same figure as Saturday. General Moore's victory signal was received and read out as the men stood ready, their tin cups and plastic mugs each charged with a well-deserved tot. That night, our toast was – *Great* Britain!

Tuesday, June 15th

A terribly cold night made that morning's task of examining the dead much more difficult, because the limbs had been set and frozen into unusual postures that were added to by the process of *rigor mortis*. This quite natural phenomenon had contributed to the unfortunate rumour that two of the dead Scots Guardsmen from Tumbledown had somehow been captured and executed by a retreating enemy. The bodies had apparently been found with 'hands tied' and 'blindfolded'. Careful examination of their wounds showed this suggestion to be nonsense. One had been killed by a long range sniper shot to the head, the other by a fragmenting mortar round. In other words, my opinion was that they had both died cleanly and quickly, on the field of battle.

The allegation of battlefield misconduct was an important one though, and so I sought advice from another professional colleague, who had also better remain nameless, but found him most unwilling to be of any assistance at all. There weren't many like him, thank goodness, but he was one of those individuals rendered completely useless by the strains of war when the pressure came on. The forensic analysis and reporting was therefore down to me – again – and I was able to describe my findings to Lt Col Mike Scott, the absolutely charming Commanding Officer of 2 Scots Guards, when he came back to Ajax Bay for his men's funerals. No more was heard of this quite unfounded allegation.

40 Commando crossed to West Falkland, and Lt Col Malcolm Hunt took the Argentine garrison's surrender in Port Howard. They also discovered three dozen or so enemy casualties over there, some with wounds that were a week old and untreated. It was just more work for our surgeons, as we expected, after the war had ended. Some of the young Argentine soldiers' stories were heartbreaking. Most were starving, indeed some had actually injured themselves deliberately in order to gain medical treatment and hospital food. Others had been shot by their officers (so they said), in the feet, to prevent them running away.

Once again our basic surgical policy, based on the time-honoured principles of battle surgery, was shown to be correct. These men had filthy, discharging and smelly wounds a week after *their* side's therapeutic philosophy of 'early closure'. The wounds of an identical vintage out on *Uganda* were not only more severe – they were also much cleaner and healthier-looking too.

It was also 'Honours and Awards' time. Ivar Hellberg had asked me to nominate the men of Ajax Bay's medical organisation who were worthy of recognition. The task of picking out those who had risen head and shoulders above the rest of a really outstanding bunch was an appallingly difficult one, and I agonised over it. The choice had then to be reinforced by a short citation, which was a written justification for the selection. This would then be scrutinised in turn by the CO, then Brigade, HQ LFFI, and then passed up the chain to HQ CINCFLEET in Northwood, and finally, presumably, to the Ministry of Defence.

I put seven names up for various awards and all were accepted, endorsed and passed on by the CO. When I finished the final drafts of the citations, one of the marines who had been watching me beavering away at the typewriter came up and suggested that everyone in Ajax Bay had already got the 'MBE'. My polite agreement that everyone in Ajax Bay certainly *deserved* Membership of the Order of the British Empire – but there would not be that many awards available for dishing out – was met with the protestation:

'No, Boss – not the medal. I mean the *MBE*...'

'MBE?' was my baffled reply.

'Yes sir – that stands for *Mind Boggling Experience!*'

Wednesday June 16th – Saturday June 19th

Port Stanley was in an appalling mess. The Commando Logistics advance party sailed around in *Fearless*, then disembarked ashore by helicopter and landed on the racecourse. I joined them, by air, at Brigade HQ's request. The town and its approach roads were ankle deep in mud and human faeces. There was no sign of any attempt by the Argentine soldiery to build field latrines, or even try to concentrate their excretory arrangements in one area. If you stepped off the road or any recognised path, or if you lifted any bush or branch, some *campesino* had left his personal and neatly coiled calling card. One of my NCOs later described the area around Government House with some accuracy as a '*Close Encounter of the Turd Kind*'!

It was no wonder that hygiene was now a serious problem for the British troops billeted in the houses. The Stanley water purification plant, fairly antiquated anyway, had been partly destroyed and damaged by shelling. An aggressive form of diarrhoea and vomiting (known, inevitably, as *Galtieri's Gallop*) was beginning to take its toll on their general health.

The Community Centre building to the west of the town had been the location of the main Argentine Field Hospital, seemingly under Air Force control. There were Red Crosses painted everywhere, although one of the outbuildings was stuffed full of belted ammunition and boxes of hand grenades.

All their surgical kit and caboodle had been centralised in one large room, where Malcolm Hazell's men from Teal Inlet were now well established. There was no need for them to provide any form of emergency medical cover in this location, because Charles Batty and his team had reinforced the civilian medical authorities in the town's hospital. These surgical gurus soon had business to do, because one paratrooper, rather the worse for wear after getting outside some looted Argentine wine, managed to fire a .45 inch Browning pistol bullet through his cheek and the adjoining eye socket.

The Argy medical kit piled in the centre of the room was a curious mixture of the old-fashioned and the thoroughly modern. A couple of the operating tables would have looked absolutely right in some gaslight-and-gaiters Victorian hospital melodrama, but the dozens of boxes of sterile theatre drapes and towels were of American origin. They looked expensive, and high quality. Most of the serious drugs were useless to us, mainly because their pharmacological standards differed from the British ones.

One of the chefs and I busied ourselves in the cold air, smashing hundreds of morphine hydrochloride ampoules for this very reason, as well as to prevent the possible abuse of their contents. After all, who could be certain just how our recent combat experience had affected some of the British troops and their judgement? There was a mood of happy — even reckless — celebration about, and I certainly wasn't going to take any chances in leaving serious drugs like morphine lying around.

I was slightly more cynical about some of the other medical stores though — such as the antibiotics. Many of the abandoned boxes were labelled with patriotic messages to the effect that their contents were being 'donated for the nation' by the drug company involved, some of them big names on the European market. On closer examination, most of these boxes contained brightly packaged salesman's samples, useless to a military surgeon, but no loss to a company loudly professing patriotism yet (in truth) ignoring it. One box that I opened measured about a cubic foot in volume. Divested of its plastic packaging, cardboard and other rubbish, the 200 tetracycline tablets that it contained just about filled a paper cup. The departing Argentine surgeons had also left a chalked message in English on a board nearby: '*Enjoy your life*'. For some reason, that really got to me.

From the Community Centre, the road led down past the War Memorial and east/west along the sea wall in front of Government House. Sitting forlornly beside one bend, covered in a camouflage net, was a Puma helicopter. The cannon shell holes in its tail pylon indicated Sea Harrier trouble and an emergency landing. Some ground-based hero had also fired smaller calibre bullets into the windscreen, filling the cockpit and cabin with glass splinters to add to the other rubbish.

Further along towards the town were a number of large freight containers, apparently broken into. There was food in quantity here, with several hundred ration boxes spilling out of their twisted doors. The paratrooper on guard to prevent any further looting recognised me from our journey south in *Canberra*. The basic ration pack was pretty dull, but the Tom guarding this food dump said that the Argentine officers were issued with something different! My request to inspect was readily granted, and two intact examples selected for me.

One of the '*oficial*' (officer) ration packs went back to Ajax Bay for the lads to see. The variety of contents in the other was astounding, all the way from superb pressed beef, plus another kind of preserved meat, through to a miniature bottle of appalling whisky – and a charmingly tinted holy picture of '*Our Lady of the Malvinas*'. I had been educated by the Jesuits at

Stonyhurst College, and although I no longer 'kicked with the left foot' (as Jack would say), I knew enough to wonder what '*Our Lady of the Falklands*' would have had to say about that!

There were many sons of wealthy Argentine families who also passed through the school; Lt Col Nick Vaux, the CO of 42 Cdo RM, was OS (Old Stonyhurst) as well. Afterwards, we regretted that because of our tiredness, we had not thought to visit the Argentine officer's PoW compound to enquire whether there were any fellow former pupils 'behind the wire' that we could liberate for dinner!

In the King Edward Hospital, another group of Falklands ladies were busy, but in a highly practical way. Matron and her nurses continued to be splendidly unaffected by their temporary experience under Argentine overlords. The medical superintendent, Daniel Haines and his wife Hilary were both doctors, and also back at work. They had been shipped out to East Falkland with their children soon after the invasion, as potential troublemakers, leaving two female medical officers to cope with all the remaining population's sickness problems.

Dr Mary Elphinstone was there by accident as a summer visitor; Dr Alison Bleaney was a pretty and tough Scots mum who, as well as suckling her child, had been a key figure in the process of persuading the local Argentine commander that the British were serious about negotiating an honourable surrender. She had received her instructions from Lt Col Michael Rose of 22 SAS, a wonderfully charismatic figure who had cut into the medical radio network one recent morning – and requested her help.

With goodwill, renewed water supplies, hard work and the loan of Charles Batty and Dick Knight's skills in the operating theatre, the hospital was soon fully functional once more.

Dr Daniel Haines then asked me if we had a gynaecologist travelling with the Task Force. As this was a subject I had trained in, I replied in the affirmative. Daniel asked where this person was, but when he learned it was me, his facial expression indicated that he found this suggestion rather unlikely! To be absolutely truthful, I did not exactly look the part with my filthy clothing, three weeks' growth of beard and a powerful surrounding cloud of body odour.

Anyway, the problem lay with, or rather *within* an absolutely lovely, silver-haired Falklands grandmother. She had a womb prolapse, a problem that was not unusual in Gynae Outpatients back home, and after rummaging in a couple of stores cupboards, I solved her difficulties quite easily. Suddenly she was comfortable again – and most grateful.

Dr Haines was impressed. His next question concerned the presence and whereabouts of any women in the Task Force. The Argentines had apparently been in occupation for over ten weeks, but had completely miscalculated their logistic resupply requirements – plus the difficulties of getting any stores across from the mainland in the face of British air and sea blockade. As a result, they had been unable to provide any sanitary supplies or supplements for the Islands' female civilian population.

I suggested that we should send a signal explaining this fact to the *Uganda*, with a copy to *Canberra*. The hospital ship had female nurses aboard, and it was also just possible that the stores from the passenger shop in *Canberra* had not actually been landed at Southampton in our hurry to get south.

Daniel and I went up to the Naval Signals Office, and an electronic message concerning various items of feminine hygiene was duly composed and sent. What I didn't know was that, at this stage of proceedings, it had been decided higher up the command chain that *every* signal originating from Stanley would be copied to *every* ship in the South Atlantic!

This request to check stores inventories for such things as 'sanitary napkins' and 'tampons' must have caused much hilarity throughout the Task Force, but there was one Supply Officer who reached for a big bunch of keys in the Stores office and went deep

down into the bowels of his ship. He then opened up a compartment that was well below the waterline of the big aircraft carrier
HMS *Hermes*.

There, he found the refugee stores that had been loaded into
the ship at Gibraltar in 1975, just before she steamed across the
Mediterranean to Cyprus, following the Turkish invasion of that
island. There were lots of British tourists in places like Kyrenia
who had to be rescued across the beaches before being flown home.
Now, seven years later, two netted pallet loads of babies' bottles,
teats, powdered milk, sanitary towels and napkins arrived by helicopter on the Stanley school playing fields, beneath a Royal Navy
Sea King! The remainder of her passenger shop stores were also
broken out in *Canberra*, then taken to West Falkland and presented to the female citizens of Port Howard and Fox Bay.

Uganda was now in the outer harbour as well, with even
more capability than Stanley's relatively diminutive medical
facilities. Men were continuing to step on mines, so the need for
surgery persisted, sadly, long after hostilities had ceased. A terrible accident involving faulty armament switches in a RAF
Harrier that was carrying two Sidewinder missiles caused some of
the worst wounds of the war. Both missiles self-launched as the
aircraft lifted off Stanley runway; one missile headed for the sun
– and ran out of propellant fuel. The other, with the perverse
malevolence so often seen in these accidents, headed straight for
the nearest heat source, which happened to be a bonfire in the
middle of the airfield. The warhead detonated in the centre of a
group of Welsh Guardsmen who were helping to clear up the
general mess. Many limbs were lost.

With Workshops, Ordnance and Transport Squadrons of the
Commando Logistics Regiment now fully established in nearby
buildings, there seemed to be very little left for Medical Squadron
to do. The Army had sent the personnel of No. 2 Field Hospital
out from England to take over garrison medical duties in the long
term. An overwhelming, aching tiredness consumed me. Every-

thing started to become an effort, decisions were difficult, and tempers became somewhat frayed.

I journeyed back to Ajax Bay by helicopter to collect my equipment and the rest of the men. The Sea King was being flown by HRH Prince Andrew, but his touchdown at Ajax Bay was so heavy that the fillings almost fell out of my teeth! Although there was very little space for us in Stanley, Ivar wanted his Regiment all there together. I was just in time to attend the last rites and burial of our '*African Queen*'. A welded joint in the fuel supply had finally parted, and her long and valuable career ended in one corner of an Ajax Bay scrapheap. I also found that my sleeping bag and certain other personal items had become attached to someone else's sticky fingers. Maybe the chap needed them more than I did, but it was all a slightly bitter note on which to end our time at Ajax Bay.

The boys gathered up all the remaining kit and packed it into the chacons, then sat quietly in the main building, now stripped of its blanket partitions, stretcher trestles and wooden tables. The air was thick with dust raised by scuffing feet, causing a ghostly halo to be visible through the gloom surrounding the three remaining light bulbs. As they waited for the call forward to our landing craft and a brief trip out to the freighter *Elk*, on whose steel cargo deck we would sleep during the ride round to Stanley, I walked down and back through the main building.

Stars shone through the ruined roof of the slaughterhouse, the damp and chill quiet a sharp contrast to the explosions and searing flame of three weeks ago. The greenish metal cylinder embedded in the refrigeration machinery still looked threatening and evil in the dim light of my torch beam. I resisted the impulse to make a hole in the barriers of white mine tape. There was no need to touch the thing once again. We were going. It would all soon be part of a jumble of busy memories.

I walked out of the building, and around the side, my breath misting in the cold air. For all the wounded in the land battles of the Falklands campaign, it had been a happy coincidence that both taxpayer and investor had been parted from their money those thirty years ago. Without their speculation, our efforts for the injured would have been much less effective.

My thoughts were interrupted as a runner came up from the Beach Unit to summon us to the waiting landing craft. We donned our fighting order, shouldered the bergens and weapons once again, and began to retrace our steps down to the shore. 'The Red and Green Life Machine' had now closed for ever, and somehow, I could not bring myself to look back.

Sunday June 20th – Monday June 21st

The journey round to Port Stanley set a new standard in discomfort for the majority. *Elk*'s steel cargo deck, with its minimal headroom and a total absence of heating, was in many ways worse than Ajax Bay. Thoughts about enemy torpedoes crossed a few minds but were quickly suppressed. Because of the watertight configuration of her internal bulkheads, there would simply be no way to get up and out in time.

Misfortune dealt me a decent card for once. My missing sleeping bag meant relative luxury because Captain John Morton invited me to doss down in the chartroom annexe instead. In return, the splendid little P&O freighter was donated a small piece of bent Pucara for her cosy officers' wardroom. This took the form of an airspeed indicator marked in *nudos* (knots), which fitted nicely into the half-open mouth of the elk trophy head mounted on one bulkhead. Thirty years later, *Elk* is still busy on the run between Hull and Gothenburg, and her master is a proud veteran of the dangerous times when the ship carried over 10,000 tons of ammunition to the South Atlantic.

Accommodation was a monster problem in Stanley when we finally got ashore. Most households seemed to have a dozen soldiers billeted with them, and some had more. Somehow the boys of Medical Squadron and our attached subunits were shoehorned in, and then, like everyone else, the lads took a stroll around the town they had come so far to free. The Cable and Wireless Office was besieged with requests to send telegrams. I took a look inside the Post Office, and was sickened by the sight. The Argentine soldiery had broken in and looted the place, strewing sheets of stamps, all bearing the Queen's head, over the counter and floor. Some of these had even been used as toilet paper, in a crude excess that was absolutely typical of demented football supporters. Our friends from the Royal Engineers Postal Unit, initially located with us at Ajax Bay, were now trying to restore some semblance of proper order — rather than 'ordure' — to the place.

As the Army had also sent No. 2 Field Hospital of the RAMC down to take over garrison medical duties, there was very little left for us to do except re-organise and clean the medical stores while waiting for *Canberra's* return. The liner had left for Puerto Madryn on mainland Argentina, carrying over 4,000 prisoners for repatriation. That turned out to be a fascinating story in its own right. We heard that the Argentine authorities had refused Brigadier General Menéndez's request for ships to transport his men back to their native land, apparently adopting the attitude '*you* surrendered, in contravention of your orders – so *you* must sort your own problems out...' Poor guy. I really felt sorry for him, but grateful at the same time that he had indeed surrendered and caused all the death and bloodletting to cease.

Later that morning, while the story was still fresh in my mind, I had an opportunity to express my feelings to the man himself. I was visiting *Fearless* to gather information (and gossip!) when I saw a fully armed Royal Marine standing outside a cabin door in a corridor just off the main passageway. He was one of the No. 14 Recruit Troop chaps who I had earned my green beret with, over ten years before. His cheerful opening remarks were typical of so many encounters that I had had with Royal around the globe: 'Allo sir, wot the bloody 'ell are you doin' 'ere? Cor, there's a lot more of you now than when you was a nod wiv us!'

Despite these ruderies I quickly established that my friend was guarding Brigadier Menéndez and two of his key staff officers. Our people were being serious about this task, because there was a full magazine of 9 mm ammunition on his sub-machine gun. Seized with a bright idea, I asked if I could speak to the former commander of the garrison in what had, for 74 days, been '*Puerto Argentino*'. The Lance Corporal's reply was quite firm and apparently negative: 'Sorry, sir – my orders are that no British officers are allowed to enter this cabin until further notice – an' the Argies ain't goin' nowhere neither...'

Then I realised that my friend was grinning at me as he spoke, his head slowly nodding up and down in contradiction to the words he was speaking: 'Don't be long, Boss –' he whispered. – I'll watch the passageway while you're in there...' Royal took up position behind me as I put my green beret on, knocked on the cabin door – and entered.

Menéndez was seated in a chintz-covered armchair, with the two staff officers standing beside him. There was a seriously worried look on his familiar, but tired face. He must have wondered what the hell was going on. A large, unshaven and grubby-looking British soldier was filling the cabin doorway. Did he think that his time had finally come, as it had to so many young men and women during his time as a particularly tough governor of Tucuman province during *La Guerra Sucia* (the 'Dirty War')? I closed the door behind me, turned, drew myself up to my full height – and saluted him. He looked totally stunned, but he was senior to me, and I was paying due respects. We are *British*, after all!

'Sir, my name is Surgeon Commander Rick Jolly of the Royal Marines Commando Brigade, and I am Brigadier Julian Thompson's medical adviser...' Before I could ask if Menéndez spoke any English, one of the staff officers answered this point for me by translating what I had just said into a rapid flow of Spanish. A look of understanding and relief now spread across the Argentine Brigadier's face. Military medical officers were not generally torturers or secret policemen, even in Argentina.

'Brigadier General, on behalf of all my medical teams, who have been very busy in the past three weeks, I would like to thank you for surrendering your forces when you did. The outcome was inevitable, but by your humanitarian action you saved my doctors a lot of work – and you also saved a lot of young men's lives and limbs – on both sides. Thank you, again – *sir*...'

I saluted again. Menéndez did not need reminding that if he had not capitulated, those same young men on the British side would have conducted a savage house-to-house clearance operation that would have involved the bayonet, the fighting knife and the *kukri*. The Argentine senior officer smiled with relief as he stood up, repeating the words: '*Si, si, si – gracias..*'

I understand that he felt able to use my honestly-expressed sentiments, in his defence, at his subsequent court-martial back in Buenos Aires. Good for him. In time to come, when these matters are reconsidered by historians as they manipulate their retrospectoscopes, his reputation as a humanitarian commander may well be restored, even if his military prowess (especially in relation to the lack of appropriate defensive preparations) might be glossed over somewhat. We were certainly grateful in Brigade HQ for the way things eventually turned out, but no-one in Argentina should ever misjudge the British determination to achieve victory in the final attack on Stanley.

The Argentine soldiery were the products of a semi-feudal conscript system, but did not have the *bushido* fanaticism of the Japanese defenders of Guadalcanal and Tarawa. Yet, if the liberation of the Falklands had required the elimination of every last-ditch defender by the attacking marines, paratroopers, guardsmen and Gurkhas, then that task would have been completed. Thank goodness – and thanks to the humanity of Mario Menéndez (aided and abetted by the practical cunning of Lt Col Michael Rose, CO of 22 SAS) – such a bloody final outcome to the land battles was successfully avoided.

Ashore, we saw our first RAF C-130 Hercules too, as it ran in low over the high ground south of Stanley. Its bulbous snout had been changed in outline by the addition of a long refuelling probe above the cockpit. This particular '*Fat Albert*' made six circuits under a low grey cloudbase before departing back to Ascension Island. The staff planners back at RAF Headquarters in UK had decided that Stanley's runway was not safe, apparently, although the gallant crews of the Argentine Hercules and Electra aircraft were using the same strip right up until the last night of the war.

Each circuit of our friendly freighter was marked by the blossoming of a number of parachutes beneath its open tailgate door – probably urgent spare bits and pieces for the Rapier missile units. With some surprise, we later discovered that part of the drop was actually for Medical Squadron! The American and British supply systems had jointly come up trumps in answer to our hot water supply problems. Sixteen examples of the American '*Heater, Water, Portable, Immersion, Field Kitchen Pattern*', were delivered beneath nylon canopies. Another four descendants of our wonderful and late lamented '*African Queen*' ended up, like their ancestor, as scrap metal when one of the cargo parachutes failed to open.

We taught our Army medical successors how to use them, and then spirited half a dozen away with us, in Medical Squadron's returning stores. Our Field Dressing Stations in Norway, high up inside the Arctic Circle, would from now on become much more comfortable places thanks to these gifts from the sky.

We had 'acquired' a captured Argentine jeep as transport, so I took a ride out to the airfield to find some of the medics who had abandoned all the stores in the Community centre. We found them huddled together, looking thoroughly miserable with their lot. Mr Angry now dumped on them. There was no need to translate. I told them all that I was deeply ashamed of their indifference. There was sickness all around them and they were doing nothing about it. I told the senior guy to start rigging some shelter for a medical aid post, and took two of the livelier looking individuals back to Stanley with me. They ferreted around in the piles of drugs and medical stores to extract medications for diarrhoea, chest infections and that sort of thing, which my boys loaded into the little truck. Our new 'colleagues' appeared grateful for the chance to do something positive about their reduced circumstances.

I was then sought out by one of the posties, handed an impressive-looking, heavy white cartridge envelope, and asked to sign for it. My heart missed a beat. It was a hand-written letter from *Red Dragon*, the Naval nickname for HRH The Prince of Wales! Inside, the seven pages told me of his pride and relief that an old shipmate was looking after his soldiers – the Welsh Guardsmen and Parachute Regiment soldiers who had been injured. We had served together in early 1975, in HMS *Hermes* during a Western Atlantic deployment when the *Red Dragon* was a Fleet Air Arm helicopter pilot. As some of his contemporaries were now 'Junglie' flight commanders, this was another great source of pride for him. I could sense that he really wished he could have been with us, although we all knew there were some other, much greater responsibilities placed on his shoulders.

Typical of his huge generosity and thoughtfulness, The Prince of Wales had added that if there was some small piece of equipment that I needed and could not obtain from official sources, I was to let him know immediately. Of course, the time had passed for that, but his kind concerns for the welfare of 'his' soldiers has never diminished. When, later on, I became the founding Chairman of the South Atlantic Medal Association (SAMA82), HRH took an immediate interest, and supported our new veterans' group in several discreet but highly significant ways. He also took me with his entourage when visiting Buenos Aires in 1999, helped me to encourage some of the injured survivors of the *Sir Galahad* incident to come on our 2002 Pilgrimage to the Islands – and then assisted them as they formed a busy and successful Welsh chapter of SAMA82.

846 Squadron then offered me a ride in one of their Mk. 4 Commando Sea Kings. The Ops officer knew that I was a complete plane spotter, and would seize this opportunity – which I did! The mission was to fly back to the area around San Carlos and pick up as many as possible of the Rapier anti-aircraft missile firing units that were still positioned up in the hills surrounding the anchorage. The pilot was an old acquaintance, and with only an aircrewman in the back to assist him, pronounced himself glad of my company.

Very soon, I was flying the easy sectors in between the more dificult load-lifting phases, during which the Rapier units could behave a bit skittishly beneath the helicopter fuselage. The weather was wonderful, the visibility fantastic, and I was completely relaxed and happy. The instructors back at Culdrose had taught me properly, and soon I was doing the take-offs and landings as well.

We refuelled in Stanley at one stage, and then flew west once more. The pilot then indicated that he would like a 'comfort stop' and the crewman chipped in that he needed one too. No problem. I asked for the pre-landing checks, completed them, and then brought the aircraft round in a gentle descending turn into wind before settling on the soft tussock grass. The pilot grinned at me, gave me a 'thumbs up' signal, unplugged the intercom, undid his harness straps and climbed out of his seat – to disappear down the back.

All the engine instruments indicated operation within normal limits, but a quick check outside revealed that I had landed just below the crest of a slight slope. As a result, I could no longer see the horizon to the west. That was the direction from which a threat might materialize, and an attacking Argentine jet on some kind of last-ditch raid could have arrived right on top of us without any warning.

The solution to this problem seemed obvious. I lifted the Sea King back up into the hover, moved forward steadily using the cyclic trim button, and put the aircraft back down on the grass again, about sixty yards away. The junction between sky and sea now stretched right across all the front cockpit windows. I sat there and waited, 'fat, dumb and happy' as they say in aviation, until I heard the pilot re-enter the aircraft. He almost ran up towards the cockpit, and looked a bit flustered as he strapped in quickly. I asked:

'Everything OK?'

'Well, yes – Doc – everything *is* OK now...' followed by:

'*Why* did you move the aircraft?'

As I began to explain, it suddenly hit me. Without the aircraft captain's permission, I had done something seriously illegal. It was time for some grovelling apologies. We took off in silence, and after reassuring himself that I hadn't bent anything, the pilot suddenly grinned, and handed control of the aircraft back to me. He thought a bit more, then announced: 'If you want your log book signed, Doc, then the minimum time of flight that I can approve is *five minutes*, and not twenty-something seconds...'

He paused: 'Congratulations on your first solo, sir. The beers are most *definitely* on you...'

Tuesday June 22nd – Wednesday June 29th

The *Great White Whale* welcomed us back on board in the best style and traditions of the Peninsular and Orient Line. A friendly crew, large amounts of cold beer, and twelve hours of sleep each day quickly restored the mental equilibrium of a full load of very tired men. Having promised my Senior Rates in Ajax Bay that my rather ugly, salt-and-pepper beard would be removed the moment we began to head north after upping anchor, I found from the compass repeater mounted in the Crow's Nest Bar that I'd actually been spoofed! We were heading out due east instead of 'up' and north, back to England. There was a good reason for this. Apparently, the Argentine Air Force had taken to rolling things that go bang out of a C-130 Hercules tailgate, and had already caused an entirely innocent (and non-British) tanker to be abandoned and scuttled because of its dangerous additional cargo of a UXB. *Canberra* therefore did not turn north until we had travelled the best part of a thousand miles to the east, and had passed well out of the *Fuerza Aerea Argentina*'s maximum range.

The paperwork began.

As the men relaxed and cleaned themselves, their weapons, and all their equipment, the staff officers and commanders tackled the exacting business of assembling reports and returns. Perhaps the biggest pressure was on John Chester, the Brigade Major. The whole military world wanted to know about the detailed conduct of the campaign, the lessons learned, the mistakes to be avoided next time, what kit worked well and which bits of equipment were failures. The signal traffic became as voluminous as it had been in the early days on the way down, only this time there were lots of congratulatory messages as well as the trivia.

From the Commando Training Centre at Lympstone came this signal: '*Bravo Zulu to all ranks 3 Cdo Bde from all ranks CTCRM. Our kit was packed, but our hearts were in our mouths.*'

Julian Thompson's reply was typically succinct – and reassuring: '*To all ranks CTCRM from all ranks 3 Cdo Bde. Thank you. Change nothing.*'

For Malcolm Hazell's Troop, *Canberra* was an eye-opening sequence of luxury features after their deployment penance on RFA *Sir Galahad*. For them, having only four to a cabin now was like being asked to occupy a penthouse suite! The system that issued replacement personal kit to survivors also caught up with them. With all their other baggage about to become part of the official War Grave that used to be the *Galahad*, none of them had any sports or training rig, or even soft shoes.

Their new white service-issue plimsolls were soon modified using coloured pens and added extras like stuck-on 'wings'. Marine Dave Gowland won the Troop competition, (first prize, a case of beer donated by me) with some rather fancy footwear that Icarus might have saved himself with. Corporal John Clare's dry sense of humour was visible too. Along the outside edge of his 'training shoes' were some 'go-faster stripes' and the blocked-in words '*NIKE LEGGIT*'...

Life settled into an easy and pleasant routine which would, depending on the cabin occupied, have cost up to £100 per day under more normal circumstances. Outside, the air temperature rose, the sea took on a welcome shade of blue, and the sun turned up like clockwork every morning to bronze the lean gods stretched out on the upper deck.

The day usually began with roll call on one of the shade decks, after breakfast, when any announcements were made, but basically we were trying to sight everyone 'formally' once every 24 hours – to make sure that no-one had fallen overboard. The boys would then disperse for the remainder of the day and, unusually in an active military organization, be allowed to behave as if they were on leave. Uniform had to be worn about the ship, except when sunbathing of course, but 'reasonable' amounts of alcohol were permitted too. A marine in one cabin abused this privilege, and his colleagues found that *their* allocation was withdrawn as well...

Each Unit had its own designated recreation area, but invitations to 'call round' (an old Navy term) were often issued and accepted. If a group of marines wanted to stay up all night and talk about shared experiences, that was fine – as long as they all 'turned to' the next morning. If someone wanted to curl up in his cabin all day, missing meals while mourning a dead friend, well that was fine too – as long as good order, as an extension of *self*-discipline – was maintained.

There was a happy, vibrant atmosphere aboard the ship. Recreation expanded to fill the time available. In slow time, the Royal Marines of 3 Commando Brigade were decompressing steadily after their short but intense experiences of war. This gradual release of tension and pressure was all a happy accident, because it really was the very best way of staving off development of a corrosive set of symptoms called Post Traumatic Stress Disorder or 'PTSD'. The benefit of sharing memories and recalling emotions honestly, in the company of those who had been through the same experiences as you, brought with it an understanding that your reactions were entirely normal.

One morning, the same young man who had asked to be drafted back to 42 Commando during the journey south (only to be refused by me) came up and asked to see me again. I reassured him that I had taken no action about his earlier request, but he shook his head and told me of an important encounter he had experienced the previous evening. He had been up in the Peacock Room, with his old rifle troop, listening to stories of the assault and capture of Mount Harriet. Apparently, one of his former corporals had done particularly well and was in line for a gallantry medal. He suddenly found the NCO looking at him and asking where *he* had been. The stretcher bearer apologised, and explained that he was located at Ajax Bay with Medical Squadron.

Apparently, a look of amazed admiration came over the Corporal's face: 'What, in that field hospital with all them unexploded bombs, looking after my injured mates?'

The stretcher bearer nodded.

'Well just you sit there, my friend...' said his hero, 'I'm going to go and get *you* a beer!'

My marine's eyes were shining as he recounted the story.

The arrangements for our return were in sharp contrast to those made for our Parachute Regiment colleagues. The authorities wisely realised that, without a war looming to get ready for, both physically and mentally, there would have been trouble between those who wore the maroon beret and those who wore green. The happy co-existence between 3 Para and 40 and 42 Commandos that we had witnessed in *Canberra* on the way down, a time in which old rivalries and jealousies had been blown away during the intense preparations for battle, could no longer be assured.

I think that this also made a big difference, in the long run, to the way that the members of each fraternity coped with the aftermath. 3 Para were instead shoe-horned into the *Norland* along with 2 Para, for a brief but uncomfortable ride up to Ascension Island. During this voyage, Airborne Forces Day was celebrated in a tidal wave of beer and lager that degenerated into the traditional punch-up between the two units. Sporting many black eyes and some splintering headaches, a similar consequence had the event been held in Aldershot, the Toms were then flown home to RAF Brize Norton, arriving long before the Commando units following behind in *Canberra*.

At the time, this was thought to be a 'good thing', and that the Paras, despite their temporary inconvenience, would benefit in the long run by getting home first. A senior Army psychiatrist was on record as stating that a man would 'soon recover his equilibrium when returned to the bosom of his family'. In the same document was the wholly accurate observation that the incidence of psychiatric casualties in a battle is related directly to the number of casualties sustained. Despite the recording of this truth (to which might have been added the multiplying factor of enemy direct and indirect fire), no special arrangements were put in place to detect those survivors of Goose Green, Mount Longdon or Wireless Ridge who would later suffer a delayed response to their ordeal. Indeed, for some reason that I have never yet seen explained satisfactorily, the Army did not even send a field psychiatric team down to the South Atlantic with 5 Infantry Brigade in the *QE2*.

The police in Aldershot braced themselves for mayhem, but all was quiet during the six weeks' leave period that followed. What trouble there was came from those who had *not* seen combat down South, such as the new recruits and Depot personnel involved in their training. There were however many 2 and 3 Para veterans to be found later on, standing at the bottom of their gardens with blank expressions on their faces, looking out on the world with what a former Vietnam journalist had most aptly described as *'the thousand yard stare'*.

In sharp contrast, the Royal Marines in *Canberra* and the other ships sailing home were slowly but steadily 'fizzing off'. They were enjoying relaxed circumstances, positively encouraged by a sense of shared adversity, and existing in a state where the grip of any lingering sense of reticence or reluctance to talk about frightening experiences, or sad personal loss, could also be loosened by a sensible use of alcohol. This was the best form of post-incident 'counselling' that there could ever be. The therapy was not being administered by some eager young 'trained counsellor' with no real grasp of the horror or terrors of war. This process was being done by the boys themselves.

The alcohol aspect was important. A daily issue of rum to the ratings of a ship's company had been a vital feature of the Royal Navy's long and glorious history. Although the 'Tot' was discontinued in 1970, Their Lordships had been wise enough to retain the possibility of a carefully-defined 'Arduous Duty' version within the Regulations. On reflection, we had simply been using Naval tradition to our advantage in 'The Red and Green Life Machine'. During the journey home, I submitted my account to the Ministry of Defence, quoting the appropriate paragraph from QRRN (Queen's Regulations for the Royal Navy). My bill from HMHS *Uganda* was for just over £350, but as this covered the issue of 'two-thirds of a gill of commercial spirit' to nearly a hundred men on eleven different occasions, it represented good value, especially as every one of the team had subsequently done his (demanding) duty without the need for a single sleeping tablet or tranquillizer. The MoD paid immediately!

The Royal Navy Medical Service were slightly less slack in their handling of their late-presenting psychiatric casualties, although with over 18,000 sailors and 3,000 Royal Marines entitled to wear the newly-announced South Atlantic Medal, they had no excuse to be complacent. The sole exception to this comment had to be the splendid figure of Surgeon Commander Morgan O'Connell. Throughout the campaign, in which he was closely involved, this combative, articulate and wholly committed consultant psychiatrist had fought a lone battle to remind us all of the corrosive effects of battle shock, how men could be broken by its effects, and that these delayed effects needed to be anticipated – and then detected and treated. My wonderful Irish colleague, friend, and fellow veteran remains a key individual within the *Combat Stress* charitable organization.

These comments are just part of many other purely subjective observations that were made in the aftermath of the Conflict, because all such issues were tackled at that time on a single Service basis, rather than from a 'Joint Force' point of view of the kind that, hopefully, now prevails twenty-five years on. Very little of this medical, surgical or psychiatric material was ever reported on formally, or analysed professionally after 1982. After OP CORPO-RATE, life simply went on as it always had, in an Army dominated by Central Front tactical planning, and a Royal Navy obsessed with the Atlantic in both its surface and subsurface modalities.

It was easy to get the impression that the South Atlantic conflict was merely an expensive little sideshow that had prevented extinction of the Royal Marines – along with the Royal Navy's amphibious capabilities. At the same time, it seemed that victory had irritated the Treasury in a rather ominous way. While the restoration of Her Majesty's Sovereignty had also saved the Government from embarrassment about its neglect for the South Atlantic region, fiscal storm clouds were already gathering over the horizon. Simply stated, the South Atlantic Conflict had cost too much. In the hour of triumph, none of us in the Task Force realised this particular truth.

Thursday, June 29th – Monday, July 5th

Ascension Island eventually appeared on the horizon again, but we did not anchor. Our fortnight here seemed a year or two ago, not seven short weeks. There was mail to bring onboard, as well as a team of tri-Service and civilian experts on clothing, equipment and weapons. Someone in the Ministry of Defence had got it right! The captive audience in *Canberra* had much to say, and not all of it was exactly complimentary. No doubt some of the stronger recommendations of the foot-sore infantry would later be downgraded as irrelevant to the plains of Northern Germany, but there was a huge fund of new knowledge to tap into.

I wondered which weapons or kit items would receive the high accolade from Royal of '*Gucci*', a descriptive adjective that combines all the qualities of leading-edge style and practicality that the marines value in their off-duty lives. The 66 mm anti-tank weapon looked like a front-runner. It was basically a disposable cardboard tube with lightweight, folding sights, which contained a rocket-propelled and high-explosive warhead. The weapon had been light enough to carry strapped to the webbing of a man's fighting order, and had that important quality, as Royal would put it, of 'making the enemy's eyes water...' I think it achieved the post-conflict ultimate award of '*Everyone Should Have One*'.

For my part, I would like to have seen every infantryman equipped, as standard issue, with a personal activated charcoal and ion-exchange drinking straw. These new technology items were designed to purify 150 litres of fresh water from whatever source, whether jungle stream or peat-sodden puddle. I heard afterwards that many of the marines had indeed bought these kit items for themselves, regardless of official attitudes. If they went to war again, the 'extras' were going to be ready in their kit lockers!

We steamed on, past the Equator; the debriefings continued. The BBC World Service was piped into every cabin, along with an endless flow of heavy-metal rock music provided by enthusiastic bootneck disc jockeys. I gave up counting how often Meatloaf's rendition of '*Bat Out of Hell*' tried to warp the deckhead speakers.

Trouble flared in the Lebanon as we passed the Straits of Gibraltar. A rumour spread rapidly around the ship that we were going to turn right, enter the Mediterranean, and then go into Lebanon to sort out this particular load of dissidents! No-one seemed particularly worried by the prospect.

Next day, the buzz changed completely. Royal Marines have 'Gibraltar' on their beret badges, so now we were going to land in Algeciras Bay, cross into Spain, annex the Costa Plenty and only hand it back in return for the uninterrupted future of the Rock! However, the Straits of Gibraltar and Cape Trafalgar were soon left astern as well, and the Canary Islands appeared next. A Spanish civilian helicopter pilot made half-a-dozen cautious circuits of a strange-looking *Canberra* before he allowed himself to be waved on to the midships flight deck. He seemed a bit unhappy there because, as soon as passengers and luggage were disgorged, our new guest simply lifted and shifted for home. The poor marshaller then got it in the neck from the Bridge for allowing him to go.

The first and last 'Annual Garden Party' of the *Canberra Medical Society* was held on another hot midday, and brought its professional and social programme to a splendid close. With a guest list that reflected our feelings for a ship that had done everything possible for the medical fraternity in their labours onboard, a lot of chilled white wine disappeared down relaxed and thirsty throats. The sunlit Captain's deck was a happy scene as I presented Dr Peter Mayner, in a short speech, with the Society's Record of Proceedings.

To my great surprise, our applause was echoed from the flight deck below, now a mass of bronzing bodies. There was none of the barracking and jeering that one might have expected. Clearly, Royal had decided that his medics were good news, and had also earned their fun.

Another Naval tradition at the end of a long passage home is the '*Sod's Opera*'. This entertainment can best be described as 'by the lads – and for the lads'. There are only two basic rules. First, the Commanding Officer has to sit in the front row and take some stick, and secondly, at some point he has to get up on the stage and participate in proceedings. Many of the boys were in fancy dress, some looking surprisingly attractive in drag, while lots of beer and even more good humour settled a few old scores. The Band were in the thick of things, as usual. Captain John Ware, their boss, even produced a piece of music entitled '*The San Carlos March*'. Cleverly inter-linking the regimental marches of the various participating units on D-Day, the composition was very well received.

Tuesday, July 6th – Saturday, July 10th

The sea grew darker again and the air became noticeably cooler. We were turning the corner into the Western Approaches. All the shore-based pressure to bring *Canberra* back into Plymouth, home of 3 Commando Brigade, had been ignored. Although Devonport would have been much more convenient for most of us because it was nearer our homes, this was to be *Canberra's* homecoming, and Southampton was her home port.

For the first time, on July 10th, we saw England again, or more correctly Cornwall, as the Lizard peninsula loomed out of an afternoon sea mist. Helicopters from the Royal Naval Air Station at Culdrose were running a shuttle service for the hordes of cameramen and journalists who now flooded on board, among them our fellow veterans, Jeremy Hands and Robert Fox. Jeremy predicted a monster welcome for us in Southampton the next day. We were all a bit sceptical about this – firstly, Jeremy was such an enthusiast (and now an Honorary Member of 42 Commando RM as well!), and secondly, the war had ended three weeks ago. Most of us had experience of Northern Ireland, and we knew that a fickle British public soon forgets.

We were buzzed by lots of aircraft of varying shapes and speeds, including a maritime reconnaissance Nimrod from RAF St Mawgan. As the big four-engined jet turned in and dived towards us, Phil Shouler and I shared the Ajax Bay rallying cry that started with WO2 Terry Moran: 'Oh no! We're *doomed*!' There was much laughter now, as there had been then. Thank the Lord, this great and noisy beast, climbing away near-vertically, was definitely one of *ours*.

We picked our way carefully through the brightly-coloured spinnakers of the multihull fleet outbound from Plymouth in the Round Britain Race. Channel 16 was busy as a number of the competitors called up to speak to their now-famous sailing chum,

Ewen Southby-Tailyour. The wistful look in Ewen's eyes as he watched them pass out of sight indicated that as far as he was concerned, we had come home from the war a week too late.

There were lots of things happening on Up Channel Night. A wonderful, and deeply moving 'Sunset Ceremony' was performed for us by the Commando Forces Band. The sound of bugles playing the Sunset Call, just after 'Eternal Father', sent shivers down most spines; while we stood to attention, the Ensign was lowered. An incredible meal followed.

Dennis Rogers, *Canberra's* chef, was retiring from P&O the next day, so he had been allowed to go completely over the top. The souvenir menu contrasted his celebratory Bill of Fare with *Menu C* of the Arctic Ration Pack. Four weeks ago it was 'chicken and bacon paste' with the dry and tasteless 'biscuits AB'. Tonight, poached *Trout Hollandaise* then followed *Pâté de Canard à l'Orange*. And who would willingly have chosen 'mutton granules and dried peas' in preference to *Fillet Steak San Carlos*? When the Loyal Toast to Her Majesty the Queen was drunk, the P&O officers shared our Royal Navy and Royal Marines' privilege of remaining seated.

The later revelries continued long past midnight as the lights of Torbay, Teignmouth and Exmouth passed slowly down the port side. Were those car headlights being flashed at us? It really did seem possible. *Canberra* was dawdling along at half-speed in order to arrive alongside in Southampton at 1030 the next morning. It promised to be a long and exciting day.

Sunday, July 11th

Breakfast was rather earlier than usual. Some of the smarter young subalterns had arranged for champagne at table with which to entertain their company commanders. A festive end-of-term spirit pervaded the air, and by the time we were up in the Solent, a growing flotilla of cabin cruisers and speedboats had joined us. The P&O ferry *Dragon* sliced along off our port quarter, her lines blurred in the growing heat haze, and her deck rails crowded with excited punters. The excitement increased as a shiny red Wessex 5 of the Queen's Flight settled smoothly on the flight deck, and the Prince of Wales arrived on board.

Later on, we met him at a large reception in the Meridian Room. He seemed keen to speak to each and every one of the 400 men and women there to greet him, but time was obviously short. I was able to thank him for his fantastic letter, and then introduce him to a number of the men from Ajax Bay. Then, modestly, and typically, he flew back to London, anxious not to distract from any of the forthcoming celebrations by his presence. Only later did we discover that he had also visited every single one of the Falklands wounded still in Service hospitals.

And what a welcome we received!

As *Canberra* entered Southampton Water, it seemed that most of southern England had emptied into Hampshire for the day. There was a sea of faces on the Hamble side, countless waving banners, tooting car horns, and shouted greetings that were almost inaudible with the helicopters circling overhead, while the liner's own deep bass whistle sounded occasionally in acknowledgement. Eventually the press of smaller craft around *Canberra's* salty and rust-stained hull became so great that we had to slow to a walking pace while the Harbour police tried to restore some semblance of order and create sufficient margins of safety.

The Royal Marines who crowded the starboard rails in their green berets also had the opportunity to savour the incredible sight. Two nubile ladies on one 'gin palace' below them stripped off their suntops and waved their splendid chest development in welcome. A section of the onlooking military cheered loudly and suggested that further developments would be welcome. The girls seemed keen to oblige, but the spoilsport at the helm stopped them.

Eventually our pier came into sight, again obliterated by signs, placards and upturned faces. Six Army Lynx helicopters droned overhead, trailing red smoke. The repeated singing of *Rule Britannia* was accompanied on certain faces by tears of joy, excitement and pride rolling down tanned cheeks. Up went the balloons, down went the gangways, and then it was back to military life as we'd always known it. Hurry up – and wait...

Medical Squadron were amongst the last in the schedule for disembarkation, but we didn't really mind that. The fighting units had priority. I wandered along the upper decks to brief the lads, and then found to my considerable amusement that they had scored again with their fantastic humour. The Royal Marines had fashioned a long banner out of four linked white bed sheets, and then constructed a telling message of thanks in black masking tape on it, with the words '*Canberra cruises where QE2 refuses*'. The Cunard liner had raced down to South Georgia, transferred her passengers to the 'Great White Whale' in Grytviken Bay, and then sped off back to England. Despite claims to the contrary in the subsequent advertising, she never came within six hundred miles of the Falkland Islands...

Four hours later, with Susie driving, I kept looking at my son James – and then out of the car window at the passing trees and fields of England. By the time we got down to Exeter, the sun had disappeared and a steady drizzle set in. Despite this, every bridge and lay-by from here on was lined with cars and people, ordinary folk out in the rain to greet their returning heroes. The road down into Plymouth itself was almost completely blocked by a crowd of over 20,000. We got through eventually, but only after much hand-shaking and back-slapping. For almost everyone else in the Task Force, the homecoming would be the same.

My house had been decorated with banners and bunting, unknown to Susie. Overwhelmed, I stood outside in the soft

Cornish rain as my neighbours left their houses and walked over, their faces wreathed in smiles. There were yet more pumping handshakes and silent, fierce embraces. In every case, the message was the same: 'Thank you, thank you all for what you've done for British pride – and *welcome home...*'

AFTERMATH

We were then sent on leave for six weeks, but this time was broken into by various summons to London, and elsewhere, in order to debrief senior staff. My RN Medical Branch leaders in High Holborn seemed more interested in the fact that I did not know who had been recommended for Honours and Awards from *Uganda* than they were in what we had all achieved together. Over 580 British casualties of the land battles had passed through the casualty evacuation chain, and only three of that number had subsequently died of their wounds. However, I had the distinct impression that one of their number, a hospital-based physician who had never been to sea or served in the front-line, would have gone to the Cross rather than agree that surgeons had an important part to play in the care of battlefield casualties.

I also telephoned the Curator of the Fleet Air Arm Museum in Yeovilton, towards the end of our leave period. Vernon Hillier burst out laughing when I told him that I had a piece of an Argentine Navy jet's fuselage to offer him, along with a Pucara pilot's helmet. Both items had been sitting out in the garage, with Susie threatening dire retribution if they ever came into the house. I was a bit offended at first – until he told me that his laughter stemmed entirely from a sense of relief. As Research Consultant to the Museum, he had been told to clear decks for a Falklands exhibition, but was then denied any chance to go south, visit the battlefields and acquire a few items to put in the display cabinets. Mine was the fourth or fifth call that he had received from a Fleet Air Arm supporter that week, and they had all described very similar behaviour by their spouses!

Although the *London Gazette* was not officially published until Monday October 11th, one weekend media leak became a trickle, and then burst into a sudden flood. On the previous Friday, a number of us were called up to Ivar Hellberg's office and handed envelopes marked '*Honours in Confidence*'. Our families could be told, but no-one else.

Like Ivar Hellberg, I had been made an Officer of the Order of the British Empire (Military Division). This entitled a recipient to the post-nominal letters of OBE. It was a huge surprise. I felt then, and I still do, that this award belonged to *all* the staff of 'The Red and Green Life Machine', and not just to me. It had been a huge honour in its own right to have actually been in charge of the Ajax Bay medical facility, as well as having done our duty well. I was really proud to have shared every detail of the Falklands experience with that outstanding bunch of men. Perhaps there was some truth in the oft-repeated assertion that the letters 'OBE' actually stood for '*Other B*gg*rs' Efforts*'!

The names of all the frigates of that resolute D-Day picket line were there, with the Commanding Officers of HMS *Antrim, Brilliant, Broadsword, Ardent, Argonaut, Plymouth* and *Yarmouth* receiving Distinguished Service Orders and Crosses for their tenacity and leadership during that vicious fight. If, along with the Fleet Air Arm Sea Harriers from 800 (HMS *Hermes*) and 801 Squadrons (HMS *Invincible*) they had failed to win what is now called 'The Battle of Falkland Sound', the landings at San Carlos might have failed, the British Government would have fallen, and we could have quite easily lost the war.

From Ajax Bay, Lieutenant Bernie Bruen, Chief Trotter and Flight Lieutenant Alan Swan were all decorated for their great courage in coping with the various unexploded bombs on ships and ashore. That arrival of a Scout helicopter outside Ajax Bay on the night of May 28th was also recognised, when Captain John Greenhalgh received the Distinguished Flying Cross. Richard Nunn was also awarded the DFC, but posthumously. And Robert Fox got the MBE! It was great news.

For Bill McGregor there was also a richly deserved OBE. I had written him up for the DSO, but as this citation then spilled over into his unexpected promotion to full Colonel, I had no reason to feel unrequited. Phil Shouler and Charles Batty were both made MBEs (Members of the Order) as was Terry McCabe for his efforts on the nursing side. Chief Medical Technician Stuart McKinley received the British Empire Medal for his devoted management of one vital Ajax Bay feature – the blood bank. A 'Mention in Dispatches' went to Marine Stephen Duggan, so naturally able as a 'medic' despite being completely untrained, that he was sent forward during the final push on Stanley to help the two Medical Officers of 42 Commando, Martyn Ward and Ross Adley. Up in the hills and also receiving 'Mentions' for their work under fire with the front line units were Leading Medical Assistants Paul Youngman, George Black and Medical Assistant Michael Nicely.

For Captain Steve Hughes RAMC of 2 Para there was only a 'Mention in Dispatches'. It was a little disappointing at first that this was not a Military Cross, but then a 'Mention' in the allocation of honours for that gallant unit was pretty difficult to get, and had to be seen in its true perspective. He had done really well; we all knew that. So had the girls of Port Stanley Hospital, with Dr Alison Bleaney receiving the OBE, and Dr Mary Elphinstone an MBE.

Some strongly recommended names did not make the final list, which was sad, although some were given 'Commander-in-Chief's Commendations' instead. Like the 'Mentions in Dispatches', these did not warrant a trip to Buckingham Palace and an Investiture by the Queen. What was more important was that each man (and woman) felt that they had given of their very best, and understood that those around them knew it.

I looked in vain for any mention of the Hospital Ambulance ships HMS *Hydra, Hecla* and *Herald*. Also, the *Uganda's* list of suggested honours did not, for some reason, get to the post on time, so it was a great disappointment initially when none of her names appeared either. This was made up for by some fast foot-work and penmanship in time for the New Year's Honours List of 1983. Surgeon Commander Charles Chapman, the plastic surgery guru, was appointed OBE, and the Queen Alexandra's Royal Naval Nursing Service also featured. The gentle kindness and tough organising abilities of Sister Jean Kidd were recognised and rewarded with the MBE. A week or so later, her engagement to Ross Adley was announced. At last, the fellow had seen sense...

Tuesday, October 12th, saw a Victory Parade in the City of London. We would all have liked to be there, but numbers were limited to an officer and six Commando Naval medical personnel. Erich Bootland and Chief Petty Officer Jethro Young took a care-fully selected group up as our representatives. They marched, as they always do on Royal Marines occasions, in Naval blue suit beneath the green beret. The Chief of the Defence Staff's eyes widened as the Corps contingent passed the saluting dais, at this rather 'unofficial' rig. To the rest of us watching on television, the boys looked very smart indeed.

On December 14th, Rear Admiral Sir John Woodward and Major General Sir Jeremy Moore were knighted at Buckingham Palace by Her Majesty the Queen. Down in Southampton on that same morning I attended, along with several other medical offi-cers, the inquest on those 64 members of the Task Force whose bodies had by then been brought back to England for re-burial. Our careful initial examination and recording procedures for the dead at Ajax Bay and elsewhere now paid big dividends.

Her Majesty's Coroner, Mr Roderick MacKean, listened closely to the testimony given by representatives of the various

Units that had 'owned' the deceased, and was then able to accept both the evidence of identity and the causes of death. In a quiet and dignified voice he then paid tribute to their memory by reading out the list of names as a Roll of Honour.

One stated cause of death, for the four crewmen killed in the Gazelle shoot-down of June 6th, really disturbed me though. According to the two 656 Squadron officers summarising the incident, the helicopter had been shot down by an Argentine 'night fighter', using a Sidewinder missile! I should have stood up in the Coroner's Court right there and then in protest at such a falsehood, but by then I had been 'busted' back down to my substantive rank of Surgeon Lieutenant Commander, and also made aware (in a number of subtle ways) that I was not exactly 'flavour of the month' with my professional heads of Branch up in London. I had yet to find out exactly why, but meanwhile I remained silent, to my eternal regret, at what appeared to be a deliberate cover-up involving the deaths of Major Mike Forge, Staff Sergeant Baker, Sergeant Chris Evans and Lance Corporal Simon Cockton.

The truth finally came out when one of the many post-Conflict books was published. The 'red top' tabloids had a field day, and the Royal Navy – in the shape of HMS *Cardiff*, the Type 42 destroyer that had fired the pair of Sea Dart missiles, was made to look incompetent and foolish. In fact, the Navy had done its duty properly; the real culpability for this incident lay elsewhere.

Night-flying 'corridors' were usually established during the hours of darkness to allow planned safe passage for friendly aircraft. The Argentine resupply by air was still getting through to Stanley, and the British were keen to disrupt this. On the night in question, the Gazelle had been sent forward with two Royal Signals experts, to repair a tactical radio rebroadcast ('rebro') unit. General Moore's HQ was *not* informed of this plan, remained unaware of the 5 Infantry Brigade commander's intentions, and so no formal clearance for the Gazelle's flight was requested or passed to the warships operating just offshore.

Mrs Winifred Cockton, the mother of the young air gunner, Simon Cockton, had to go all the way to the House of Lords to get the Coroner's verdict of 'death by enemy action' struck out and corrected. It was eventually Dr John Reid, of the (new) Labour Government, who authorised the payment of her (considerable) legal expenses.

However, there was still much to look back on with quiet pride. I think that the last paragraph of Admiral Sir John Field-house's official Despatch of Tuesday, December 14th 1982 summed it all up rather well:

Major contributory factors to the survival of the wounded were the supreme physical fitness of our troops and the exemplary medical attention given to casualties of both sides. First aid matched the professional expertise of the field and afloat medical teams. Equally vital was the skill of the helicopter pilots in speedily evacuating casualties. Casualties were transferred to the Hospital Ship SS Uganda. *Once fit for further travel, they were transferred to the three casualty ferries HM Ships* Hydra, Hecla *and* Herald, *and conveyed to Montevideo for onward aeromedical evacuation to the United Kingdom by RAF VC10. These operations were all con-ducted with great efficiency and great concern for the comfort of the wounded. I could not have been better served.*

My first Naval appointment post-Conflict allowed me to for-malize my professional relationship with the Fleet Air Arm, by attending the Diploma in Aviation Medicine course with the RAF at Farnborough. I'd also finished the first draft of a book about our time at Ajax Bay, and sent it to my friend Patrick Janson-Smith, who had edited my first efforts at writing – a Corgi paperback novel about Belfast during the Troubles, called *For Campaign Service.* He'd written to me down South, and now became involved in a package deal with the team at Century Pub-lishing. I gave each and every one of my men his own signed copy.

I then returned to the Commando Training Centre at Lympstone, followed by another two years in Medical Officer recruiting, which was also a succesful and happy time. I was based in London, but spent a lot of time touring the country, giving illustrated talks to medical schools about 'The Red and Green Life Machine'. *We* gained some excellent young doctors as a direct result. After that came another appointment to HMS *Seahawk*, the Fleet Air Arm base in Cornwall. Both my Captains had served with distinction in the Conflict, and liked me to fly with all the Pilot and Observer training squadrons whenever I could. No problems there!

During the long summer evenings, the airfield had to remain open for night flying, with the Duty MO actually on base. I now took the opportunity to collate the contents of a shoe box containing all the amusing words and expressions that I had ever heard during my service. The wonderful cartoonist 'Tugg' brought these to life, and *Jackspeak* has now passed through three editions and is currently also published by Conway.

More writing followed with a Defence Fellowship at University College, London in 1988. My thesis was concerned with the role of '*Personality, Individual Experience and Command in War*' and was subsequently published in the *Journal of the Royal Naval Medical Service*.

The appointing system was very kind to me at this juncture. A Central Staff requirement had come in to look at the problems of protecting commercial ship crews against Biological and Chemical Warfare agents (BCW). This was especially important for the crew and medical teams of any future Merchant Navy vessel requisitioned as a Hospital Ship. I was selected to do this study while attached to the staff of the Surgeon Rear Admiral (Operational Medical Services) based in Plymouth.

I realised that there could be a cross-pollination of ideas and methods from the land-based BCW concepts that I was familiar with, from service with the Royal Marines. The British Army had studied the problem carefully, and had developed a special system of tailored tent liners that were protected by airlocks. The Royal Navy, in contrast, tended to think in terms of steel 'citadels' and unlimited electrical power for air pumps and filters. The answers to our problem lay somewhere in between.

Unknown to me at the time, Saddam Hussein was plotting to invade Kuwait. Suddenly, after the deed was done, there was an urgent need to turn theory into practice, without any 'proof of concept' or test phase. My proposed solution was based on a new type of modular building made in York by the Portakabin people. It looked better and better each time the facts were examined, and eventually the buttons were pushed to make the forward hangar of a Royal Fleet Auxilliary 'aviation training ship' (RFA *Argus*) available for casualty reception and treatment. The ship was in fact a Falklands War veteran, then serving as the *Contender Bezant*. She had taken and treated two dozen of the burned Welsh Guardsmen who we had been unable to deal with at Ajax Bay.

Twenty-two such modules arrived one sunny morning down in Devonport, on a similar number of big HGV lorries. The frames were lifted up, swung inboard, and carefully lowered onto the forward aircraft lift. With the same hard graft and flexibility that the dockyard mateys had shown in 1982, the 'hospital complex' was soon bolted together. The two-storey, L-shaped building was then secured by anti-sway bracing to the adjacent hangar walls, and powerful air filtration units fitted as the interior was made gas-tight by lining every vertical and horizontal 'seam' with long strips of an impermeable material.

It all worked really well, and the ship went on to do great things, including accepting casualties from two US Navy ships that were mined during the war. *Argus* was right in close to them, whereas the brightly-lit and huge American hospital ships had to remain hundreds of miles further down the Gulf.

With that interesting project completed, it was time to return to the front line again, this time as PMO of the Dartmouth Training Ship, HMS *Bristol*. We actually deployed to the Mediterranean just before the final push against the Iraqi forces in Kuwait, and also took female officer cadets to sea for the first time. A training cruise to the Baltic followed, before the ship returned to Portsmouth for paying off, to become a Harbour Training vessel for Sea Cadets. It was a very happy time for me; I was in amongst all the keenness and enthusiasm of those young officers, so I volunteered to follow my Commanding Officer, Richard Hastilow, to his next appointment as Captain of the Britannia Royal Naval College itself.

After finishing this two year stint at Dartmouth, I returned to the Royal Marines, a privilege which was granted in late 1993 when, in the Acting Higher Rank of Surgeon Captain, I became the Corps Surgeon, based in Portsmouth. On settling down to all the background reading, including a large quantity of documents and files relating to the events of 1982, I found a letter that had been misfiled. It was a nasty, factually incorrect piece of mudslinging written by 'Not Entitled' – about *me*! There was no mention of the fact that Brigadier Julian Thompson had written these words about his medics in the wonderful book *No Picnic*, his masterly account of the Falklands campaign: 'No Brigade has ever been better served by its Senior Medical Officer and the teams that he led'. Instead, there was a recommendation that I should be placed on Quarterly Special Report! What a bummer...

Now I understood why certain senior officers in the medical hierarchy had been so lukewarm in their post-Conflict attitudes to me. It was too late to do anything about it though, because by then the lock gates to promotion were closing. A new series of 'Defence Cost Studies' had been initiated by the Treasury, and the then Conservative Government had signed up to a massive reduction in the provision of medical services to the Armed Forces. When fully implemented, the cuts of *DCS 15* closed all the Service hospitals in the United Kingdom, apart from Haslar, near Portsmouth. This historically important facility had been completely modernised, but was almost useless as a tri-Service asset because of its geographical isolation on a south coast peninsula.

The writing was on the wall, and my name was certainly not visible on the list of those who were adjudged to pee lavender water. Without consultant status or Staff College training on my record, it was time to go. I applied for redundancy, and was released from the Royal Navy at the start of 1996, in the Honorary rank of Surgeon Captain.

Of course, the depth of all this cutting was seriously misjudged by the Ministry of Defence, who then discovered that you could not hire the right medical experience from *Yellow Pages*! So, I spent the first year of my retirement helping out, on a part-time basis, with the care of recruits at the nearby Naval training establishment, HMS *Raleigh*. It was another piece of serendipity, because this enabled me to minimise the shock of disconnection from the Royal Navy. As an Acting Surgeon Captain I'd been a VIP in the hierarchy; now I'd become a 'FIP', or *Formerly Important Person*!

Meanwhile, I continued lecturing on the 'Realities of War' at Sandhurst and the Army Staff College, watching with interest as people like Hew Pike (3 Para in '82) and Michael Rose (CO of 22 SAS) were appointed to command these institutions as they rose steadily in rank. Major General Pike wrote to me and asked for help with one of his paratroopers who wanted to start a Falklands veterans' organsation, in much the same vein as the private soldier who first suggested the British Legion in the early 1920s. Hew's chap had been one of our customers during the fight for Mount Longdon, and had been lucky to survive the artillery shell that blew his right leg off, and all but wrecked his left leg as well.

Denzil Connick survived a horrid convalescence after that, which included the mental torture of some serious PTSD symptoms. The love and devotion of a good woman, his soon-to-be wife Teresa, got him through that and onto the path to recovery, and now here he was trying to help others who were still in transit.

We first met in Hew's office at the HQ of United Kingdom Land Forces, and I took to Denzil immediately.

At this initial formal get-together we agreed to form the South Atlantic Medal Association (1982) as of April 2nd, 1997, the fifteenth anniversary of the Argentine invasion of the Islands, and then appointed the 'founding officers' of SAMA82. I became Chairman, Denzil was appointed Secretary, and Tony Davies, the former RSM of 1st Battalion of the Welsh Guards brought his wisdom and life experience to the post of Treasurer. Our motto was agreed as '*Freedom, from the Sea*'.

I was still looking for a job though, and salvation came through the good offices of a friend from Culdrose days. I was appointed as the Ship's Surgeon of the Royal Mail Ship *St Helena*, a wonderful, compact 6,500 ton passenger ship and freighter that sailed between Cardiff and Cape Town. She is the current lifeline and sole connection to the outside world for the little South Atlantic island whose name she bears. The Napoleonic artefacts and buildings there were absolutely fascinating. Some of the ship's crew had helped the British mine-clearance operations at sea after the Conflict of 1982, while others were working throughout on the airfield at Ascension Island.

I enjoyed the sea time so much that I also took an appointment on the *Saga Rose*, a lovely ex-Cunard cruise liner with predominantly British passengers and officers. The South Atlantic connections of 1982 continued here too. Martin Reed, one of her two Captains, had been Chief Officer of the *Canberra*. The Security Officer was a former Royal Navy Master-at-Arms called Rob 'Whacker' Payne, who also wore the South Atlantic Medal and became a very good friend. We organised 'Armed Services Reunions' on each cruise for anyone who had ever worn the King's or Queen's uniform in their time, and included any American guests who had served their country *after 1777*! We also raised charitable monies for SAMA82, and made sure that the Battle of Trafalgar was remembered properly whenever we passed through the waters off Cadiz in the month of October...

Meanwhile, SAMA82 itself grew apace, and by 1998 we had a 9:1 majority mandate from our growing cohort of members to develop contacts with the Argentine veterans of 1982. Accordingly, I wrote to Mr Tony Lloyd at the Foreign Office and stated that SAMA wished to support Her Majesty's Government with regard to the forthcoming State visit of the Argentine President, Carlos Menem. This initiative was gratefully received, and resulted in a summons to the Crypt of St Paul's Cathedral on October 28th, to witness his laying of a floral tribute to the 258 British dead of the South Atlantic conflict.

In order to ensure that everything went smoothly on the day, we also asked the Foreign Office if all the Argentine veterans accompanying the President (five in total) could be our guests for dinner the previous night. SAMA82 thought it would be a smart and hospitable move if we took our guests to the Argentine restaurant in the Chelsea Farmers' Market, *El Gaucho*. The evening was a splendid success, with the delighted owner, Luis Seygas, only complaining that we had not given him enough notice to prepare and serve a really first-class feast! Some excellent *chorizo* sausages and the huge steaks made those Brits present wonder what on earth he was talking about.

The *vino rioja* was also *muy fantastico*, and Denzil Connick, who had been feeling a bit under the weather, suddenly burst into Celtic song, much to the amusement of our three officer guests. Commander Alvaro Lonzieme, a survivor of the crúiser *General Belgrano*; Major Eduardo Elmiger, a veteran of the Mount Longdon battle in which Denzil lost his leg, and Lieutenant Colonel Gustavo Aguirre Faget, a Dagger jet pilot, were all giggling at the full throated and endless repetitions of *Men of Harlech*.

The other two veterans had both been conscripts, called up for *Operacion Rosario*. Señors Hector Beiroa and Luis Ibanez had declined our invitation to dine, saying that they were wary of meeting anyone from the Press! In fact, they weren't really interested in the reconciliation process at all, as I was to discover later. The rest of us had a good time, although Gustavo fell silent when I told him how unpleasant it was to witness the death of a brave pilot. He asked me for names. When I told him of Pedro Bean, the Dagger pilot 'splashed' by a Sea Wolf missile on Friday May 21st 1982, his face became very sad. He put his loaded fork down and whispered:

'Sir, I was on that mission, and he was my best friend…'

The service at St Paul's the next morning was an impressive success, especially in the effect it had on the two former conscripts. Although they had declined to dine with us, they now found themselves standing with us down in the Crypt, and in a place of honour. Hector Beiroa, my Argentine counterpart, was a bit stunned to find that he and I were the nearest people to President Menem. It was a wonderful occasion, made memorable for me by Mrs Rita Hedicker's presence. This lovely lady's son was killed on Mount Longdon. She had been there when the memorial was first dedicated – but could not look at her late son's name during that service. Now, her heart was bursting with pride during this remarkable event.

President Carlos Menem grasped my hand warmly after the service, but I didn't get to embrace or hug his daughter Zulemita, who looked millimetre-perfect in her classic *haute couture* outfit. The Foreign Office wrote us a nice letter of thanks.

Earlier in the month, I had also been surprised to receive an invitation to attend the 50th birthday celebrations at Buckingham Palace for HRH The Prince of Wales. That Saturday (November 13th) was another splendid occasion, with 850 guests gathered in from every aspect of HRH's diverse interests and charitable involvement. It was impossible to see everything and enjoy all the entertainment laid on in a variety of rooms within the Palace, so Susie and I stuck to the Grand Ballroom. This was full of memories for us, as it was where I'd been invested with the OBE back in February 1983.

I caught HRH's eye at one point, shook his hand and bowed in the usual manner – whereupon he amazed me with the announcement: 'Rick – we're going to Argentina and the Falkland Islands next March. Can you come too?' My positive response was registered by his long suffering Private Secretary, Stephen Lamport, and his Equerry, Lieutenant Commander John Lavery. The two men were smilingly trying to extract The Prince of Wales from the ever-growing throng of his admirers.

Three months later, all the details were confirmed. I arranged for my CV (resumé in American parlance) to be translated into Spanish and e-mailed to the British Embassy, and was also contacted by Nick Tozer, an Anglo-Argentine journalist who we had met at St Paul's. I e-mailed him a list of the 79 Argentine wounded who had general anaesthetic operations whilst in our care. Five of them were labelled 'unknown' due to lack of identification tags whilst unconscious. This e-mail caused some consternation with the Argentine authorities. They sent a return message that all the wounded were fine, but what had this fact got to do with me?

I replied that we had taken them in, operated on them, and then passed them all back to the British Hospital Ship *Uganda*, from whence they were transferred to the Argentine *Buque de Hospital Bahia Paraiso*. The response to this, after a short delay, was a statement that the Argentine doctors were denying this, and claiming that they had been responsible for *all* the care of their injured! By this time I had become slightly cheesed off. I e-mailed back with the killer suggestion that would settle this issue once and for all.

I told them to ask the *wounded* exactly what had happened!

Monday, March 8th

In the evening, we were taken by coach from St James's Palace to Heathrow. After passing through security at a side gate, we arrived at the steps of a gleaming, newly-minted British Airways Boeing 777. If you travelled with The Prince of Wales you went in some style! The Household occupied the Club section, while the 'media mob' of journalists and TV crews had three seats each at the back of the plane. I recognised a couple of them. Nicholas Witchell fronted a very good commercial video of the 1982 Conflict, but I was a little bit puzzled as to why Ms Jenny Bond was chewing gum. Could she really be the BBC's Royal Correspondent?

There was a surprise in store, shortly after take-off. I was standing in the aisle, minus shoes and tie, talking to the official artist, a lovely lady called Susanna Fiennes. She was laughing at my newly minted nickname for her – the '*Daily Sketch*'! Then the Prince's valet called for me, with an invitation to have supper with HRH up in his 'apartment'. I noticed some sly grins on various faces as I hurriedly got dressed again – I'd been stitched up!

The Prince's section had been set up as a combined office, sitting room, dining room and sleeping facility. There were two other guests – Peter Westmacott, 'Director Americas' at the FCO, and Colonel Robert ffrench-Blake, HRH's polo manager. The conversation was wide-ranging, and terrific, but must remain private. Later on, as the big jet slid quietly through the night, it was easy to fall asleep in the fantastic reclining seats, especially after a couple of brandies with Robert Hardman, the *Daily Telegraph* columnist.

Tuesday, March 9th

The shutters came up; there was bright sunlight and a hot towel for my bleary eyes. What looked like the Amazon rainforest was unrolling beneath us, a vast expanse of green that soon turned into the cultivated fields of Uruguay, and then the muddy water of the River Plate estuary. The landing in Buenos Aires was impossibly smooth, but Captain Mike Bull regarded himself as a failure for being two seconds early. The Prince of Wales disembarked with the key members of his Household, and we watched from the cockpit as he boarded a smaller jet for a flight into the city centre's *Aeroparque*.

The rest of the team stayed back, before following by road in a minibus. Traffic around the Plaza St Martin and the Monument to *Los Caidos* (the Argentine fallen) was very dense, and it was a struggle to get through and on to the British Embassy in order to drop off our luggage. Here I met Ian Mason, the very pleasant Third Secretary who was to be my minder and escort during the visit. He was a pleasant, thoughtful Yorkshireman with a dry and quick wit that made him excellent company.

The diplomatic plates on the embassy car helped us get back to the Monument with some despatch. There was already a big crowd watching the action, which included several lines of impressive ceremonial infantry of the Argentine Army's 1st Regiment. Some of the civilian veterans were there and again I was confused by the existence of two main groups, the FVGRA (*Federation de Veteranos de Guerra Republica Argentina*) and AVeGAS (*Agrupacion de Veteranos de Guerra Atlantico Sud*). The FVGRA chairman, Hector Beiroa, was a little bit distant, perhaps still sad at having lost Luis Ibanez, his Vice Chairman, to a heart attack two months ago. He accepted my condolences, then wandered off to talk to some thirty or forty veterans gathered just behind us.

I then met the chairman of the other lot, a cheerful civilian called Carlos Humberto Croci. Here was someone who I could instantly warm to. Carlos spoke quite good English, and was to be my host in the coastal town of Mar del Plata on Wednesday. He was a veteran of the submarine *Santa Fe*, which was caught on the surface by HMS *Endurance's* helicopter in April 1982, and now lies half-submerged in the bay at Grytviken, South Georgia.

The other people in the planned line-up were in uniform, but I did not recognise either of the two *Ejercito* (Army) veterans or the *Armada* (Navy) chaps in their smart white uniforms. The two Air Force officers however were very interesting. One was President Menem's personal pilot, and was in Tomba's Pucara squadron during the Conflict; the other had an interesting name, Major Guillermo Dellepiane. He took part in the attack on HMS *Glasgow*, and put a bomb through the ship without it exploding. He also smacked a cannon shell through one blade of my friend Commodore Simon Thornewill's Mk. 4 Sea King helicopter. When I told him that Major Tomba's helmet used to be on display alongside the holed section of that very same rotor blade, he smiled bravely and expressed a wish that he might inspect it some day!

The ceremony appeared to go well, with HRH laying the big laurel wreath in silence, helped by a rather stern-faced Army officer. There was a minute's pause for reflection, overlaid with the playing of a slow and sad march, presumably the Argentine equivalent of *The Last Post*. The Royal Party then returned to the waiting line of veterans. It was my job to introduce them to HRH, a task which went fairly smoothly, apart from Beiroa's presentation to The Prince of Wales of a document that HRH promised to 'pass on'. More of that later.

There was an amusing hiccup when I introduced Commander Leandro Gurino, the Naval officer from the destroyer ARA *Hercules*, because obviously my words were not spoken clearly enough. The Prince started to compliment him as being one of the brave Argentine C-130 Hercules pilots that he had heard so much about! My fault.

After the Royal Party had gone, the veterans behind us moved up to the main Monument, which consisted of a series of grey slate plaques arranged in a semi-circle and engraved with the names of the dead. On the open marble platform before these chiselled names, they started to sing patriotic songs about the war, culminating with an episode of collective hopping about and shouts of '*If you can't jump up and down, you must be English*'. It was some sort of football supporter behaviour, which I did not quite understand. It also seemed rather undignified and inappropriate for this location, even sacrilegious.

As individuals however, the veterans were all very friendly when I moved amongst them – before being ambushed by a *mobillero* crew, a TV team with a blonde lady front of camera. The interview went well until she said quite pointedly:

'Why is it that an Argentine passport holder can go anywhere in the world except the Malvinas?'

This question got a straight bat, right into the block hole:

'Why ask me? I'm just a retired old warhorse!'

Her face registered much disappointment with this reply.

I then got to look at a copy of the FVGRA document. It was in perfect English, but downright insulting. It stated that Prince Charles was not really welcome in Argentina, that his 'royal blood' was just the same as anyone else's, and that in Argentina all men are equal. How could they justify being so offensive to an important guest of their country? Had the author ever seen the two quite different field ration packs for Argentine officers and men? *Equal?* Time for a reality check, *amigo*!

We moved on to the hotel to check in, and then it was time to proceed, without lunch, to the Naval Hospital in the northern suburbs. I was delighted to be travelling with Rear Admiral Rodolfo Moreno, head of the medical branch of the Argentine Navy. It was ironic that his British opposite number, Surgeon

Commodore Ian Jenkins, who had just been appointed Medical Director General of the Royal Navy, was presently in close attendance on The Prince of Wales.

The hospital was a huge building and I was rather happy to discover that it was commanded by a four-ring Marine Captain who was a Malvinas veteran having encountered the Scots Guards on Mount Tumbledown. His name was Hugo Santillan. There was a brief press conference, and lots of photographs, followed by a nice surprise. One of the Navy doctors, Surgeon Commander Jose Alberto Montivero, produced a framed X-ray of Corporal Nigel Peters' bullet-smashed left arm. This Royal Marine was injured in South Georgia, and well cared for by the Argentine medics. I promised to try and find Nigel when I got back to England. We then filed into the main auditorium, and then I began to tell, for the umpteenth time, the story of 'The Red and Green Life Machine'.

Our little facility in the Ajax Bay mutton processing plant, plus its twin subordinates at Fitzroy Cove and Teal Inlet, treated nearly 200 Argentine casualties, of whom 78 or so underwent major surgical procedures. Captain Santillan translated fluently as I went through the story. Over half of the tri-service audience were themselves veterans. Then, after we stopped for a cup of tea, they told me what it was like for them! The doctors were a charming, thoughtful and pleasant lot. I did not envy the Air Force chap who had to endure the RAF Vulcan bombing raid. Twenty-one 1000 lb bombs, descending onto Stanley airfield at four o'clock in the morning, apparently had a rather marked effect on one's intestinal functions...

They also showed me pictures of Jeff Glover, the RAF Harrier pilot who was shot down, on May 21st 1982, with a British Blowpipe missile fired by an Argentine Army officer. Jeff ejected at high speed and very low level, sustaining an unpleasant arm injury. He almost drowned, but was saved and treated well by his captors. They were now delighted to hear that their patient had recovered so well that he had gone on to fly with the Red Arrows.

One thing puzzled me though. None of the Argentine doctors mentioned the British input to their wounded, and there was no reference to us at Ajax Bay, or to the hospital ship *Uganda* in a little book that I was presented with. It must all have been a bit embarrassing for them.

Then it was back to the hotel, and barely time to change for the President's banquet. The gracious furniture and fittings of the Alvear Palace Hotel looked superb under the glittering chandeliers. I got ambushed by Jenny Bond, who was still relentlessly chewing gum. She lined me up for a radio interview against a charmingly smooth Argentine Congressman. Careful words were exchanged, then it was in for dinner, which was excellent – and very stylishly served. Eyebrows went up on our table as the Prince's wishes for harmony between an 'old but small democracy offshore' and the 'new and bigger mainland one' were also digested.

I was sitting next to a beautiful banker's daughter who, when I ventured an opinion as to the charm and attractiveness of Zulemita Menem, stated very firmly that in Argentina, she was not really considered beautiful at all! Having sighted some of the loose-limbed and languid specimens of Argentine womanhood on the streets of Buenos Aires, I could see her point, but couldn't possibly have agreed!

I missed the subsequent tango demonstration, because we had to leave early and go to the television studios of Channel 13 for a live programme hosted by a chap called Santo Viasati. I had lent his production team some video of Ajax Bay taken during the Conflict, and had also been told to await some surprises. Brigadier Tomba then strode on to the set, a compact, handsome man, with his lined face wreathed in smiles. He was followed by the tall, impressive and familiar figure of Colonel Horacio Losito, who I last saw with a gaping bullet wound in his right leg seventeen years before.

The other guests were Hector Beiroa, Doctor Julio Municoy, a civilian intensive care specialist who volunteered for military service in 1982 and ended up as a PoW, and a chap called Hector Cisneros – whose brother died in the war – and who now chaired the 'Malvinas Families Assocation'. Nick Tozer was also present. He had a fantastic appetite and memory for detail concerning the Conflict. I liked him, and formed the same good opinion of his friend Colonel Tomas Fernandez, the chap who did for Jeff Glover's Harrier during the Conflict, and who also rescued him from the sea.

The programme began, I was introduced to the viewing audience and then had the enormous pleasure of returning Major Tomba's helmet to its rightful owner. I had 'borrowed' this item from him in 1982, and for the past sixteen years it had been on display at the Fleet Air Arm museum. The Brigadier was obviously well pleased and proud, and gave a very moving statement to endorse this.

Like all the combatants in the war, he was proud to have done his duty, but still felt in his heart that the Malvinas belonged to Argentina. Nonetheless, he understood that his British opponents took a different view. He then recounted how my initial request for his help with translating in Ajax Bay led him to think that he was being squeezed for military intelligence and information! When he realised that our efforts were purely humanitarian on behalf of the Argentine *heridos* (wounded), he was proud to help. Colonel Losito said much the same thing, and Doctor Municoy too.

Señor Cisneros, however, was of the opinion that the Argentine dead were pushing them on to ultimate victory, but seemed unsure when I later asked him (privately) what he thought the British dead were doing from the same celestial position! He gave me that blank look that I always seemed to get when asking my Argentine friends any awkward questions. I was not quite sure whether it was tactical deafness or selective amnesia at work, but it tended to slow the discussion process down.

Señor Beiroa, receiving whispers in his ear at each break from an unsmiling individual who was the FVGRA Treasurer, by name of Gonzales Trejo, was of the opinion that there should be absolutely no dialogue or reconciliation between veterans until Argentine sovereignty over the Islands had been restored. I pointed out to him that, as Chairman of SAMA82 I was not exactly in a position to meet his wishes, but that as long as we were speaking, the process of reconciliation was actually taking place.

After the final break, Santo Viasati read out transcripts of the phone calls and e-mails that had been received while we were on air. One of them was from Colonel Losito's children: '*Thank you Doctor Jolly, for saving our father's life so he can be with us today – and we send you lots of love…*'

Straight to the heart that one, and it almost reached the lacrimal glands too. The conversation proceeded pleasantly – but Santo Viasati ended with his back to us, face to camera, signing off by stating that the 'Islas Malvinas' were a sacred cause to the Argentine people…

Pretty knackered by then, I was driven back to the hotel and fell asleep with the bedside light still on.

Wednesday 10th March

It was another bright and sunny day. The air was cool, which was a welcome relief for the citizens of Buenos Aires. I was to have a magazine interview with *Gente* at 11 o'clock, so there was time to walk around, sit down over a coffee and watch the passers-by. The girls were simply beautiful, skinny and tightly clothed. Any (male) close inspection was usually met with a quick check to see if you really *were* looking, followed by a disdainful sneer.

It was also apparent that this nation respected its grandparents and loved its children. The strength of family feelings, and the way that these were integrated with patriotic sentiment for the Motherland were strongly featured. What a paradox it was then that, prior to 1982, in *La Guerra Sucia* (the 'Dirty War') families could be destroyed on the merest suspicion of subversion. The sight of a white Ford Falcon sedan, of the type used by the security police, still provoked deep-seated and unpleasant memories. No one knew how many of *los desaparecidos* ('the disappeared ones') actually went missing. Some say it was 10,000, while others put the figure at nearer 16,000. I had seen some of their faces staring out from an internet site that was linked circumstantially to SAMA's on the World Wide Web. If those bloodied walls in the cellars of the Navy Mechanic's School could speak, what horrors they would recount.

The *Gente* interview was in panel format, and went reasonably well, with strong and patriotic sentiments being expressed once more from Brigadier Tomba, still proudly clutching his flying helmet. I really liked him, and Colonel Losito too. Doctor Julio Municoy claimed that there was never any objectionable behaviour by Argentine troops in *Puerto Argentino* (their name for Stanley). Horacio Losito backed this up, stating quite firmly that such misbehaviour would have been very severely punished.

I had to agree that, to our knowledge, there were no serious crimes such as assault or rape, although there were certainly some unpleasant incidents like guns being pointed at people who refused to take down Her Majesty's portrait from their walls. However, I then went on to say that the internal state of Stanley Post Office was a memory that would remain with me for the rest of my life. Some very angry young conscripts had defaecated in several places there, and then used sheets of stamps bearing the Queen's head as toilet paper. They all looked shocked at this story, and fell silent. I finished with the observation that, if reconciliation was to be successful, then we would have to be honest with each other, since openness and truth were the preludes to forgiveness.

The taxi ride back to the Embassy was a real eye-opener. Juan Fangio, the Argentine who was the greatest racing driver of all time, appeared to have had many sons, all of whom were now taxi drivers in Buenos Aires. Forward velocity is one thing, but the side-to-side lane changing and gap-spotting was combined with remarkable speed over the ground, to create a rather breathtaking experience. The driver grinned at my shocked expression and explained that he liked high speed 'very good...' I could certainly testify to that!

Thursday, March 11th

Those lovely mornings were becoming routine. The skies above Buenos Aires appeared devoid of pollution as we drove to the Aeroparque near the city centre, and boarded a Boeing 737 for the flight to Mar del Plata. Here we were met by a group of veterans of a different hue, the *Agrupacion de Veteranos de Guerra Atlantico Sud* (AVeGAS), led by Carlos Croci. His was the submarine caught on the surface by HMS *Endurance's* helicopter. The British pilot's attack was made more difficult by the fact that he had been the dinner guest of the sub's CO, Commander Horacio Bicain, only three weeks before! Holed through its conning tower, the submarine could not dive. Her crew were taken prisoner, returning to Uruguay via the hold of RFA *Tidespring* and a roundabout journey from South Georgia to Montevideo, via Ascension Island.

Those chaps were wonderful; they were proud, open and friendly. I was taken to the War Memorial in the centre of the town, then stood and listened as a roll call was made of the eleven residents of Mar del Plata who died in the Conflict. Each name was met with a collective shout of '*Presente!*' from all the veterans. I laid the floral tribute and stood back, with my panama hat removed and held against my chest. I felt just as sad as I do on every Remembrance Sunday at the Cenotaph in Whitehall, or at home. It was obvious that the Argentine veterans could sense this grief and found it to be genuine, because they all shook my hand with warmth and affection.

From Señora Artuso, widow of the Petty Officer who was killed in the tragic accident while the submarine was being moved later across Grytviken harbour, there was a warm embrace. She was desperate to visit the place where her husband died. I really did wish that I could help her. We were then whizzed off to meet the Mayor in his parlour, and then be taken up to the bluff behind this lovely city for a look at the submarine base. Targets everywhere! I had to remind myself that I was now a civilian.

Half an hour's drive then brought us to the Estancia Coronel Vidal, now the home of a wonderful man called Felix Pedro Imaroni. He had been a civilian administrator in the Islands during the Argentine occupation. Our most gracious host wore the traditional *gaucho* outfit of embroidered shirt, loose black trousers, and knife hanging from a waist belt. He and his wife could not have been more genuine or profound in their welcome. We all sat down to a traditional *asado*, an open-air barbecue held under a sunlight-dappled canopy of trees. The tables were arranged in a T-shape, with my position in the place of honour in front of joint British and Argentine flags. There were over three dozen people here, all enjoying the family friendship that was such a feature of these typically Argentine gatherings.

The wine flowed, and great chunks of delicious meat arrived with surprising regularity as I tried to eat and talk at the same time. Particularly important to me was a conversation with Carlos Cachon, a small, dark, former Argentine air force veteran who led the A-4 Skyhawk attack on RFA *Sir Galahad*. Our little facility at Ajax Bay received 160 casualties that evening, and when I showed him some pictures of the pitifully burned and Flamazine-covered casualties, his eyes wrinkled with pain. I tried to reassure him that we had no anger or enmity towards him, because he was only doing *his* job. He was obviously a brave and sensitive man, and had apparently visited Simon Weston at his home in Wales.

We whizzed into town in the mayoral limousine, with a motorcycle escort efficiently clearing the traffic in front of us. After a brief stop in the Mayor's parlour for the inevitable TV and radio interviews, watched by his gorgeous twin daughters looking upward through the forest of microphones, it was time to lay another wreath. I was helped in translation by a Danish lady, married to an Argentine, who later on suckled her babe at the breast during one of the interviews.

Reconciliation between military men is a matter that *could* be independent of the subject of sovereignty. We'd simply got to try. My hosts all spoke of the pain inflicted on them by being ignored by the Argentine masses following their return from the Islands. Some of them even had stones thrown at them. Their anguish was matched only by their readiness to blame the United States for helping us, the British, to defeat them.

One of their spokesmen was very keen to ask for help from the British in the Argentine programme for dealing with PTSD (Post Traumatic Stress Disorder). The veterans also thanked me for using both terms 'Malvinas' and 'Falklands' interchangeably when speaking of the Islands. It was a sensitive point, and maybe I was not subtle enough to worry about it; one is a Spanish word and the other English. It was not a sticky problem for me, but I suspected the Falkland Islanders themselves would disagree most strongly! Then it was off to the airport again, with that million-aire feeling as our own private jet whisked Ian Mason and me through a clear night sky, back to Buenos Aires.

Saturday, March 13th

After a free day for sightseeing, it was another sunny afternoon in Paradise. I took a walk down across the city to the *Carrefour* hypermarket, where the meat counter was difficult to believe, with 6 pesos per kilo (about £2 per lb) the charge for some really excellent-looking beef. The wine was cheap too, with brand names like '*Colon*', and even '*Menem*'! Later on, it was time for supper, at the unusually early hour of 9 o'clock, with Carlos Doglioli. He brought along a great pal who he called 'Luchita', a retired journalist from the mass-market newspaper, *Clarin*, plus his wife. The four of us made noisy company as we recounted the tales of 1982 to each other.

Because of his excellent English, Carlos had been one of the joint deputies to Brigadier General Menéndez, in his role as the temporary Governor of the Islands between April 2nd and June 14th 1982. He'd shared these duties with a Major Guillermo Buitrago, the last Argentine army officer to attend the British Army Staff College at Camberley. How excited Major Buitrago must have felt when he heard some politician (probably that cerebral toad John Nott) state, in a 1981 lecture to the course, that the 'British would never again conduct an amphibious landing...' Guillermo and Carlos were both the British military's guests, under rather different circumstances, the following summer.

I told them how disappointed I was that some of the Argentine veterans had adopted a stance which linked sovereignty to any process of reconciliation. We wondered how we might have actively tackled this business of reconciliation, before parting company at 3 am. As we left, I noticed a couple just starting into their dinner. These Argentine people were simply amazing!

Sunday March 14th

After a good breakfast I took a stroll round the nearby park, then at midday was picked up by Admiral Santiago Moreno and his wife Adela. I'd already met this tall, thin and elegantly greying man, the Medical Director of the Argentine Navy; his lovely, sparkling wife spoke excellent English. We had a terrific time in a restaurant converted from the old British warehouses down on the river. The restaurant was all cool elegance and filtered sunlight; the food started with a huge smorgasbord display, and ended up with brochette after brochette of meat from the wood fire. It seemed as if every part of the bullock was served to us during this Sunday *asado*, even its barbecued thyroid (which was really delicious!).

We then moved on to the pork and finally a piece of mountain goat! These warm and generous people also gave me a leather purse for Susie, to add to a beautiful coffee table book on the ARA *Libertad*, the sail training ship with both an important past and present in the Argentine Navy. Then it was back to the hotel again for a *siesta*, thank goodness.

At 6 pm, it was time for yet more hospitality, this time from Naval Aviation. I was picked up from the hotel by the retired Captain Jorge Colombo, whose Super Etendard squadron was, pound for pound, the most effective unit of either side in the whole 1982 Conflict. With only five aircraft and six Exocet missiles, he and his men sank two ships, and tied the British fleet defences up in knots. It seemed rather unlikely that this charming, sleek and grey-moustachioed man was also one of the finest carrier aviators ever to draw breath. He was also thoughtful and witty.

We returned to his house in the suburbs and there met Rear Admiral Roberto Agotegoray, in charge of Argentine naval aviation, who had been Colombo's Operations Officer back in 1982. He was of Basque origin. We talked long into the night, yet again.

The Admiral was disappointed that I could not go with him to Espora naval airbase the next day, to look around the Museum and perhaps sit in a Super Etendard. Of many generous invitations, this was the one that I didn't really want to refuse – but I had to. He had heard that I was giving my own flying helmet to his museum, and was keen to get hold of other British pieces of naval flying kit if possible. 'Like a Sea Harrier?' I asked, innocently. The Admiral chuckled, especially as I had just told him of every SHAR pilot's dream from 1982 – to be in the 'six o'clock position' behind an Argentine Navy Super Etendard, with the Sidewinder infra-red seeker heads growling in his headphones...

Monday, March 15th

This was my last day in Argentina. Chacho Munoz, the editor of *Soldados* magazine, arrived at the hotel to interview me. Our discussions were a little more technical than those in the meeting with *Gente*. They centred on how the spirit of reconciliation and a new professionalism in the all-volunteer *Ejercito* (rather than the hapless conscripts of 1982) had seen a good relationship develop recently between a British and Argentine battalion on UN service in Cyprus.

Ian Mason then came to collect me with Ugo, the splendid Embassy driver; we proceeded just after midday to the Palacio San Martin, where I was met by the *Chef de Protocol* and escorted upstairs into a chandeliered waiting room. Here we were joined by the British Ambassador, Mr William Marsden CMG and his deputy, Dominic, a nice man who bore the distinguished surname of Asquith.

There were some familiar faces amongst the Argentine military uniforms out in the main reception area. These were suddenly joined by a dimly-remembered visage. To my astonishment, I was looking at the former *Teniente* Luis Bruin. This great bear of a man had sustained multiple gunshot wounds of his legs in the fight for Top Malo House, on 31st May 1982. I had despaired of ever seeing him again, having been told that he had been 'cashiered' (sacked) from the *Ejercito* for involvement in an officer's revolt against both Presidents Alfonsin and Menem. Apparently, he'd teamed up with his old boss in the Islands, a strange chap called Sein-eldin, and they became the *carapintada*, or 'masked ones'. This insurrection failed, and they were all chucked into outer darkness. Yet here he was now, large as life and grinning happily. I was subjected to a series of classic Argentine bear hugs. His wife kissed me much more gently in her grateful thanks...

Eventually we were ushered in to a rather grand hall where about fifty of the Argentine veterans, most of them wounded war veterans who had passed through Ajax Bay, were standing in a hollow square. The citation was read out. My lady interpreter had a weak voice and I could barely hear her explain that, in recognition of all the efforts by British medical personnel to assist wounded Argentine citizens in 1982, the Government had directed that I was to be made an *'Officer of the Order of May, with Merit'.*

The Foreign Minister, Señor Guido di Tella, a most charming and rather donnish figure, then took an ornate ribbon and medal from its bright red velvet box and pinned the thing to my jacket pocket. He then addressed the group in Spanish, followed by my contribution in English, which again suffered in its translation because of the interpreter's quiet voice. Also, when I used a term that she did not understand, she simply ignored it. When, for instance, I referred to all the British medics in the various 'echelons' of medical care who must share in this award, there was an empty silence.

Nonetheless, I tried to point out to my audience that we had not cared for our Argentine patients because of some military command or international convention, but simply because we were human beings who respected life. Furthermore, I stated the hope that our countries would never again go to war over this particular issue. Knowing Señor Di Tella's professional interest in history, I also repeated Winston Churchill's dictum that '*jaw, jaw*' was always better than '*war, war*'; Ian Mason had already translated this for me, and it came out as '*habla, habla – no peliar, peliar*'.

Everyone smiled at that, then it was champagne, more embraces and lots of photographs. One of the wounded NCOs asked me to sign his medical discharge papers, confirming that he had indeed been under my care in Ajax Bay! The whole episode passed in something of a blur. I would have liked it to go on longer, but we had to take our leave. British Airways was calling. Slowly, we retraced our steps to the entrance, and then Ugo took us in the Embassy Rover to the Monument of the Fallen in the nearby Plaza San Martin, the place where our visit had begun just six days before.

After a short interval, we were joined by the veterans who had been at the Palacio. A photographer lined us up, and Ian took some good pictures as well. We all stood, in the blazing sunshine, in a curved line. Then I stepped forward, and laid a chaplet of scarlet poppies down at the monument's centre, between the two guards who presented arms in salute. There was a moment's silence amidst the roar of passing traffic, all the uniformed officers saluting as we thought quietly about the dead. But timetables and departure schedules were pressing, so I had to leave for the airport. I took hurried goodbyes of all my new found friends. I did not really want to go, but a Club Class upgrade eased the sadness. It was the dream ending to an amazing trip, all thanks to the thoughtful kindness of The Prince of Wales.

After Easter, I wrote to Her Majesty the Queen to inform her of the Argentine award, and requested her instructions as to what I should do with this medal. I had by now discovered that the grade '*Oficial*' (Officer) within the '*Orden de Majo*' (Order of

May) was analogous to the OBE which she had invested me with in February 1983. The reply was swift. Her Chief Clerk informed me by letter that she had '*the honour to inform* (me) *that The Queen had granted me Unrestricted Permission to wear the insignia...*'

It all makes for a rather unusual medal group. I don't know if anyone else has ever been decorated by both sides for their services in the *same* campaign! I wear this Argentine tribute on behalf of all the British paramedics, medical and nursing officers who looked after the Argentine wounded in 1982.

Each and every one of us could be proud that we fulfilled the wishes expressed by Vice Admiral Lord Nelson in his Prayer written before the 1805 Battle of Trafalgar – and his death in action just a few hours later:

'*May humanity, after the Victory, be the predominant feature of the British Fleet...*'

I was also hearing good things about many 'Red and Green' veterans. Jim Ryan, for instance, the charming Irishman with endless energy and a delightful sense of humour seemingly unaffected by personal experience of the bombing of *Sir Galahad*, became a leading light behind the new 'Diploma in Medical Care of Catastrophe' awarded in London by the Society of Apothecaries, and combined this with the distinction of an appointment in the University of London as the Leonard Cheshire Professor of Post-Conflict Recovery. He was also Director of A&E Services at University College; the new Accident & Emergency Department opened just a few days before the July 7th bombings of 2005.

His Army colleague, the redoubtable Mike von Bertele, stayed in the Service, made it to Major General, and is still serving. Erich Bootland broke through the previous promotion ceiling for RN Medical Service officers and reached the rank of Captain before retiring. Howard Oakley became a world-ranking guru in the subject of 'Trench Foot' (Non-Freezing Cold Injury), as well as a national authority on everything to do with Apple

Mac computers! Corporal John Clare, one of my 'steady men', also did well. He was commissioned in the Royal Marines, reached the rank of Lieutenant Colonel, and finished his time in an important NATO appointment. Hooray for all of them.

Early in 2002, I decided to retire from the sea, my hand forced by having developed the early signs of insulin-dependent diabetes. By sheer luck, I found a wonderful job doing medicals for applicants in the Plymouth region intent on joining the Royal Navy, Royal Marines, and Royal Air Force. It was also time to step down as Chairman of SAMA82, and my friend Martin Reed, who had also just retired from sea service, agreed to take over. However, before I went, I was determined to fulfil a long-cherished ambition – which was to organise, raise the money for, and then lead a Pilgrimage to the Falkland Islands to coincide with Remembrance Sunday that year.

Chartering a suitable aircraft was a problem, at least until I encountered a man called John Romo, who worked for Air 2000 at Gatwick. John was a real enthusiast, who subscribed wholeheartedly to what I was trying to do. Not only was one of their Boeing 757s made mine for eight days, he also ensured that all the flight crews were ex-Service, including three pilots who were veterans of the Conflict. Nothing was too much trouble as our 215 passenger slots started to fill. The Royal Navy Benevolent Trust supported the deserving RN and RM cases, while the Army Benevolent Fund swung in behind the Paras (mainly) and other veterans who were in need. I was handling all the cheques and donations personally since I'd chartered the aircraft in my own name. It meant that on one occasion I had to dip into my own savings to meet a stage payment, but that was the only real hiccup! The readers of the *Sunday Express* also kicked in, thanks to a fine article by their chief reporter Anna Pukas about Jim Davidson's involvement.

Eventually we gathered at Gatwick, and were waved off by Lady Thatcher. Some of the Welsh Guards veterans were really nervous, and reluctant to board the aircraft. One of them was a chap called Neil Wilkinson, who got off at the train station which is part of the airport, and then returned there twice before he was spotted, and then gently steered through the check-in process. As a group, the Welsh Guardsmen sat together in the middle of the aircraft, with my former Naval colleague Dr Morgan O'Connell (now of *Combat Stress*) in amongst them. I read everyone a bidding letter from HRH The Prince of Wales after take-off, then introduced Chris Greaves, our co-pilot, who in 1982 had been flying one of the Navy Sea Kings that lifted the Welshmen off *Galahad*. After that, everything went really well.

There were refuelling stops at Banjul and Rio de Janeiro (where the *Girl from Ipanema* failed to turn up with coffee), and we arrived in the Falklands at some ungodly hour, long before dawn. There to greet us (with a handshake for each and every Pilgrim) was the Military Commander, Commodore Richard Ibbotson DSC. He then provided a 'full Monte' English breakfast for us all.

We were staying, in the main, with the Islanders themselves, and soon became submerged in a tidal wave of love and gratitude that had a profound effect. All the major battlefield sites were visited, including Ajax Bay after a tough and bumpy drive. For safety reasons, the galley area had been partially demolished by explosive charges, and it was all looking rather sad in the afternoon light, but the holes made by two of the bombs that penetrated into the roof space were now clearly visible in an adjoining wall. It was almost impossible to imagine the wet and dark inner compartments behind this as being associated with a 'House of Healing'...

The return of our Welsh Guardsmen and Royal Fleet Auxiliary personnel, in company with about 60 other Pilgrims, to Fitzroy Cove was also very moving. There is a memorial here that overlooks the anchorage where the two logistic landing ships, RFAs *Sir Galahad* and *Sir Tristram*, were bombed and set on fire on June 8th 1982. As two of the Pilgrims were a priest and a Medical Officer who had been involved on the day, a short account was given by these eye-witnesses. Then an impromptu memorial service was conducted, which ended with the sounding of *The Last Post*, played by another of the Pilgrims (a *Scots* Guardsman!) who had brought his cornet. Most of the Welshmen were overcome with emotion, and many shed tears, some for the first time in over twenty years. Their general physical demeanour also changed, and they began to look much happier.

The wonderful Steve Hughes of 2 Para, now a consultant orthopaedic surgeon, operated on a young Islander with a complex leg fracture. We had brought the instruments down with us! This saved huge amounts of time and money in that the patient did not need to be flown back to England, but what was really interesting was the fact that Steve had also treated the lad for D&V as a baby, following 2 Para's liberation of the population of Goose Green.

The Memorial Services also had a positive impact, and were attended by our aircrew as well. The Governor held a Reception, spread over two evenings, to which everyone was invited. The media got their in-depth stories, and I renewed acquaintance with many other old friends, including some of the St. Helenian catering staff with whom I'd previously served in the Royal Mail Ship.

As an additional aspect to our visit, I had arranged for two pairs of South Atlantic Medal facsimiles to be struck at the Royal Mint, in gold and silver. The latter pair was presented by the Pilgrims to our hosts, as a token of heartfelt thanks (and can now be seen in the Stanley museum). The gold set returned to England with us. They had toured all the major battlefields, been to sea in the South Atlantic guardship – and then been flown above Sovereign British territory in a RAF Tornado F3 fighter. All too soon it became time to leave.

In the Departure Lounge at Mount Pleasant, I saw Neil Wilkinson again. Twenty years previously, he had been the second worst burns casualty after Simon Weston, and was now a bright pink colour, with a large grin on his previously grey and lined face. We had warned everyone about the powerful effects of the sun resulting from depletion of the ozone layer in these southern latitudes, but Neil had obviously been out every single day. I remarked that he was looking a bit different just a week on from Gatwick (referring to his cheerful, smiling face), but he misunderstood me, thinking I was talking about his pinkness: 'You know, Doc, I've only been to the Falklands twice – and both times I got ruddy burnt!'

My heart turned over in my chest. Neil was *better*, and laughing at himself with the military black humour that shows an intact mental coping strategy at work. We eventually rotated from the runway at Mount Pleasant after a very long take-off run, thanks to the extra baggage now loaded on board, mostly rocks and stones being taken home for friends...

The journey home was characterised by a lot of quiet and reflective thinking, plus a general atmosphere of satisfaction and feeling that the financial outlay and fund-raising efforts had all been worthwhile. Many individuals commented how the positive welcome by the Islanders themselves had been critical in helping them to come to terms with their memories.

A burst tyre at Banjul airport, due to debris on the runway, then led to an unplanned seven hour delay. This interval was put to good use by the *Combat Stress* team, who held an impromptu clinic in the airport buildings for all their clients. A further eight Pilgrims approached them there, and asked to be registered with the organisation for future treatment and psychotherapy.

I tried to assess the Pilgrimage's effectiveness with a 'snap-shot' questionnaire; 137 of the 180 forms were returned for marking, giving a response rate of 76%. The subjects asked about were 'sleeping', 'flashbacks', feelings of 'contentment and happiness', 'alcohol intake' – and a wife or partner's perceptions. Four out of five responding Pilgrims had improved, in that they judged their feelings of contentment to be 'better' or 'much better'. The validity of this assessment was endorsed by three out of five spouses or partners confirming that such an improvement had indeed occurred.

Although responders were instructed not to append additional comments on the questionnaire sheet, some did. It was interesting to note how many of these reflected a sentiment expressed in the many 'thank-you' letters, most along the general lines of '*Op CORPORATE was like a huge jigsaw puzzle – bewildering and a bit frightening. Now I know that I've been back, seen the ground and met the other veterans, I've got much more understanding of exactly where I fitted in...*' I also felt uplifted by one wife's letter – '*Thank you for returning to me the man that I remember from before the Conflict...*'

It would be appropriate here to record another unique (and quite unexpected) benefit. The majority of Pilgrims had seen the Task Force's ultimate destination, Stanley, in an unpleasant and filthy mess when they arrived there on or after June 14th 1982. The streets were full of discarded rubbish, most of it deposited by the Argentine military, and the amount of human ordure (from the same source) was appalling. Nearly twenty-one years later, the streets were clean and well-paved, there was a plethora of new buildings, the citizens were cheerful and welcoming and, perhaps most important of all, there were children everywhere, all of them knowledgable about the '82 Conflict, and grateful to the visiting veterans for securing their freedom and their future.

The Pilgrimage had a positive effect on the Islanders too. They decided that funds would be made available each year for half-a-dozen veterans to fly down to the Islands in November for Remembrance Sunday. Repeat Pilgrimages have subsequently been organised, and just before the 30th Anniversary events commence, plans are well in hand for the 2012 journey.

I also found myself thinking along strategic and global, rather than *national* lines. What if the balance of military power in the Pacific began to change? Would a certain Asian nuclear power seek to expand its hegemony into the Atlantic? If so, would it not be a good tactical move to have an 'aircraft carrier' permanently moored down near the 'choke point' between Antarctica and Cape Horn? Could the Falkland Islands, with its 10,000 foot long runway, become that Free World 'carrier' asset? No doubt, somebody in a much higher pay grade than mine, is thinking about all this...

In December 2002, Her Majesty the Queen gave four of us an audience at Buckingham Palace, where we presented her with our Golden Jubilee tribute and an album. After photographs were taken, she asked about our Pilgrimage. We said that we had heard that she was not best pleased to be told that all her portraits and photographs had been taken down, at gunpoint, by the Argentine forces that had invaded the Falklands in April 1982.

Furthermore, we understood that she had summoned Her Armed Forces that same day, and issued instructions for us to get down there and put all those pictures back up again!

Her Majesty's voice tinkled with laughter at this rather unusual analysis of the Conflict. We then told her how proud we had been that she had sent her second son to help us in the fight. That important fact had also made her the senior South Atlantic Mum! The Queen seemed a little taken aback at first, but then smiled again, and her voice was tinged with pride when she replied: 'Do you know, no-one has *ever* said that to me before – and *thank you!*'

THE MEN OF THE
RED AND GREEN LIFE MACHINE

Medical Squadron,
Commando Logistic Regt,
Royal Marines

Headquarters Troop (21 May–19 June) Ajax Bay
Surg. Cdr Rick Jolly RN
Lt Fred Cook RM; Surg. Lts Martyn Ward, Graham Briers RN; FCMA Bryn Dobbs RN; WO2 Terry Moran RM; CPOMA 'Scouse' Davies; POMA Eddie Middleton; Cpls 'Gigs' Worthington, 'Sigs' Rennie; L/Cpl Billy Noble; Mnes Charlie Cork, John Naughton, 'Radar' Shields, Mark Cridland and Pete Pearson.

No. 1 Troop (21 May–3 June Ajax Bay, then Teal Inlet)
Sub Lt Malcolm Hazell RN
Surg. Lt Howard Oakley RN; CPOMAs John Smith, 'Nutty' Edwards; Sgt John Simmonds RM; POMA 'Jacko' Jackson; LMAs Jock Winton, Andy Ellis, Rod Cain, Dave Cook; Cpls Tom Robinson, Cy Worral, John Clare; MAs Taff Barlow, Nick Vrettos, 'Porky' Greaves, Derek Whitfield; Mnes Fraz Coates, Gene Jago, Scouse Currall, Jock Ewing, Jim Giles, Dave Gowland, John Nelson, Taff Price, Ray Whittaker, Robby Robinson, Chris Thornton, 'Tojo' Hughes, Kev Frankland, Taff Evans, John Thurlow, Dougy Duggan, Neil Blaind and Steve Gosling.

No. 3 Troop (from SS *Canberra* 2 June–19 June) Ajax Bay
Lt Erich Bootland RN
CPOMA 'Jethro' Young; Sgt Paul Demery RM; POMAs Roger
Beck, Jack Sibbald; Cpls Andy Christy, 'Pusser' Hill; LMAs Terry
Andrews, Phil King; L/Cpls Jan Mills, Jock Inglis; MAs Dave
Burdett, Derek Taylor, Chris Penney, Col Glover, Andy Blocke,
Mnes Mark Bunyan, Jock Cordiner, Gav Fleming, Roy Finbow,
Dave Gooding, Col Hewitson, 'Spud' Hudd, Gerry O'Donovan,
'Bumble' Hollis, Tim O'Keefe, Dave Needham, Jeff Phillips,
'Smudge' Smith, Garry Treacher, 'Timber' Woods and Bungy
Williams.

No. 2 RN Surgical Support Team (RN Hospital, Plymouth)
(21 May–19 June) Ajax Bay
Surg. Lt Cdr Phil Shouler RN
Surg. Cdr George Rudge RN; Surg. Lt Cdrs Andy Yates, Nick
Morgan and Tim Douglas Riley RN; FCMT Dave Price RN;
MT1s John Davis, Steve Davies, Trevor Firth, Stu McKinley,
Tony Byrne; MT2 Bob Griffin; POMA Chris Lloyd; L MAs John
Billingham, Phil Evans, Ken Parkin, Dave Poole, Kev Dooley,
Alec Pickthall; MAs Geoff Evans, Tom Boyd, Simon Judge, Kevin
Shore and Al Wallace; MT4 Steve Garth.

RN Task Group Surgical Team (7 June–19 June)
Surg. Lt Cdrs Tony Mugridge and Sean Tighe RN; MT1 Malcolm
Wotton; LMA Steve Walsh

Elements No. 1 RN Surgical Team (RN Hospital, Haslar)
(30 May–19 June) HMS *Hermes*, then Ajax Bay
Surg. Lt Cdr Ian Geraghty; CMT Murray Bowden; POMA Bob
Johnson; LMAs Steve Moutrey and Carl Rich

Elements of No. 3 RN Surgical Team (from SS *Canberra*)
(3 June–19 June) Ajax Bay
Surg. Cdr John Williams RN

Parachute Clearing Troop, 16 Field Ambulance RAMC
Headquarters, Reception, Resuscitation and Holding Sections
Ajax Bay, then Fitzroy
Maj. Peter Lansley; Capt. Terry McCabe; WO2 Brian Apperly+;
Staff Sgt Jed Newton; Sgts Tich Davies, Chris Fowler; Cpls Stan
Wright, Roly Young, Colin Hudson, Neil Parkin; L/Cpls Sweeney
Lea-Cox, Dave Donkin, Mick Jennings, Mac Macleod; Ptes Tam
Craine, Jock Wilson, 'Fozzy' Foster; Dvr Ally Alich.

No. 5 Field Surgical Team Ajax Bay, then Teal Inlet
Majors Charles Batty, Dick Knight; Capt. Rory Waggon; WO2
Fritz Sterba; Staff Sgt 'Webby' Webster; Cpls Jim Pearson, Gary
Seabrook; L/Cpls Rick Saunders and Roy Haley.

No. 6 Field Surgical Team Ajax Bay, then Fitzroy
Lt Col. Bill McGregor+; Maj. Malcolm Jowitt; Capt. Mike Von
Bertele; WO2 'Phred' Newbound; Sgt Russ Russell; Cpls Caddy
Cadwell, Colin May; L/Cpls 'Doc' Holliday and Bob Murdy.

Elements 16 Fd Ambulance RAMC (from RFA *Sir Galahad*
9 June–20 June)
No. 2 Field Surgical Team
Lt Col. Jim Anderson; Majs Jim Ryan, Jim Aitken; Sgt Cleverly-
Parker; Cpl Wright; L/Cpls Robson, Lawrence and Elsey

INDEX

UPPER FALKLAND SOUND
& SAN CARLOS WATER

WEST
FALKLAND

FANNING
HEAD

EAST
FALKLAND

SAN CARLOS WATER

FALKLAND SOUND

HMS
Antelope

AJAX
BAY

FIELD HOSPITAL

HMS Ardent

SUSSEX MTS

HOSPITAL SHIP
Uganda

GRANTHAM
SOUND